# Women in antiquity: new assessments

The study of gender in classical antiquity has undergone rapid and wide-ranging development in the past two decades. This collection of new assessments has been written by some of the most influential experts in this field from all over the world. The contributors reassess the role of women in diverse contexts and areas, such as archaic and classical Greek literature and cult, Roman imperial politics, ancient medicine and early Christianity. Some offer original interpretations of topics which have been widely discussed over the last twenty years; others highlight new areas of research.

*Women in Antiquity: New Assessments* reflects and expands on existing scholarly debates on the status and representation of women in the ancient world. It focuses on methodology, and suggests areas for research and improvement. It is invaluable and engaging reading for all students and teachers of ancient history.

**Richard Hawley** is a Lecturer in Classics at Royal Holloway College, University of London. **Barbara Levick** is a Fellow of St Hilda's College, Oxford.

# Women in antiquity

## New assessments

Edited by Richard Hawley and
Barbara Levick

London and New York

First published 1995
by Routledge
11 New Fetter Lane, London EC4P 4EE

Simultaneously published in the USA and Canada
by Routledge
29 West 35th Street, New York, NY 10001

Reprinted 1997

Selection and editorial matter © 1995 Richard Hawley and
Barbara Levick
Individual chapters © 1995 the contributors

Typeset in Baskerville by Florencetype Ltd, Stoodleigh, Devon
Printed and bound in Great Britain by
Biddles Ltd, Guildford and King's Lynn

*British Library Cataloguing in Publication Data*
A catalogue record for this book is available from the British Library

*Library of Congress Cataloguing in Publication Data*
A catalogue record for this book has been requested

ISBN 0–415–11368–7
    0–415–11369–5 (pbk)

# Contents

# Plates

# Figures

# Tables

# Journal abbreviations

| | |
|---|---|
| *ABSA* | Annual of the British School at Athens |
| *AC* | L'antiquité classique |
| *AClass* | Acta Classica |
| *AD* | Ἀρχαιολογικὸν Δελτίον |
| *AE* | Ἀρχαιολογικὴ Ἐφημερις |
| *AHB* | The Ancient History Bulletin |
| *AHR* | American Historical Review |
| *AION* | Architettura e storia antica. Annali Istituto Università Orientale Napoli |
| *AJA* | American Journal of Archaeology |
| *AJAH* | American Journal of Ancient History |
| *AJPh* | American Journal of Philology |
| *AncSoc* | Ancient Society |
| *AncW* | The Ancient World |
| *ANSMusN* | American Numismatic Society Museum Notes |
| *APhs* | American Philosophical Society |
| *BICS* | Bulletin of the Institute of Classical Studies of the University of London |
| *CJ* | The Classical Journal |
| *ClAnt* | Californian Studies in Classical Antiquity |
| *C&M* | Classica et Mediaevalia |
| *CPh* | Classical Philology |
| *CQ* | Classical Quarterly |
| *CRDAC* | Atti del centro ricerche e documentazione sull'antichità classica |
| *CW* | Classical Weekly/Classical World |
| *EMC* | Echos du monde classique (Classical Views) |
| *G&R* | Greece and Rome |
| *GRBS* | Greek, Roman and Byzantine Studies |

| | |
|---|---|
| *HSPh* | Harvard Studies in Classical Philology |
| *HThR* | Harvard Theological Review |
| *ICS* | Illinois Classical Studies |
| *JHS* | Journal of Hellenic Studies |
| *JRS* | Journal of Roman Studies |
| *LCM* | Liverpool Classical Monthly |
| *MDAI(A) (I) (R)* | Mitteilungen des Deutschen Archäologischen Instituts (Abteilung Athen) (Istanbul) |
| *MH* | Museum Helveticum |
| *MPhL* | Museum Philologum Londiniense |
| *NC* | Numismatic Chronicle |
| *OJA* | Oxford Journal of Archaeology |
| *PACA* | Proceedings of the African Classical Association |
| *PAPhS* | Proceedings of the American Philosophical Society |
| *PCPhS* | Proceedings of the Cambridge Philological Society |
| *PP* | La Parola del Passato |
| *QUCC* | Quaderni Urbinati di Cultura classica |
| *RA* | Revue Archéologique |
| *RBN* | Revue Belge de Numismatique et de Sigillographie |
| *REA* | Revue des Etudes Anciennes |
| *REG* | Revue des Etudes Grecques |
| *RhM* | Rheinisches Museum |
| *RIDA* | Revue Internationale des Droits de l'Antiquité |
| *RSA* | Rivista storica dell'Antichità |
| *SO* | Symbolae Osloenses |
| *TAPhA* | Transactions and Proceedings of the American Philological Association |
| *WS* | Wiener Studien |
| *YCIS* | Yale Classical Studies |
| *ZPE* | Zeitschrift für Papyrologie und Epigraphik |

# Preface

The first international conference on Women in the Ancient World to be held in the United Kingdom took place on 1–4 September 1993, at St Hilda's College, Oxford. It coincided with the celebration of the College's centenary at a time when the College had become the only women's college in the University.

The Conference was a product of the seminar, 'Women in Antiquity', which had been devised and run by a graduate student, Susan Fischler, and by Leonie Archer, Fellow of Wolfson College, since 1986,[1] and which we had taken on when they left the University in 1989. The theme of the conference – New Assessments – had two sources: the changes that a theme naturally undergoes when it is treated over a number of years, and our own awareness that the emphasis of the seminar was also changing, and rightly, away from 'women' towards 'gender studies' (and that is the title it has borne since the Conference).

There is no need to recapitulate here the topics dealt with so lucidly in the papers we are printing; our contributors can speak for themselves. Many papers treat explicitly the changes that have come about in the decades since scholars began to interest themselves in women and gender in antiquity. Beryl Rawson's paper surveys the current landscape and offers suggestions for new directions. Some suggest revisions and amendments to particular views, received or controversial. Mary Beard indeed returns to the topic of Vestals to reassess her own standpoint. The volume accurately reflects current debates, as several scholars within it interact with one another's views.

Discussion at the Conference was also full and open, with the atmosphere as conducive to fruitful thinking as it could be. This was due to the friendly spirit in which speakers and audience approached the work, and we thank everyone for their contributions. Not all the papers are represented in this volume; there was a fine off-the-cuff contribution done almost entirely from slides, and excellent papers, on the Middle East, on Egypt, and on Anglo-Saxon England, which had to be excluded in order to give the volume its Classical unity. Those papers will surely appear elsewhere, and we are appreciative both of the contribution of the speakers at the Conference and of the speed and efficiency with which those whose texts are printed here have prepared them for publication. There was also a series of visually stimulating poster presentations by scholars in a wide variety of fields, from Classical Greek religion to Anglo-Saxon Britain. In this, as in the range of speakers and delegates, the Conference presented a truly international perspective. One of the most striking sessions was a group presentation by four women from Finland, who are currently advancing the study of gender in their country; Liisa Savunen's paper represents one facet of their present research.

Other thanks are due: first to the Oxford University Faculty Board of Literae Humaniores which has generously supported the expenses of the seminar for a number of years, and to the Oxford University Craven Committee for defraying costs of the Conference itself. The seminar has lately been held in the Social Studies Faculty Centre, and we should like to take this opportunity of expressing our thanks for their hospitality. Next we should mention the work put in for the Conference by the staff of St Hilda's under the Assistant Bursar, Mrs Sarah Griffiths, and the last-minute adjustments and anticipatory measures of our miraculously efficient Secretary, Ms Annabel James, then entering her final year as an undergraduate of the College. The College Librarian, Ms Maria Croghan, and representatives of Thornton's Booksellers and Oxbow Books generously put books on our subject on display. It was a particular pleasure that Dr Richard Stoneman was present, and we were delighted when at the end of the Conference he invited us to publish the proceedings with Routledge. That invitation he has followed up by taking a personal interest in the volume's progress towards completion. We should like to express our warmest thanks for all that he has done to ensure that the papers given at the 1993 Conference should be available to as wide a public as possible, and as soon as possible. Especial thanks must go to Routledge's Editorial Assistant, Ms Victoria Peters, who has kept a firm but fair control over the whole editorial process and has made our tasks much easier; so too has all that has been done by way of transferring and processing discs by the Oxford University Computing Centre and by Mrs Toni Ross, St Hilda's Computer Officer.

Richard Hawley and Barbara Levick
*November 1994*

## NOTE

1  Papers from the seminar series have been published: L.J. Archer, S. Fischler and M. Wyke (eds), *Women in ancient societies: 'an illusion of the night'* (London: 1994).

# Notes on contributors

**Mary Beard** is a Lecturer in Classics at the University of Cambridge and a Fellow of Newnham College. She has written widely on Roman culture and religion and (with John Henderson) has just finished *A Very Short Introduction to Classics* (Oxford University Press).

**Susanna Braund** is Professor of Latin at Royal Holloway, University of London. She is author of books on Roman satire, including *Roman Verse Satire* (*Greece & Rome New Surveys in the Classics* no.23, 1992), a commentary on Juvenal *Satires* 1–5 (Cambridge University Press forthcoming); of a translation of Lucan's *Civil War* (Oxford, 1992); and co-editor of *The Passions in Roman Literature and Thought* (forthcoming, Cambridge University Press).

**Mireille Corbier** is Directeur de Recherche at the Centre National de la Recherche Scientifique in Paris. She was trained in epigraphy and is the author of *L'Aerarium Saturni et l'aerarium militare: Administration et prosopographie sénatoriale* and *Indulgentia Principis* (forthcoming) and the editor of the periodical *L'Année épigraphique*. She has written extensively on public finances, family, literacy and food in the Roman Empire.

**Ken Dowden** is Senior Lecturer in Classics at the University of Birmingham. He is the author of *Death and the Maiden: Girls' Initiation Rites in Greek Mythology* (Routledge, 1989) and *The Uses of Greek Mythology* (Routledge, 1992), as well as of *Religion and the Romans* (1992) and various articles on the ancient novel. His next book will be *European Paganisms* (forthcoming, Routledge).

**Elaine Fantham** is Giger Professor of Latin at Princeton University. A graduate of Oxford, she emigrated to Canada in 1968, where she taught at the University of Toronto before moving to Princeton in

1986. She is co-author with H. Foley, N. Kampen, S. Pomeroy and A. Shapiro of *Women in Classical Antiquity: Image and Text* (Oxford University Press, 1994) and author/editor of five books and over forty articles on Latin literature and aspects of women's sexuality and status in Greece and Rome.

**Lin Foxhall** is Lecturer in Ancient History in the School of Archaeological Studies, University of Leicester. In addition to several articles on gender, she has written *Olive Cultivation in Ancient Greece: the Ancient Economy Revisited* (London, 1995), and will shortly publish *Studying Gender in Classical Antiquity* (Cambridge) and *When Men were Men: Masculinity, Power and Identity in Classical Antiquity* (Routledge).

**Danielle Gourevitch** is Directeur d'Études for medical history at the Ecole pratique des hautes études (4ème section, Sorbonne, Paris). She is author of *Le Mal d'être femme* (1984), *Le Triangle hippocratique* (1984); editor of Daremberg's *Diary of his travel to Italy* (1994); co-editor of Soranus of Ephesus' *Gynaecology*, I–III (1988–94); she is preparing a methodological handbook to the history of medicine (Ellipses, Paris, 1995).

**Richard Hawley** is Lecturer in Classics at Royal Holloway College, University of London. His doctoral thesis was on gender in Attic drama. Publications include: contributions to *The Bloomsbury Guide to Women's Literature*; articles on women philosophers, Athenaeus, Aspasia, Greek declamation. He is currently finishing *Greek Drama: A Sourcebook* and *Greek Drama: An Introduction* (both Routledge). Since 1988 he has co-organised the Oxford 'Women in Antiquity' seminar series.

**Marilyn A. Katz** is Professor of Classical Studies at Wesleyan University in Middletown, Connecticut. She is the author of *Penelope's Renown: Meaning and Indeterminacy in Homer's Odyssey* (Princeton, 1991) and of numerous articles on Homer, Hesiod and women in ancient Greece. She is currently completing a manuscript on 'Women and the Polis in Classical Athens'.

**Helen King** is Senior Lecturer in History at Liverpool Institute of Higher Education and an Honorary Research Fellow at Liverpool University. She has held research fellowships at Newnham College, Cambridge and the University of Newcastle, and has published widely on ancient Greek gynaecology and midwifery, and their transformations in later Western medicine. With Sander Gilman, Roy Porter, George Rousseau and Elaine Showalter, she published *Hysteria Beyond Freud* (1993).

**Voula Lambropoulou** teaches courses including 'The Philosophy of Plato' at the University of Athens. She is the author of *Women in Pythagorean Societies* (1972), *Female Dances in Ancient Greece and their Philosophy* (1985), *Pregnancy and Childbirth in Art* (1986), *Women in Papadiamantis' Works* (1992), amongst others. Since 1984 she has also edited the journal *Hypatia*.

**Barbara Levick** is a Fellow and Tutor in Literae Humaniores at St Hilda's College, Oxford and she is a vice-president of the Society for the Promotion of Roman Studies. Her publications include works on imperial Roman history, the government of the Roman Empire and the antiquities of Asia Minor. Since 1988 she has co-organised the Oxford 'Women in Antiquity' seminar series.

**Lucia Nixon** is co-director of the Sphakia Survey and College Lecturer in Archaeology at Magdalen College, Oxford. She has taught classics at Queen's University at Kingston and the University of New Brunswick at Saint John, and was a Visiting Scholar at Wolfson College, Oxford in 1994–5.

**Sarah B. Pomeroy** is author of *Goddesses, Whores, Wives, and Slaves: Women in Classical Antiquity; Women in Hellenistic Egypt from Alexander to Cleopatra; Xenophon's Oeconomicus: A Social and Historical Commentary*; co-author of *Women's Realities, Women's Choices: An Introduction to Women's Studies* and of *Women in the Classical World*; and editor of *Women's History and Ancient History*. She is Professor of Classics, Women's Studies, and History at Hunter College and the Graduate School, City University of New York.

**Beryl Rawson** is Professor of Classics and Head of Department at the Australian National University, Canberra. Her research interests lie in the social and political history of Rome – the late Republic and the Empire – especially 'the Roman family'. Her publications include *The Politics of Friendship: Pompey and Cicero* (Sydney University Press, 1978) and, as editor and contributor, *The Family in Ancient Rome: New Perspectives* (Routledge, 1991), *Marriage, Divorce and Children in Ancient Rome* (Oxford University Press, 1991) and *The Roman Family: Status, Sentiment, Space* (forthcoming). She is currently working on *Children and Childhood in Ancient Rome*.

**Liisa Savunen** is a Scholar of Ancient History at Renvall Institute of Historical Research, University of Helsinki. As part of a research project *Women in Roman Society: Female Networks and the Public Sphere*, she is preparing a study of the women of Pompeii.

**Anna Wilson** is a former Lecturer in Latin at the Queen's University of Belfast and in Classics at the University of Birmingham. She has written on Latin poetry and on Late Antique Christian literature and is joint editor with Margaret Mullett of *The Forty Martyrs of Sebasteia* (forthcoming, *Belfast Byzantine Texts and Translations*).

**Froma Zeitlin** is Ewing Professor of Greek Language and Literature at Princeton University. Co-editor of *Before Sexuality: The Construction of Erotic Experience in the Ancient Greek World* (1990), *Nothing to do with Dionysos?: Athenian Drama in its Social Context* (1990), and editor of J.-P. Vernant, *Mortals and Immortals* (1991), she is also author of *Under the Sign of the Shield* (1982) and *Playing the Other: Gender and Society in Classical Greek Literature* (1995).

# Chapter 1

# From 'daily life' to 'demography'

*Beryl Rawson*

The period since the 1960s has been described as 'that Golden Age of historiography'.[1] In the historiography of ancient societies (especially Roman) there has been both a revolution and an explosion. There has been an enormous amount of new writing relevant to the study of women in antiquity. Not only has there been specific and specialised scholarship on women (new examples of which follow in this volume), but there has been much progress in related fields, e.g. in family studies and in the archaeology of domestic space. This enables the study of women to be contextualised better than it has ever been.

This paper therefore takes a broad perspective and begins with general histories rather than specialised works. Indeed, there are few single-authored, comprehensive studies specifically on women in antiquity. There was, of course, Pomeroy's pioneering work of 1975 with its emphasis largely on the Greek side, and there have been many useful collections since then[2] – always including more work on the Greeks than on the Romans. (That is perhaps surprising, in view of the range of evidence available and the great volume of writing on 'the Roman family' as compared with the family in Greece.) For Rome, there has been only Balsdon's 1962 book, *Roman Women* – a very unsatisfactory book published just before the wave of new scholarship. There have been important books on some aspects of ancient women,[3] and there has been a lot of writing in the scholarly journals; but the general reader, the undergraduate and even the Classics/Ancient History scholar in other fields will reach first for an introductory book, and first impressions from such books, which have been for a long period of the 'daily life' type, can be lasting.

The great success story of 'daily life' books has been that of Jérome Carcopino, published in English as *Daily Life in Ancient Rome* in 1940

after its original appearance in French in 1939.[4] It has had phenom-
enal sales. It caught readers' imagination by drawing on the exciting
archaeological work which had been going on in Italy in the 1930s,
and it also used a variety of other evidence – not only literature but
also inscriptions, architecture, the law – to recreate the physical
aspects of the city of Rome. Yet when he gets to the topic of Marriage,
Woman and the Family (in the section on 'The Moral Background')
Carcopino does not continue to exploit the material evidence: he
deals only in formalities, literary *exempla* and conventional value
judgments. Moreover, Carcopino provided no photographic illustrations to enable readers to make some assessment of the material
evidence for themselves. The English-language edition in 1940 added
illustrations, but the paperback editions by which most people know
the book dropped them.

I make these points not as antiquarian comments on the publication history of one book but as fundamental judgments on the nature
of historical understanding (as we have come to perceive it). Material
evidence, material culture, must be integrated with other aspects of
cultural history and the reader/student must be brought as close as
possible to first-hand familiarity with such evidence. Short of seeing
the archaeological evidence in situ, the student will be best served by
two things: good photographic illustrations with enough annotation
to make them basically intelligible, integrated with the text; and
training in methodology in how to understand and interpret such
evidence.

The publication history of Philippe Ariès' book, *Centuries of Childhood: A Social History of Family Life* (a book with obvious relevance for
the study of women), reversed the Carcopino story in that Ariès
included in his French edition illustrations (of works of art) which
were integral to his arguments, but the English translation omitted
these. Recently there has been a revaluation of Ariès' thesis, with
criticisms of his interpretation of the visual arts evidence.[5] But how
can one assess this without having the illustrations?

Handsome illustrations are provided in volume 1 of *A History of
Private Life*,[6] but the text of the first section, 'The Roman Empire', is
disappointingly superficial. This is surprising in that its author, Paul
Veyne, was closely associated with *Annales* scholars and the *Annales*
school, which has done much to advance the study of the material
world and non-elite society. Veyne had in 1978 published an
article (much cited since but unconvincing) on relations between
husbands and wives in imperial Rome and had foreshadowed a more

ambitious publication that would provide details and documentation. The *History of Private Life* volume offers no detailed documentation and may have an unfortunate influence because of the quality of the physical production and the prestige of the series.[7] Specialist scholars might recognise its defects but those working in comparative fields might not.

Much of the innovative work in social and cultural history is being done by comparativists.[8] With the increasing use being made of archaeological evidence we ourselves have to rely on methodologies and findings from cognate disciplines. Architecture and iconography are now important areas of study: we can learn much about women in past societies by studying their relationship to physical space and the representations of women in public and private art. The question of separate living quarters for women in Greece is still a subject of lively debate and studies of Roman architecture are being integrated with studies of family life and studies of women and children.[9] In the analysis of images and of the use of physical space we have much to learn from art history and from prehistoric ('new') archaeology.[10]

The material evidence, especially epigraphy, has led some to hope that we might become more numerate in answering questions about cities and their populations. Instead of superficial questions of dress, food, 'habits', we might ask about fertility and mortality rates, age at marriage, women's life cycles, to try to understand women's roles at a deeper, more structural level. In other words, can we move from 'daily life' to 'demography'? Tim Parkin's book *Demography and Roman Society* (1992), has provided a masterly statement of possibilities and limitations.

The limitations, the disappointments and the dead ends in these demographic excursions are undeniable. And I believe[11] that to some extent we have been asking the wrong questions of the epigraphic material. Inscriptions (even the numerous and demographically detailed ones of the western Roman Empire) cannot be taken as a representative sample of the whole of the population in the Roman or Greek world. We cannot extrapolate from these data average age at death, percentage of slaves or women or other groups in the population, or similar quantifications. The inscriptions are better used as cultural artefacts, to reflect *mentalité*, and this is where some real progress has taken place.[12]

The Greek and the Roman epigraphic data differ greatly in scope, frequency and type. The cultural implications of this deserve closer examination. But let me first say that terms like 'Greek' and 'Roman' are usually too general to be useful. It is important to differentiate regionally and chronologically, e.g. fifth-century BC Athens, Bronze Age Mycenae, Greek-speaking provinces of the Roman empire in the second century AD; the huge city of Rome, or country towns in Italy, or other parts of the empire which had different cultural traditions. These differentiations are too often ignored. Perhaps because of the paucity of some of our evidence we are tempted to agglomerate it.

Having said that, let me use 'Greek' and 'Roman' for the moment as a kind of shorthand to ask why Greeks should have left so much less personal detail on their tombstones and other memorials than Romans did. There were, of course, periods of Athenian history when funerary commemoration was severely limited by law (e.g. the first two-thirds or so of the fifth century BC and the first couple of centuries of the Hellenistic period). But even when private, individual monuments exist, they tell us very little about personal relationships. The basic problem is that there are few monuments where text and 'picture' reinforce each other.

Consider, for example, one of the earliest classical grave reliefs, *c.* 420–410 BC, the stele of Mnesagora and Nikochares (Plate 1.1), whose iconography seems obviously that of mother and child: it is only the fairly rare occurrence of an inscription that tells us that these are brother and sister. Also late in the fifth century a stele was erected to Ampharete and an infant (Plate 1.2) – surely a mother and child, but the inscription tells us that this is a grandmother, with her daughter's child.[13] There is much to be explained here about idealisation, about lack of fit between representation and reality.

By contrast, consider some examples from Italy of the early Empire. Diana Kleiner's work (1977, 1987) provides excellent collections of such examples. Iunia Venusta, an ex-slave, was the sole dedicator of a handsome marble altar of the late first/early second century AD (Plate 1.3). In the inscription she lists all her beneficiaries before her own name: patron (ex-master) M. Iunius Perseus, husband M. Iunius Satyrus, children M. Iunius Iustus and Iunia Pia; and at the end she names her own freedman, Pharnaces, as a collaborator in the dedication. We can identify a whole household and network of relationships with this woman at the centre. The sculpture represents members of her group, and although she is not herself represented in the sculpture she is the driving force in this monument.

Even without iconography, the text of an inscription like that set up for Gauia Chrysis by her son M. Gauius Socrates (Plate 1.4) can

Plate 1.1  Stele of brother and sister Mnesagora and Nikochares,
          c. 420–410 BC

Source: Athens, National Museum 3845; *IG* II/III² 12147

Plate 1.2 Stele of grandmother Ampharete and infant, late fifth
century BC

Source: Athens, Kerameikos Museum, *IG* II/III² 10650

Plate 1.3  Altar, lunia Venusta and *familia*, late first–early second century AD

Source:  Rome, Capitoline Museum: Museo del Palazzo dei Conservatori, Museo Nuovo, room VI, no. 13, inv. 2886; *CIL* 6.20819

Plate 1.4 Epitaph of a mother, Gauia Chrysis, first–second century
        AD, from Rome

Source: Classics Department Museum, Australian National University,
        Canberra, inv. no. 71.03; *CIL* 6.18920

tell us a good deal. The nomenclature (son taking family name from
mother) suggests that the child was not born of a legal Roman
marriage and that Gauia was a sole parent. We can place this in a
whole contextual web: conditions of slavery, concubinage and illegitimacy,[14] and legal changes which in the second century recognised
(in some circumstances) the rights of mothers and children to inherit
from each other.

Without such reinforcement from text, can Greek iconography
nevertheless be used to illuminate other developments in Greek society
or to be illuminated by them? It is a methodological question – and
a challenge.[15]

These Greek and Roman illustrations come from societies five
centuries apart. Can we identify forces of acculturation when Greek
and Roman intersect? Are there some periods which lend themselves to this more than others? For example, in the early Roman

Empire did 'Romanisation' of the east Mediterranean lead to different forms of relationship and commemoration? There is a great deal of epigraphic and iconographic material available from this area in this period: there was a 'Renaissance' of Greek society at work, but I know of no study of women or families in this society (of the first two centuries AD). This is a result of the periodisation of history and the privileging of classical Greece (and Athens) in the study of Classics and Ancient History. By turning our attention to different periods we might deepen our understanding of 'Romanisation' and 'Hellenisation' and of women's role in a changing cultural context.[16]

The culture of the city of Rome itself in this period (early Empire) must have reflected the changes in its population – multiracial, host to diverse religions, beliefs and social practices. The growing interest, nowadays, in religion, death, ethnicity and sexuality might help us penetrate this world further. In the matter of funerary practice, cultural traditions seem to have retained their own character for a long period. In Imperial Rome children had a much better chance of being commemorated than in most other parts of the Mediterranean (Saller and Shaw 1984). But Greek-language funerary inscriptions from Rome show a quite different pattern from Latin ones: for Greek speakers the emphasis is more on the elderly end of the population curve, for Latin speakers on the young end. However, on a graph the two lines do come closer together as time passes,[17] raising the question of possible Christian influence.

If we can get this far with the epigraphic evidence for children, surely there is something to be said about ways in which women commemorate and are commemorated in such a multicultural society. Funerary commemoration is especially important, as infant and child mortality rates were high in this society: how did this affect women's lives and outlooks? Here as so often we can learn from anthropology, where studies make clear that even in societies with high infant mortality rates real grieving takes place, and especially by mothers: theories of indifference to children until they have survived some years seem to have little support.[18]

Some progress has been made in population studies of ancient Greece and Rome. Contraception, abortion, infanticide and abandonment, pregnancy and childbirth have all received attention in recent years.[19] We are now better informed on ages at marriage and the implications of such information.[20] Females of non-elite families in Rome and Italy of the first two or three centuries of the Christian era probably married in their late teens.[21] This counteracts earlier arguments (about exceptionally young brides) based on a few scattered sources, mostly literary (e.g. Tacitus), generalised from the elite to all social classes. The age at which a woman first married, and the age-gap between her and her husband, had implications for her health, her education, her property, her relationship with her children, husband and other relatives, her prospects of divorce, widowhood and remarriage and so on.

Moreover, a computer simulation based on work done for other pre-modern societies by demographers with the Cambridge Group for the History of Population and Social Structure has produced a plausible picture of inter-generational relationships. We can get a fair idea, for example, of the probability that a woman had one or both parents alive at the time of her first marriage. (More than half had probably lost their father by their late teens.[22]) More generally, tools such as model life tables can be useful 'in showing us the way population dynamics work' (Parkin 1992: 90).

Population dynamics, relationships, *mentalité*: these all interact. Work of the last twenty to thirty years has confirmed, and revealed in more detail, that the 'nuclear family' was a core institution in Roman society – in symbolism (exploited particularly by Augustus in visual and other propaganda: Zanker 1988) and, where possible, in actual practice. Indeed, for pre-modern western European societies in general, the Cambridge Group has shown that as far back as their records exist, 'the household' has been based on a nuclear rather than an extended family. There is little evidence of extended family groups in Roman households (but slaves and ex-slaves could be a kind of surrogate extended family). The focus on the conjugal group (two parents and their young children) has implications for the role of wives and mothers. Moreover, from the late Republic (first century BC), relationships between agnates became less important (in law and in practice) than those between cognates. This is a different picture from the old one derived from a narrow reading of *patria potestas*, the powers of the *paterfamilias*.

Some scholars find the term 'nuclear family' unacceptable because of the frequency of divorce and death and therefore of changing relationships and households.[23] We cannot ignore the effects which death and divorce must have had on women. For propertied families, in both Rome and classical Athens, a woman's dowry was protected, thus making a further marriage possible – a marriage in which she might have more say in choice of partner than when she first married at a young age. But any children of a marriage belonged to the father.

In theory, they remained with the father and, if he remarried, a step-mother. We do know, however, of cases in Rome where after a divorce a child was reared by the mother or by some other relative.[24] In any case, in Roman society there was considerable movement of all family members (in propertied circles) from one physical location to another: from city base to rural villa to coastal retreat (Cicero and Pliny are well attested examples). Children probably shared in this movement, perhaps staying with different parents at different times and getting to know different sets of step-siblings. For non-propertied families, dowry and villas were irrelevant or much less important and divorce was probably correspondingly rare.[25] For a variety of reasons, then, the familial focus at any particular time for any individual in Roman society[26] was the conjugal unit, even if membership of that unit changed from time to time.

Archaeologists have contributed to the demographic picture with new techniques of bone analysis. Bisel worked on skeletons found at Herculaneum in 1982. She took advantage of new discoveries to apply methods used by pre-historians to make judgments on nutrition and fertility levels (Bisel 1986, 1987). I would have said until recently that this was a rare opportunity unlikely to be replicated elsewhere. But what Dyson[27] says about the potential for physical anthropology in Italy may be true also of Greece: 'a long tradition of inhumance burial with a high level of osteological preservation'. And I have only recently come upon a study (Schlörb-Vierneisel 1964) which has a skeleton and grave goods to complement a stele (sculpture and inscribed name) of late fifth-century BC Athens. Is there more of this hidden away in archaeologists' notebooks? The question underlines two urgent aspects of our study: first, the need for archaeologists and historians to work more closely together, to share data and insights and to develop cooperatively what are the important questions; and second, the need to study any evidence in context, in particular to consider all aspects of any monument (inscription, sculpture, decora-tion, construction material, . . .) as a whole, and to correlate the mon-ument with its find-spot, associated grave goods, skeletal remains, etc.

One area of study which is ideal for contextualising, for drawing together the whole range of evidence available, is 'the city'. This has become a popular topic, and there are many ways in which the urban environment affected women in antiquity (as now) and was affected by them. It is often said that the majority of people in antiquity lived in 'the country' as opposed to 'the city'. 'The country' might, of course, mean smaller towns rather than farms, in which case urban factors still apply. I do not see how we can recapture the population 'on the land' in any gender-differentiated way.[28]

Two matters in which cities took a keen interest were, first, the law and second, status/citizenship of individuals. Recent work, with new approaches, has shown how these matters can shed light on women in antiquity – far beyond the narrow sphere of property rights and legitimacy of children. For this we have again to thank cross-fertilisation between legal scholarship and other disciplines – social history, anthropology, epigraphy.[29] In earlier handbooks of classical law, matters such as dowry and divorce were technical legal problems; now questions are also asked about the social impact of these, what they meant to individuals and groups (including women).

Status is a particularly useful classification in discussing Roman society, since that society was characterised by both sharp hierarchy and considerable social mobility. Women were agents, beneficiaries and victims of this system. Analysis in this area is assisted by the elaborate system of Roman nomenclature, and much progress has been made in understanding the implications of the Roman name. This helps us see the frequency with which slaves of the imperial household 'married' (formed marital-type unions with) free, Roman citizen women. There were mutual benefits in such unions: the imperial slaves often had prestige, power and wealth[30] and the prospect of becoming imperial freedmen (with even more of these commodities), whereas the women's free status conferred its own prestige and ensured that any children born of the relationship would be free-born.

Women's legal status was relevant to marital status in another way. Roman marriage was based on cohabitation and marital intent rather than formal ceremony, so the relationship between two free citizen partners was normally marriage (*matrimonium, iustae nuptiae*). There were some vetoes on marriage across status boundaries, but not many (e.g. members of senatorial families could not marry ex-slaves). Concubinage was not a harem relationship; it was monogamous, the concubine was in many respects treated by the law as wife, and she commanded a certain degree of respect and standing. The emperors Vespasian, Antoninus Pius and Marcus Aurelius, all respectable figures, each took a concubine after being widowed. Those women were ex-slaves, so the emperors – as senators – could not marry them. In most other relationships with freedwomen the wish for legitimate children surely led to marriage rather than concubinage.[31] All of the relationships attested (directly or indirectly) as concubinage can be explained as originating at a time when at least one partner was ineligible to marry (e.g. as a slave, an alien, a soldier). Even then they often borrowed the terminology and symbolism of full marriage. The implications of all this for *mentalité*, for moral and social climate, are great.

The epigraphy and archaeology of 'the city' can also give evidence of women's independent role beyond family and household. In Italy under the Empire and in Greece and Asia Minor of the Hellenistic and Roman periods, women not infrequently were responsible for endowing public works and their names can be found on a variety of monuments, e.g. a portico, baths, and monuments recording beneficence such as games or food distribution.[32] There is thus a female dimension to euergetism (an increasingly prominent scholarly topic) which should not be neglected or underestimated.

It is worth developing this aspect, in order to give women an appropriate place in public life. It is tempting to focus on the private sphere because it was there that women lived much of their lives. But much of ancient life was lived in public, more than nowadays. The public-private opposition was not absolute. We therefore risk distorting women's experience if we go too far in de-emphasising the public sphere. We should try to reconstruct women's relationship to the city and the state, to see how city and state looked through women's eyes. This will mean extending our understanding of public history, to encompass not only politics narrowly conceived but ritual, religion, slavery, citizenship, social and moral legislation, public works.[33]

Historiography, ancient and modern, has been uncomfortable in dealing with women who did not fit the dominant pattern of 'normal' women. Women have often been used as markers of moral and political breakdown (Wyke 1992: 111), exemplifying sexual misconduct or appropriation of male political power. Part of the explanation for this has been the privileged position of High Literature in the study of Greek and Roman antiquity. This influence is changing, with the growing use of a wider range of source material and with the new, largely feminist readings of those literary texts (but again these changes may not have infiltrated the non-specialist world very far).

Another reason for the widely perceived stereotypes is, I suggest, the power of images, the visual evidence. It is not the ancient images to which I refer here but modern art, especially eighteenth and nineteenth century European painting. Historical scenes were very popular, and antiquity was perceived through a miasma of literary and artistic sources.[34] Post-Renaissance painting dressed up historical characters in modern garb appropriate to the artist's own time and culture. Thus we can trace representations of Cleopatra as a 'blonde

Plate 1.5a  Cleopatra and son Caesarion as Isis and Hathor, Temple
of Hathor, Dendera, Upper Egypt, first century BC

Source: Donald McLeish/Robert Harding Picture Library, London

*Plate 1.5b* Cleopatra on Roman coin, Alexandria 32–31 BC, as Queen of Kings

*Source:* H.A. Grueber, *Coins of the Roman Republic in the British Museum*, II, British Museum, London, p. 525, no. 180

*Plate 1.6* Roman coin of Sabina Augusta, wife of emperor Hadrian, AD 128–138; reverse has Pietas and children

*Source:* Classics Department Museum, Australian National University, Canberra, inv. no. 69.02; H. Mattingly and E.A. Sydenham, *Roman Imperial Coinage*, II, p. 478, no. 1041.

nordic beauty', e.g. in Tiepolo's frescoes, as Victorian England's perception of an eastern seductress in Alma-Tadema's painting, and, in the twentieth century, through a variety of representations in cinema.[35]

Representations of Cleopatra in her own day are very different from the historical reconstructions of later times, e.g. on a frieze on a temple of Isis and Horus and on her coins she is a powerful religious and national leader (Plate 1.5). The Roman women of the imperial family were also presented to the world as serious individuals associated with national symbols, e.g. those of family virtues, in the second century (see Plate 1.6 for Sabina).[36]

One of the most influential 'historical' paintings must have been that of the Frenchman Thomas Couture, often reproduced under different titles but best known as *Les romains et leur décadence* (Plate 1.7). The whole theme of 'decadence' and its association with women would be well worth pursuing. In Couture's banquet scene women play a prominent part. The painting belongs to 1847, when Couture was a member of the prestigious Académie. It is no wonder that painters in the latter half of the nineteenth century turned away from such subjects of historical reconstruction towards direct experience and 'natural' life. But, I would argue, so-called 'classical' art continued to have influence and to affect the perceptions of historians writing in the nineteenth century. It has taken classical scholarship a long time to shake off these effects. That is why it is so important to provide students and other readers with the wide range of representations in original sources such as tombstones, dedications, sculpture, coins. It is important too because of the ubiquity of the visual evidence in ancient Greek and Roman societies – people could not have been oblivious to it, and it must have influenced their perceptions. Present-day students, more image-oriented than print-oriented, are well placed to appreciate this.

Many of these contemporaneous images help to illuminate women of lower status. In recent years we have had excellent collections by Kampen (1981) and by Kleiner (1987), drawing particularly on Ostia. This opens up the question of the direction of social change and influence. What model did these newly-arrived, newly-achieving members of Roman society have for their monuments? Kleiner believes that in the first century AD the Ara Pacis and Augustus' other propaganda were very influential and that this provided the model for the freedmen and freedwomen who were making good in the Julio–Claudian period and who set up most of the funerary friezes

*Plate 1.7* Thomas Couture, *Les romains et leur décadence*, 1847    *Source:* Paris, Musée d'Orsay

which we have: these friezes and their inscriptions celebrate the family – spouses, parents, children (cf. Zanker 1988). This would be consistent with the so-called 'trickle-down' principle of sociology: lower classes usually mimic their 'betters', rather than the reverse, in matters of fashion and social custom. That may well have been the stimulus. But this self-perception, this 'sentimental ideal', must also have become self-generating. New members of society – immigrants, slaves and ex-slaves – lacked most other networks and support systems except the *familia* and immediate family. The large capital city of Rome and its port of Ostia give us the most notable evidence of this, and Saller and Shaw have shown that urbanised communities with large numbers of slaves leave most evidence of such family bonds. These were also the communities most receptive to Christianity. The potential for more fruitful contact between classical studies and studies of early Christianity is great, and it provides another opportunity to look at the intersection of Roman, Greek and Near Eastern cultural traditions.

It is not only ordinary women and families whom we want to rediscover, but also the ordinary physical setting and utensils of their daily lives. Archaeologists and art historians of earlier generations were preoccupied with aesthetics, the beautiful *objet d'art*, but how many people saw and enjoyed such items in the everyday domestic situation? (Public art is a different matter.) Everyday, ordinary artefacts are now taking their place in contextualising women in antiquity (and other members of ancient societies).[37]

So, contextualisation is one of the ways forward. I have suggested that this will have to take serious account of the material evidence and that we must present this evidence as an integral part of our argument – at a scholarly level to specialist colleagues and in more accessible form to others. We will need to draw on comparative studies, and contribute to them, to exploit the full range of cross-disciplinary insights and skills. We will have to review our classification of significant periods and respect the cultural traditions of different regions. This might help us identify and interpret the forces of acculturation.[38]

## NOTES

1  Stone 1987: xii.
2  For example, those of Foley 1981; Cameron and Kuhrt 1983 and 1993; Peradotto and Sullivan 1984; Blok and Mason 1987; Pomeroy 1991; Pantel 1992; as well as the special issues of *Helios* in 1987, 1989, 1990,

1992. The methodological collection of Rabinowitz and Richlin 1993 became available to me after the oral presentation of this paper: it offers heartening support for some of the views expressed here.

3 Especially incorporating the law, e.g. Gardner 1986; Treggiari 1991a; Just 1989.

4 Carcopino remains superior to more recent 'daily life' books by French authors: Flacelière 1964 and Dupont 1992.

5 For example, by Burton 1989.

6 1987; general editors P. Ariès and G. Duby; vol. 1, *From Pagan Rome to Byzantium*, ed. Paul Veyne. The illustrations range widely in period and geographical location and although they are well placed on pages throughout the book they are not systematically integrated with the text.

7 As pointed out by R. Saller in his review in *AHR* 94, 1989: 705–7.

8 Shaw and Saller have written for such scholars in *Man* 1984 and Saller in *Continuity and Change* 1986.

9 Note Andrew Wallace–Hadrill's conference on 'Domestic space in the ancient Mediterranean' at the University of Reading, 25–7 March, 1994.

10 R.E. Park, a prominent American town-planner in the 1920s, wrote in 1952,

> The city is a state of mind, a body of customs and traditions and of organised attitudes. . . . The city is not . . . merely a physical mechanism and an artificial construction. It is involved in the vital processes of the people who compose it; it is a product of nature and particularly human nature.
> (quoted by R.A. Raper, p. 194 of *Spatial Archaeology* 1977, ed. D.L. Clarke, London: Academic Press, 1977.)

On living space in Greece see Walker 1983 and Jameson 1990.

11 As does Brent Shaw, e.g. in Kertzer and Saller 1991: 66–90.

12 N.B. Saller and Shaw 1984.

13 Clairmont 1970: 22, 23.

14 In the lower classes the mother-child link could be strengthened by the very forces of family instability (slavery, death). On children of irregular unions, see Rawson 1966 and 1990.

15 See Ridgway 1987 for possibilities in Greek art. Burial rituals and grave goods may reflect different gender roles: note the sex-specific grave-markers in Attica (Boardman 1988). Cf. McManus 1990.

16 But note van Bremen's *prolegomena* to such a study, 1983, and Nevett's study of domestic space in Roman Greece, 1994.

17 Macmullen 1982; Ery 1969.

18 For example, Scheper–Hughes 1987 and A. Macfarlane's review of L. Stone in *History and Theory* 18, 1979: 107, 115–16.

19 For example, by Valerie French (1986) (1988), Danielle Gourevitch (1987, 1990), John Boswell (1988).

20 Saller 1987; Shaw 1987.

21 For elite families, as in many other societies, betrothals and marriages were at earlier ages for both females and males – probably very early teens for females and up to ten years later for males.

22 Saller 1986 and 1987.

23  See Bradley 1991, balancing Treggiari 1991 and Corbier 1991.
24  I hope to look more systematically at this question in my current study of Roman children and childhood.
25  Kajanto 1969 is the only article of which I am aware to deal with the question of divorce in the lower classes. Arguments from silence suggest that divorce was not a frequent phenomenon among such classes.
26  Jameson 1990 accepts this for classical Athenian society.
27  1992a: 385. Cf. Garnsey 1988 for evidence of nutritional stress on women and children.
28  Dyson (1992: 38) says that it might be possible to engender the archaeological record by 'more precise and thoughtful archaeological techniques' which would 'allow us to identify female activity within the rural household'.
29  For example, Crook 1967; Gardner 1986 and 1993; Just 1989.
30  Their position was such as to override what seems to have been a general distaste for women 'marrying down'. On imperial slaves and their unions see Weaver 1972.
31  Rawson 1974 made two things clear: it is rare for any children to be attested from relationships which are explicitly concubinage; and there is no incontrovertible evidence that any of these relationships was between free partners who were eligible to marry. Such findings have had no impact on M. Foucault's *History of Sexuality*, 1986.
32  Forbis 1990; von Bremen 1983.
33  Recent studies of 'the city' which include such aspects are Murray and Price 1990; and Rich and Wallace–Hadrill 1991.
34  There may also have been influence from the discoveries at Pompeii. The discoveries at Ostia in the twentieth century have resulted in a different picture.
35  Hughes–Hallett 1990 discusses representations of Cleopatra in detail, with numerous plates to illustrate.
36  An analysis of such symbols and values would be useful. Cf. Bradley 1991a on *concordia* and *moderatio*.
37  This is consistent with the movement away from the Beazley approach to Athenian painted pottery.
38  There are implications in what I have been saying not only for research but for the undergraduate and postgraduate curriculum – and indeed for academic institutional structures. Postgraduate students in our field already need a wide range of skills and understanding: they will increasingly need more interdisciplinary skills, and we must help them open a dialogue with other disciplines. I would like to think that we would not only enrich our own studies in that way but would also have something to offer other disciplines as well.

# Chapter 2

# Ideology and 'the status of women' in ancient Greece

*Marilyn A. Katz*

Is a 'History of Women' possible? Does Woman exist? The first of these provocative questions was the title of a 1984 collection of essays by French feminists;[1] the second was addressed by the British feminist, Denise Riley.[2] With some exceptions, such challenges to the category of research have not disrupted the smooth surface of the study of women in antiquity, which, as Marilyn Skinner observed in 1986,[3] was incorporated readily into the field of classics and defined according to existing parameters of scholarly investigation.[4]

The dominant research question in the field, centered around the 'status' of women in ancient Athens, has, in fact, only recently been redefined fully, but without developing an adequate historiographic basis. That is to say, we now know that the status question is the wrong one, but we have not made clear why this is so, nor do we have a clear understanding of why the study of women in Greek antiquity was originally formulated around this issue. The object of this paper is to provide this missing historiography, to identify the ideological parameters that informed the constitution of the original research question, and to suggest that the new reformulation, centered around women in Greek society, must itself be modified in order to incorporate an analysis of female sexuality in ancient Greece.

I first investigate the constitution of the dominant research question in the field, under the heading of 'Patriarchy and misogyny'. I trace the origins of this question back to the late eighteenth century, and I take note of the continuing force of this paradigm. Under 'Women in civil society' I examine the ideological basis of this hegemonic discourse, arguing that it derives from the eighteenth-century debate over women's place in civil society, where the example of the women of ancient Athens served a legitimating function within a wider political framework. I conclude with a section discussing 'Recent challenges' to the traditional interpretive paradigm for the study of women in ancient Greece and the 'Future directions' of current research in the field.

## PATRIARCHY AND MISOGYNY

The hallmark of the approach I shall examine is its focus on 'woman' as a category and its preoccupation with the question of status. I have classified it under the heading of 'Patriarchy and misogyny' in order to highlight the concern with dominance and subordination which informs it throughout, but which is often hidden from view.

In a famous 1925 polemic the historian A.W. Gomme[5] described the then prevailing orthodoxy as the view that the status of women in ancient Athens in the classical period was an 'ignoble' one by comparison with their position in the Dorian states of the same period, and with that in the earlier, archaic period (89). Most contemporary discussion of the question has taken its start from this essay and from the similar chapter on 'Life and character' in Kitto's *The Greeks*.[6]

A more complete account of the common opinion of the time, however, may be gleaned from the sections on 'Die Frauen' in the second edition of Beloch's 1893 *Griechische Geschichte*.[7] The Ionians, according to Beloch, under the influence of the neighboring peoples of Asia Minor, inaugurated the exclusion of women from the public sphere and their confinement to the home and to the company of female friends. The Athenians adopted the practice from their fellow Ionians, but among non-Ionian Greeks women retained the freedom they had enjoyed in Homeric times. Prostitution – inspired by the example of the Lydians – sprang up among the Ionians as the inevitable corollary to the seclusion of well-born women, and the practice of homosexuality developed along with it (1.1: 406–408).

The Ionian practice of seclusion became more widespread in Athens during the fifth century BC, at just the time when democratic ideals of liberty were institutionalized: 'it was as if the women had wanted to devise a counterweight to their husbands' boundless strivings for freedom' (2.1: 159). Athenian men now turned to the company of hetairas ('female companions') for the female intellectual stimulation which they had 'sought at home in vain'.[8] These 'emancipated' women flourished especially among the Ionians, their aspirations toward freedom nourished by the Ionian exaltation of learning and instigated by the cloistered lives of ordinary free women (ibid.: 160).

By the fourth century, under the influence of their fathers and husbands, a few women rejected traditional roles and turned to the study of philosophy; the notion of marriage for the sake of children began to yield to an ideal of companionate union for mutual fulfillment. This development was resisted vigorously, and it gave rise to expressions of misogyny, but mostly from 'crybabies [whose] wives were too good for them'. Hetairas continued to play an important role, and functioned as companions for almost all of the important men of this period (3.1: 434).

In the Hellenistic period the lives of ordinary women remained restricted, and hetairas retained a prominence in Athens which was later transferred to Alexandria. But the hetaira in her role as symbol of female emancipation was eclipsed by a new type of woman – the Hellenistic queen of the Macedonian and Alexandrian realms (4.1: 416–420).[9] The example of her life of complete freedom within the court influenced the Greek world at large, leading to such developments as the extension of citizenship rights (proxeny), the institutionalization of education for women, the possibility of un-accompanied travel abroad, and the refinement of manners in social intercourse between the sexes.

This was, then, the 'orthodoxy' on the status of women in ancient Athens which prevailed in the early twentieth century and which Gomme was concerned to challenge. But how did it come into being, and on the basis of what evidence? In my search for an answer this question, I came across a long essay by a classical scholar who was prominent in his time, but who has been remembered since primarily as the editor of various Hellenistic Greek texts.

This man was Friedrich Jacobs who, in a long essay on 'The History of the Female Sex' published in 1830, challenged, in terms similar to those of Gomme, what he regarded as the prevailing orthodoxy on the matter of women's status among the ancient Greeks.[10] Jacobs remarked that in his own time this question was a debated issue:

> Some have regarded women's position in Greece as demeaned, in the manner characteristic of barbarians; others have disputed this interpretation; and a third group thinks that the housewife was little esteemed and loved, but that hetairas by contrast, because of their education, enjoyed love and respect.
>
> (161)

Jacobs divides his own treatment of the issue into an introductory section on marriage, followed by a discussion of 'The Greek woman', and concludes with a lengthy section on 'The hetairas'.

In disputing the claim that ancient Greek, and especially Athenian, women were regarded with contempt, secluded, uneducated (with the exception of the hetairas), and unfree and unequal until the advent of Christianity (228), Jacobs cites evidence of 'Christian' sentiments among the pagans, and expressions of misogyny by the Church fathers. Thus, he argues, the disparagement of women was no more characteristic of pagan thinking than was their high regard inherent in Christianity. Jacobs goes on to discuss Homer and Hesiod, characterizing the *Odyssey* as 'a love song to Penelope' (234), and arguing in general that the archaic picture gives us representations of both good and bad women. If the latter predominate in Hesiod, this has to do both with the poet's view of life, in which evil predominates over good, and with 'the nature of things', rather than with 'a contempt for the gender predominating in his time' (241). It is in 'the nature of things', Jacobs argues, that as long as there are two sexes there will be two kinds of women, but praise of the good woman will be remarked less frequently than blame of the bad (229, 242).

Concerning the claim that women in ancient Greece were secluded and uneducated, Jacobs argues that restriction to home life was a matter of custom rather than law (254, 273), and that similar practices have been the rule all over western Europe up to the present time. Furthermore, if seclusion originated in the Orient, it was nonetheless consistent with Christian belief and practice, albeit in a milder form (255). The housebound life of the Athenian matron, and the tradition, attested to in Thucydides, of silence about even her virtues, means that we have little evidence about women's education. But girls' training was in all likelihood entrusted to their mothers who instructed them in the domestic arts and 'womanly wisdom'; and their education was completed by their husbands, as Hesiod and, above all, Xenophon make clear (248ff.).

Overall, Jacobs insists, the Greek woman's intelligence and moral sensibility was sufficiently developed so that she was not an object of her husband's contempt (251), and he cites Xenophon's *Oeconomicus* in defense of his claim that the Athenian wife was regarded with respect (205–206). While recognizing the existence of a misogynistic and antimarriage tradition,[11] he nevertheless concludes that the ancient Greeks, in Athens and elsewhere, recognized the moral worth of wives and marriage and honored the 'sanctity' of this union (314).

The interpretive framework which guides Jacobs's judgments on ancient Greek women is set forth in his first chapter, 'A general view of marriage', in which he defends the general proposition that marriage is ideally a social institution representing 'a union and inter-penetration of the physical and moral strivings of human nature' which finds its fullest and most complete realization in society at large, but whose first elements are represented by the marital union (165–166). To the man belongs the right of rule, derived from the fact of his physical and intellectual superiority, and to the woman, on account of her sense for order and beauty, as well as her capacity for detail, belongs both 'the authority and duty to execute the laws set down by the man' (167–168). And he concludes: 'it is a general rule that it is proper for the woman to obey the man' (187).

If one compares the premises and conclusions of Jacobs's essay with those of Gomme and Kitto, the similarities are striking. All agree that, as Gomme puts it, 'Athenian society was, in the main, of the normal European type'.[12] Jacobs would not have disputed Gomme's contention that 'there is no reason to suppose that in the matter of the social consequence and freedom of women Athens was different from other Greek cities, or the classical from the Homeric age' (Gomme 1937: 114). And Jacobs would have subscribed to Gomme's view that 'Greek theory and practice [did not] differ fundamentally from the average . . . prevailing in mediaeval and modern Europe' (115). Gomme claims, 'when Theognis said, "I hate a woman who gads about and neglects her home", I think he expressed a sentiment common to most people of all ages' (115). This is similar to Jacobs's comments on a fragment of Menander in which a husband admonishes his gadabout wife that the courtyard door is the customary limit of a free-born woman's realm: 'in Berlin and Vienna, in Paris and London a husband in such a situation would say to his wife: "within the limits of your house your tongue may have free reign; beyond the door your realm ends"'.[13]

Kitto remarks, '[t]he Athenian had his faults, but preeminent among his better qualities were lively intelligence, sociability, humanity, curiosity. To say that he habitually treated one-half of his own race with indifference, even contempt, does not, to my mind, make sense'.[14] Jacobs found the view that ancient Greek women were tolerated only as a necessary evil, and that romantic love was directed only toward the educated hetaira, similarly incredible:

such is the harshness then, with which, it is claimed, the stronger sex exercised its mastery; such is the ignominy that the weaker sex tolerated in a land which we have been accustomed from childhood to revere as the cradle of culture, among a people whom we have learned to regard as the patrons of all that is beautiful, great and masterful.[15]

The so-called 'orthodoxy' on the question of women's status among the ancient Greeks, then, was already dominant in the early nineteenth century when Jacobs argued against it. And there is a striking continuity in both the tone and the terms in which the argument against the orthodoxy of women's seclusion in ancient Athens was formulated over the course of the century that lies between Jacobs and Gomme. I shall suggest in what follows that this continuum is even longer, stretching across the two hundred years from 1796 to 1971 and beyond. But we must first still attempt to answer the question I posed above: how did the orthodoxy itself come into being, and on the basis of what evidence?

Jacobs in 1830 was concerned, at the most general level, to refute the contention of Christoph Meiners that 'Homer makes it incontestably clear that women in the earlier period were as little regarded as in the later, and no less secluded [then] than later', a notion which Meiners explained on the basis of a postulated kinship between Greeks and Slavs.[16] Jacobs regarded as similarly misguided Thöluck's idea that 'the female sex, whose status among the pagans was low, was first through Christendom accorded a human dignity similar to that of men' (224). And he objected as well to de Pauw's claim 'that the hetairas, who were accustomed to attend the schools of the philosophers, were infinitely better educated than the women of standing, who perhaps never spoke [their] language correctly' (246), and to Böttiger's contention 'that Athenian men kept their wives secluded; that this was a dominant custom; that Athenian women sighed under "oriental harem-slavery"' (224).

Karl August Böttiger, who served as director of the Museum of Antiques in Dresden in the early nineteenth century, was also one of the first classical scholars of the modern period. In one of his earliest contributions to the genre of classical scholarship, 'Were Athenian Women Spectators at Dramatic Festivals?',[17] Böttiger took the opportunity to address the question of women's status in ancient Greece overall, and to do so with reference to what he called 'das neumodische right of Women [sic]', citing Mary Wollstonecraft.

He argued that the question of women's attendance at dramatic performances should be addressed from within the framework of the Greeks' general practice of secluding their women and confining them 'to oriental harem-slavery'.[18] Böttiger thus became the first classical scholar to articulate the 'negative' view which achieved canonical status in the nineteenth century – namely, that ancient Greek women were in general less well off than their modern counterparts.

Böttiger's views on women in Greece and Rome were subsequently popularized in a historical novel, *Sabina, or Morning Scenes in the Dressing-Room of a Wealthy Roman Lady* (Leipzig 1806), through which he became the founder of the genre of 'antique domestic literature'.[19] His novel was adapted to the Greek situation in 1840 by Wilhelm Adolf Becker, who in *Charicles* recounts the adventures of an Athenian youth of the same name who, in the waning years of the fourth century BC, having been ensnared as an adolescent by a hetaira in Corinth, goes on as a young adult to marry the young and beautiful heiress, Cleobule.

Becker appended to *Charicles* an excursus on 'The Women', in which he acknowledged that

> a variety of views have been entertained on the social position of the Greek women, and their estimation in the eyes of the men. The majority of scholars have described them as despicable in the opinion of the other sex, their life as a species of slavery, and the gynaeconitis [women's quarters] as a place of durance little differing from the Oriental harem; while a few writers have stoutly contended for the historic emancipation of the fair sex among the Greeks.
>
> (462)

While arguing overall that 'the truth lies between the contending parties', Becker goes on to defend, on the basis of an extensive consideration of the evidence from the poets, orators, and philosophers, and from vase-paintings as well, the view that the women of the classical period 'were less respected and more restrained [than in the heroic era], and that the marriage relationship was less tender and endearing' (462).

Becker's picture, although tempered in many cases by qualifications, may be summarized as follows: in the classical period

> the women were regarded as a lower order of beings, neglected by nature in comparison with man, both in point of intellect and

heart; incapable of taking part in public life, naturally prone to evil, and fitted only for propagating the species and gratifying the sensual appetites of the men.

(463)

The only *arete* [virtue] of which woman was thought capable . . . differed but little from that of a faithful slave.

(464)

[Women's] education from early childhood corresponded to the rest of their treatment . . . their whole instruction was left to the mother and the nurses, through whose means they obtained, perhaps, a smattering *en grammasi* [of letters], and were taught to spin and weave, and similar female avocations. . . . Hence there were no scientific or even learned ladies, with the exception of the hetaerae.

(465)

The gynaeconitis, though not exactly a prison, nor yet an ever-locked harem, was still the confined abode allotted, for life, to the female portion of the household.

(465)

Marriage, in reference to the procreation of children, was considered by the Greeks as a necessity enforced by their duties to the gods, to the state, and to their ancestors. . . . Until a very late period, at least, no higher considerations attached to matrimony, nor was strong attachment a frequent cause of marriage. . . . Sensuality was the soil from which . . . passion sprung, and none other than a sensual love was acknowledged between man and wife.

(473)

As to the wife's household duties: 'the province of the wife was the management of the entire household, and the nurture of the children; of the boys until they were placed under a master, of the girls till marriage' (490). At another point, he notes: 'still it is an unquestionable fact that in many cases the wife was in reality the ruling power in the house, whether from her mental superiority, domineering disposition, or amount of dower' (493). Becker concludes with a consideration of the 'double standard': 'the law imposed the duty of continence in a very unequal manner' (494), noting that 'infidelity in the wife was judged most sharply', and that the law required an adulterous wife to be divorced (494).

This is, then, the nineteenth-century orthodoxy on the status of women in ancient Greece, formulated on the basis of an extensive consideration of the evidence. The matter was, of course, far from settled. In the second half of the nineteenth century and in the first half of the twentieth, articles, dissertations, and monographs on the subject of women's status proliferated, and a complete bibliography on the topic for this century would run to more than fifty items.

I shall argue that beneath both the question of women's emancipation in ancient Greece and that of their purported seclusion we can detect the operation of a specific politico-philosophical framework. The lineaments of this ideological perspective, however, particularly in the years after 1850, have most often lain hidden from view. This, I suggest, is because, once the orthodoxy gained widespread currency, its origins in a specific philosophical discourse were ignored, and the scholarly dispute was conducted on the basis of its particulars. Before proceeding to a discussion of this framework, however, I want to turn my attention to some works by the current generation of scholars in the field of women's studies in Greek antiquity.

Pomeroy's 1975 *Goddesses, Whores, Wives and Slaves* was the first full-length study of this generation to take the question of women in antiquity seriously as a scholarly issue. In the decades immediately preceding, in the anglophone world at any rate, the discussion had degenerated into a succession of articles repeating Gomme's arguments of 1925 and upholding his views, always with the same reassurances that 'the attitude toward women among the Athenians was much the same as among ourselves',[20] and sometimes with patronizing references to 'a healthy strain of misogyny and misogamy running through Greek literature' or 'a quite normal measure of husbandly jealousy' on the part of Athenian men, defended as reasonable on the basis of ancient Greek women's supposed sexual licentiousness.[21] Otherwise, research on women had become confined to the dissection of the minutiae of quotidian reality, in a manner reminiscent of Plato's remarks about women's familiarity with 'weaving and watching over rising cakes and boiling pots' (*Republic* 5.455c), or of Böttiger's study on the use of pocket-handkerchiefs by Greek ladies.[22]

Pomeroy divided her treatment of women in ancient Greece into a discussion of the female divinities of the Olympian pantheon, followed by chapters on women in the Homeric period, in the Archaic

Age (800–500 BC), and a section on women in ancient Athens, divided into chapters on women in Greek law, private life, and images of women in literature. As the chapter headings indicate, Pomeroy did not call into question the historiographic validity of the category 'woman', nor did other scholars in the field who took up research on this subject. In the discipline of history, by contrast, Natalie Zemon Davis had suggested already in 1976 that 'we should be interested in the history of both women and men, [and] we should not be working only on the subjected sex any more than a historian of class can focus exclusively on peasants'.[23] But in the field of classics, surveys conceptualized similarly to that of Pomeroy have continued to appear and now exist in the major European languages.[24]

Pomeroy did, however, raise a number of important questions about how to conceptualize the study of women, and some of these have continued to dominate discussions of theory and methodology in classics. First, she noted the presence of male bias or of the masculine point of view in many of the sources, both primary and secondary. This indisputable fact about ancient sources – of material authored by women we have only the fragments of a few women poets – has even led to the recommendation that the study of women in antiquity be refocused away from literature to culture more generally, on the grounds that 'the study of women in ancient literature is the study of men's views of women and cannot become anything else'.[25]

The notion that texts authored by men represent a 'male' point of view is widely shared.[26] This idea, however, not only introduces an artificial distinction between text and culture, but also implicitly relegates women to an entirely passive role in patriarchal society – a view which could hardly be substantiated with reference to our own culture, and which is furthermore easily discredited through the comparative study of women in contemporary traditional, patriarchal societies.[27]

Second, Pomeroy took note of the tendency in the scholarly literature to 'treat women as an undifferentiated mass', without introducing distinctions having to do with 'different economic and social classes' and with 'categories of [citizenship]' (that is, full citizens, resident aliens, and slaves).[28] This was often, but by no means always the case. Radermacher, for example, had specifically remarked that his conclusions applied only to citizen women, and that women of the lower classes lived a very different kind of life.[29] And the debate overall, as we have seen, was generally constructed with reference to a status difference between hetairas (non-citizens) and legitimate wives. In addition, almost no information survives on women of other classes, and it is this that accounts for the absence of studies discussing them in the scholarly literature. But in any case, the historiographical difficulties in writing the history of women are not met simply by accounting for the factor of class or status, as the following discussion will show.

Finally, when addressing herself to the question of 'the dispute over status', Pomeroy argued that 'the wide divergence of scholarly opinion' resulted from 'the genre of the evidence consulted'.[30] The same argument informed an essay by Just published in the same year, who remarked that 'the real basis of the divergence of opinion is, however, an evidential one', and was subsequently taken up by Gould in 1980 who, despite his recognition that 'the explanation . . . is largely a matter of methodology', goes on to discuss women in classical Athens under the traditional rubrics, law, and custom/ myth.[31]

I argued against this view in 1976, suggesting instead that 'the shifting currents of opinion' should be attributed to the influence of ideology, namely that 'behind the debate on women's status in Athens there can be detected an apologia both for the patriarchal bias of modern society and for the liberal pretensions of the ancient and modern democratic ideal'.[32] As the present study makes clear, I continue to subscribe to that view, believing now, however, that a less simplistic understanding of ideology and its functions must be applied to the question. In addition, it is even clearer now, as I also argued in 1976, that radically different assessments of the same material abound in the literature and indeed continue to proliferate.

To cite just two examples from current literature: Eva Keuls, in *The Reign of the Phallus*, assembles a formidable array of evidence to demonstrate that:

'In the case of a society dominated by men who sequester their wives and daughters, denigrate the female role in reproduction, erect monuments to male genitalia, have sex with the sons of their peers, sponsor public whorehouses, create a mythology of rape, and engage in rampant saber-rattling, it is not inappropriate to refer to a reign of the phallus. Classical Athens was such a society.[33]

Mary Lefkowitz, by contrast, finds that '[Greek] myth portrays marriage and motherhood, with all the difficulties they involve, as the best conditions most women desire, and in which women can be best respected by society and happiest in themselves', and goes on to suggest that 'Greek men may not have been so concerned with repressing women as protecting them.'[34]

The question of women's status in ancient Athens, then, as well as the character and interpretation of their 'seclusion', continues to be debated in the scholarly literature,[35] and surveys on women in ancient Greece continue to appear, as noted above. But the question of the historiographic adequacy of the category 'woman' has not been addressed by classicists in the anglophone world. I raised it myself tentatively, in 1982,[36] concluding that 'the problem . . . is not so much that we are coming up with the wrong answers as that we are asking the wrong questions'.[37]

But it was Pauline Schmitt-Pantel who first posed the question in a trenchant and challenging manner, in her contribution to the 1984 volume edited by Perrot, *Une histoire des femmes est-elle possible?* In her essay, Schmitt-Pantel contended that 'an assessment of the last ten years' great profusion of studies demonstrates, in my view, that any treatment of Greek women as an isolated category leads to a method-ological impasse'.[38] I shall return to Schmitt-Pantel's discussion of the *sortie* from this impasse (p. 36). But now I want to turn to the histo-riographic issue which she raised, and which has only recently been theorized adequately for the field of Greek antiquity.

Josine Blok in 1987[39] and Beate Wagner-Hasel in 1988 and 1989[40] both argued that, in Blok's words, 'the 19th century provided the paradigm that was to define inquiry on women in antiquity until far into the 20th century'.[41] Blok's analysis is important; it deserves further discussion and debate from the perspective of the historiog-raphy of woman as a category in history. But her interpretation is insufficiently particularized to the specifics of the history of women in Greek antiquity to make it useful in the present context.

In this respect Wagner-Hasel's recent interventions – based on her 1980 Berlin dissertation[42] – are more compelling, in that they are organized around a specific critique of the nineteenth-century oppo-sition between the public and private spheres and its applicability to the ancient Greek social order. I want to draw attention here in partic-ular to a remark that Wagner-Hasel makes in passing and on which she does not expand: the debate over the status of women in ancient Greece, she says, 'is not only an attempt to reconstruct a bygone way of life, it is also a discourse over woman's place in modern bourgeois society which had its beginnings in the Enlightenment and has continued up until the present time'.[43]

## WOMEN IN CIVIL SOCIETY

In recent years, feminist political scientists like Carole Pateman[44] and Susan Moller Okin[45] have argued that the theory of the liberal democratic state, the study of which has flourished recently in mainstream political science, has remained unaffected by feminist theory. This is not to say that 'women's issues' have not been addressed. But, as Pateman notes, 'the underlying assumption is that questions which have been taken up as "women's issues" can be embraced and incorporated into mainstream theory'.[46] She goes on to argue that feminist theory introduces a new and challenging perspective into this discourse. For 'feminism does not, as is often supposed, merely add something to existing theories and modes of argument'.[47] Rather, feminist theory demonstrates that 'a repressed problem lies at the heart of modern political theory – the problem of patriarchal power[48] or the government of women by men'.[49]

To be more specific, classical social contract theory, on which the contemporary theory of civil society is based, is founded on the Lockian premise of freedom and equality as a birthright. This birthright constitutes men as individuals possessing a natural political right, and 'as "individuals" all men are owners, in that they all own the property in their persons and capacities over which they alone have right of jurisdiction'.[50] These free and equal individuals form a political association through a social contract which establishes obligations and to whose authority its members accede by means of their consent to be governed.

Women, by contrast, are understood to agree to subordinate themselves to their husbands, a subjection which has 'a Foundation in Nature',[51] and though husband and wife 'have but one common Concern; . . . it being necessary that the last Determination, *i.e.* the Rule, should be placed somewhere, it naturally falls to the Man's share as the abler and stronger'.[52] As Pateman observes:

> the contradiction between the premise of individual freedom and equality, with its corollary of the conventional basis of authority, and the assumption that women (wives) are naturally subject has . . . gone unnoticed. . . . [Yet] if women are naturally subordinate . . . then talk of their consent or agreement to this status is redundant.[53]

Locke did not specifically theorize women's subordination, but Rousseau's theory of the social contract, based on the premise that man, in passing from the state of nature to civil society, loses his natural liberty but gains both civil liberty and moral freedom,[54] did explicitly justify it. Rousseau, who like other Enlightenment thinkers, as Wagner-Hasel says, 'developed the theoretical foundations for the interrelationship between ancient and modern democracy, and regarded as their models Attic generals like Pericles or Roman Senators of Cicero's kind',[55] modeled his 'people's assembly' on the *comitia tributa* ('tribal' or popular assembly) of the ancient Romans, drawing certain additional features from the constitution of the Spartans.

Rousseau generally regarded ancient Sparta as 'the example that we ought to follow'.[56] But in *Emile*, published, along with *The Social Contract*, in 1762, it was classical Athens that provided the paradigm for the incorporation of women into the ideal state. There, Rousseau expanded upon arguments that he had first advanced in the 1758 'Letter to M. d'Alembert on the Theatre', where he remarked that 'the ancients had, in general, a very great respect for women'.[57] And he explained in more detail:

> Among all the ancient civilized peoples [women] led very retired lives; they did not have the best places at the theatre; they did not put themselves on display; they were not even always permitted to go; and it is well known that there was a death penalty for those who dared to show themselves at the Olympic games. In the home, they had a private apartment where the men never entered. When their husbands entertained for dinner, they rarely presented themselves at the table; the decent women went out before the end of the meal, and the others never appeared at the beginning. There was no common place of assembly for the two sexes; they did not pass the day together. This effort not to become sated with one another made their meetings more pleasant. It is certain that domestic peace was, in general, better established and that greater harmony prevailed between man and wife than is the case today.[58]

Among others, Mary Wollstonecraft, in *A Vindication of the Rights of Woman* (1792), argued against Rousseau's views. There she insisted that the confinement of women's instruction to such frivolities as Rousseau had envisioned, would produce 'weak beings . . . only fit for a seraglio!'[59]

The question of women's status in ancient Greece, and of the extent and meaning of their 'seclusion', then, did not originate in the nineteenth century, nor was it raised first by scholars of classical antiquity. Rather, as the above citations indicate, it formed part of the intellectual currency of the eighteenth century, and played an important role in the general debate over the form and nature of civil society. (Böttiger, as we saw on p. 26, cited Wollstonecraft less than admiringly when he first turned his attention to the question of women's status in ancient Greece.) Furthermore, some of the specific terms of this discourse were set in the eighteenth century. Rousseau, for example, had remarked in 1758 that women in the ancient world were 'respected' and that this was connected with their having led 'very retired lives'. What is more, the formulation of the question itself relied on a certain circular logic: Rousseau in 1758 cited the example of women in ancient Athens to substantiate his views on women's nature; Jacobs in 1830 relied on the eighteenth-century view of women's nature to authenticate his interpretation of the ancient evidence.

## RECENT CHALLENGES AND FUTURE DIRECTIONS

It is only in the last ten years or so that the 'status' model has been challenged as a research paradigm, and this has been achieved principally by introducing a discontinuity between the ancient conception of the relationship between *polis* (city-state) and *oikos* (household) and the analogous modern distinction between 'public' and 'private'. The landmark 1979 study on the question, Sally Humphreys's '*Oikos* and *Polis*', treats the opposition in Athenian society and culture overall, showing that such modern distinctions as that between the political and economic spheres are misleading when applied to ancient Athens. Humphreys forgoes discussion of women's status as such, but treats aspects of women's incorporation in and exclusion from the functioning of the sociocultural totality. In addition, she makes the important observation that 'the separation of men and women in social life meant that in a sense the public world of the city reached into the house'.[60]

Others have followed Humphreys's lead. Beate Wagner–Hasel, in an equally important 1982 full-scale study of women in early Greek society, proceeds from the premise that 'the first question of determining the status of the particular members of a society must always be [constituted] first as the question of the character of this society itself – its social, political, and economic structure'.[61]

Both Humphreys and Wagner–Hasel emphasize the importance of applying ethnographic and anthropological models to the study of ancient Greece, and in 1981 and 1982 I used analogies drawn from the anthropology of contemporary traditional Mediterranean societies to redraw the conceptualization of women in ancient Greece under the heading of 'a divided world'.[62]

Helene Foley in 1981 drew attention to the inadequacy of interpreting ancient Greek tragedy in accordance with a concept of *oikos* and *polis* as equivalent either to nature and culture or private and public, and proposed a reading overall in which *oikos* and *polis* 'are mutually defining institutions; order in one sphere is inextricably related to order in the other'.[63] Froma Zeitlin, in an important 1985 study, extended the analysis of Greek drama to embrace the generation of the categories 'masculine' and 'feminine'.[64] And Giulia Sissa has carried out an investigation of the construction of sexual difference in the philosophical works of Plato and Aristotle.[65]

The study of women in antiquity, then, has evolved over the last ten years or so from 'the history of women' to the 'history of gender', as Schmitt–Pantel has observed, adding that the concepts 'sexual asymmetry, social relations between the sexes, and gender' now serve as the 'basis for further progress'.[66] But there are other dimensions to this history which are not adequately comprehended through the reorientation around the newer categories. I am referring in particular to questions regarding the constitution of the self, or, more specifically, the constitution of the gendered or sexual self.

These questions in the field of classics have been addressed recently by scholars working within two separate subfields, those of ancient Greek medicine and ancient Greek sexuality.[67] Ancient Greek and Roman medical writers discussed the matter of female physiology at great length, and in a series of gynecological treatises developed an extensive discourse on the subject of the female body. Some aspects of their theories – for example, Galen's notion that the female reproductive structure was equivalent to that of the male turned outside in – survived into the Renaissance and served as the basis for theories of human physiology which remained unchallenged until the late eighteenth century.[68]

The Graeco–Roman medical writers, however, concerned themselves almost exclusively with the reproductive aspects of female physiology. As Ann Hanson observes, even when they acknowledge the existence of female orgasm, the medical writers' concern is with its relation to the woman's capacity to conceive: 'the Hippokratic gynecologies center attention not on woman's desire or pleasure, but on whether or not she has taken up the seed'.[69]

Recent discussions of ancient Greek sexuality have centered on male sexuality, and in particular on questions having to do with the character of male homosexuality in ancient Greece.[70] This work has given rise to a lively debate on whether there exists a discontinuity between 'the Greeks and us' in the conceptualization of sexuality, and on whether Greek culture, like our own, constructed a distinction between 'homosexuals' and 'heterosexuals'.[71]

The issue is itself a historiographic one, formulated principally around Halperin's contention that the category 'homosexual' was itself a product of the late nineteenth-century discourse on sexual pathology. But the matter of woman's sexual desire and the question of female erotics have, by and large, received little attention, in this or other literature.[72]

What is, in fact, the nature of women's *eros*? And what was the character of female sexuality in Greek antiquity? The answers to these questions remain an unfinished project for the study of women in ancient Greece.[73] To undertake it would require both a historiography of the question and a consideration of ancient Greek laws on adultery and of ancient conceptualizations of such phenomena as prostitution, rape, and pornography. Some important new research in these areas has appeared, for example, Cohen's chapters on adultery,[74] Zeitlin's and Scafuro's essays on rape in Greek myth,[75] and a new volume on pornography edited by Richlin.[76] But a full discussion that takes into account distinctions between our own notions and those of the Greeks awaits formulation.

It has been the overall point of this section to argue that our own understanding of sexuality and of the difference between the sexes has been critically mediated by the nineteenth- and twentieth-century discourses on this same subject. Thus, however much the ancients may appear to resemble or anticipate us, in this as in other areas, such as their notions of 'woman's place', they were also working within a radically different cultural framework which has been illegitimately assimilated to our own. And it is, therefore, no less important to the project of understanding our own values than to that of comprehending theirs that we reconstruct the divide which separates the 'Greeks' *from* 'us'.

Such a project would require also that we reconstruct the point at which the history of the construction of sex and sexuality intersected with that of the construction of race. From the perspective of the history of women in ancient Greece, that point is marked by Meiners' coinage of the term 'oriental seclusion' to characterize the condition of the women of ancient Greece. Meiners, in his *History of the Female Sex*,[77] published 1788–1800, found that the ancient Greeks, who 'in certain respects so nearly resembled the most spirited and magnanimous nations of our division of the globe', seem more like Slavons or Orientals: 'in other points, and especially in its general conduct to the sex, and its laws concerning women, [the Greeks] appeared much more closely allied to the Orientals and to the Slavonic nations of Europe' (1: 260).

The metaphor of the seraglio or harem originated in the seventeenth century, developed a widespread currency in the eighteenth century, and forms part of the general history of what Edward Said has called 'Orientalism'.[78] Thus, when Mary Wollstonecraft, in her discussion in 1792 of women's education, referred to the 'seraglio', she was drawing on an idea that was current in the popular culture of the time. Its application to the condition of the women of ancient Greece continues to be debated,[79] but it is now generally discussed under the heading of 'seclusion'.

The very term 'oriental seclusion', however, should have warned us against attempting to interpret it outside the ideological context in which it arose – a context which cannot be eliminated simply by dropping the adjective and referring to 'seclusion' instead, as we have all been inclined to do, in recognition of the now embarrassing overtones of the phrase. But adjustments in usage, while salutary from a political point of view, also constitute evasions from the historiographic perspective.

Thus, an adequate historiography of the history of women in ancient Greece would require that we discuss the formulation of the question of women's seclusion in ancient Athens in the light of the history of Orientalism generally, taking note of such issues as its origin in the linguistic theories of the time, and its subsequent evolution, in the late eighteenth and nineteenth centuries, into a generalized theory of racial difference. Such an investigation would also reveal an important further historical point of intersection – between the theories of racial and sexual difference – on the basis of which the theory of sexual pathology was constructed in the late nineteenth century.[80]

Recent challenges to the 'status' model, then, have served to redefine and reorient a research paradigm which, as I have attempted to demonstrate, is now almost two hundred years old. The new directions in research that have been marked out offer the promise of adding important new dimensions to our understanding of the ancient Greeks' cultural particularity. But much remains to be done in order to integrate this new history with the old, and to redefine and reformulate the character of the continuities and discontinuities which both connect and separate them.

## SUMMARY AND CONCLUSIONS

The burden of this paper has been, first, to show that the question of women's status in ancient Greece has continued to be addressed in contemporary scholarship in much the same terms as it was formulated in the nineteenth century. Scholars generally, even when they have acknowledged this history in long and ponderous footnotes, have generally stopped at this point, availing themselves of what I shall call the 'European seclusion theory' – the notion that their nineteenth-century predecessors developed the foundations of classical scholarship alone in their studies with their books. (One need only think here of the frontispieces frequently prefacing biographies, depicting the scholar poring over his voluminous tomes in solitary concentration.) In the second section, I have attempted to demonstrate that the formulation of the question of women's status in ancient Greece has a far more complex history, and that its terms were intimately bound up with the eighteenth-century discourse on freedom, the individual, and civil society.

This history is well known, but within the field of classics it is generally relegated to the subdiscipline known as the history of the classical tradition or the classical heritage.[81] Within this framework, not only are the ideological specifics of the tradition widely overlooked,[82] as Martin Bernal has made clear,[83] but the discussion of women and their history is largely left out of account, except where it touches on themes having to do with Greek mythology and religion.

What I have tried to show, with reference to the study of women in antiquity, is that its history and historiography are in fact constituted through a complex intersection between classical scholarship and the classical tradition, and that this interpenetration was itself significantly conditioned by the contemporary discussions on language, nationalism, and race. To evaluate this history properly, we must take into account, therefore, not only Rousseau's reading of antiquity, but such further considerations as his contribution to the formation of political theory, and the contemporary rereading and critique of his influence.[84] Furthermore, the exemption of women from civil society in political theory should be understood, not only in terms of the perseverance of patriarchy and a motivated nostalgia for the ancient Greek past, but within the context of eighteenth-century medical inquiry, its rereading of the ancient theory of biology, and its eventual intersection in the nineteenth century with the discourse on language, race, and nationality.

It should be clear that what has interested me here is not the history of ideas, although I do regard it as important to know that a certain continuity can be found among the ideas of, for example, Rousseau, Jacobs, and A. W. Gomme, and that this continuity is based on a shared notion, inherited from the eighteenth century, of women's proper sphere and its correlation with their 'nature'. Rather, I have been concerned to make clear how the terms of the discussion themselves came into being, and to identify their ideological valences.

Thus, from the historiographic point of view, there is not a 'history of women' as such. But there is a history of women in society, as Wagner-Hasel and others have shown, and there is also a history of the gendered individual, as recent studies on sexuality in ancient Greece have demonstrated. In this paper, I have concentrated on the history of the history of women, which, as I have argued, still awaits reconstruction in its fullest particulars. This can only be achieved, not by dismissing as outdated what has gone before, but by exposing the ideological foundations of a hegemonic discourse that has dominated the discussion of ancient women and that continues to make its powerful influence felt in the discussion of women generally as part of civil society at the present moment in history.

## NOTES

1  Perrot 1984.
2  Riley 1988.
3  Skinner 1987.
4  I have not attempted to be comprehensive in this paper: some books or articles are discussed in detail; many other important items are omitted altogether. My discussion is restricted to works that I consider representative of the principal analytic approaches and that are useful for demonstrating the theoretical and ideological premises of the various interpretive methods.
5  Gomme, 1925, here cited from the 1937 reprint.
6  Kitto 1951.
7  Beloch 1912–1925, 2nd edn, here cited from the 2nd edn as follows: 1.1, Strasbourg 1912; 2.1, Strasbourg 1914; 3.1, Berlin 1922; 4.1 Berlin 1925.

8  The term is the feminine of *hetairos* meaning 'companion'; the Greek plural is *hetairai*, sometimes Latinized to *hetaerae*. Gomme 1937: 105 suggests the translation '*demi-mondaine*'; and Beloch renders *hetairai* as 'Damen der Halbwelt' (3.1: 434).

9  For the most recent discussion of these women, see Pomeroy 1984.

10  Jacobs 1830.

11  See especially his discussion of Meiners, 1830: 206–210.

12  Gomme 1937: 99, n. 2.

13  Jacobs 1830: 264. Compare Gomme's statements about this same fragment, 1937: 99.

14  Kitto 1951: 222.

15  Jacobs 1830: 243–244.

16  ibid.: 224. I discuss briefly the 'racial' aspects of Meiners's formulations on p. 38.

17  Originally published in 1796, reprinted 1837.

18  ibid.: 295. On the concept of 'oriental harem-slavery,' see p. 38.

19  According to Frederick Metcalfe, in the 'Translator's preface' to Becker 1866: vii. All subsequent citations of *Charicles* are from this translation.

20  Hadas 1936: citation p. 100; cf. Shero 1932; Seltman 1955; Richter 1971.

21  Richter, 1971: 5, 7. Cf. Richter's view that 'the young wives [of ancient Athens] were as undisciplined a bevy of nymphs as Hellas ever reared', ibid.: 7.

22  An exception to this general rule was the study of women's status in ancient law, which the nature of the subdiscipline obliged scholars to discuss in a wider sociocultural context.

23  Davis 1976: citation p. 90.

24  Mossé 1983; Cantarella 1987; Schuller 1985; Clark 1989; Just 1989 (1991).

25  Culham 1986: citation p. 15.

26  For example, Just 1975: esp. 154, and 1989 (1991): 4; Gould 1980: esp. 38.

27  Cf. Nicole–Claude Matthieu's critique of the anthropologist Edwin Ardener's notion of women as a 'muted group' (Ardener 1975a (1972)), and of the biological essentialism implied by the concept: 'there is no "autonomous female way of seeing"; there is no woman's way of seeing on the one hand and man's way of seeing on the other; there is only that of the society as a whole': Matthieu 1973: citation p. 112. Both Just and Gould draw freely on Ardener in constructing their own analytic paradigms.

28  Pomeroy 1975: 60.

29  Radermacher 1928: 16.

30  Pomeroy 1975: 60.

31  Just 1975: 154, cf. 157; Gould 1980: citation p. 39.

32  Arthur (= M.A. Katz) 1976: citation p. 383.

33  Keuls 1985: 1.

34  Mary Lefkowitz, 'Epilogue', in Lefkowitz 1986: citations pp. 133, 134. Cf. also Lefkowitz 1981 *passim*.

35  For example, D. Cohen 1989; see also D. Cohen 1991c.

36  Arthur (= M.A. Katz) 1982b.

37  ibid.: 535.
38  Schmitt–Pantel 1984: 105.
39  Blok 1987, first published in Dutch in 1984.
40  Wagner–Hasel 1988, 1989.
41  Blok 1987: citation p. 2.
42  Published in a revised and expanded form as Wagner–Hasel 1982.
43  Wagner–Hasel 1989: 19.
44  Pateman 1989. For a recent discussion of Pateman's work overall in the context of political theory, see Phillips 1992.
45  Moller Okin 1979b.
46  Pateman 1989: 2.
47  ibid.: 14.
48  I shall not embark here upon a definition of the term 'patriarchy', an understanding of which, despite its widespread popular currency, requires a thoroughgoing historiographic and political analysis. For some preliminary remarks on a contrast between 'paternal' and 'fraternal' patriarchy, see Pateman 1989: 35–36.
49  ibid.: 2.
50  ibid.: 10.
51  Locke 1967: 191–192 (I.47–48).
52  ibid.: 339 (2.82).
53  Pateman 1989: 213. Cf. also her chapters, 'Women and consent' and 'Feminism and democracy', 71–89, 210–225. For a theoretical critique of John Stuart Mill's theory of sexual egalitarianism, see Moller Okin 1979a: 197–223.
54  Rousseau 1978: 64–65 (book 1, ch. 8).
55  Wagner–Hasel 1988: 26.
56  Rousseau, 'Letter to M. d'Alembert on the Theatre', in *Politics and the Arts*, trans. Allan Bloom, Glencoe, Ill. 1960: 133.
57  ibid.: 48.
58  ibid.: 88–89.
59  Wollstonecraft 1988 (1792): 10; cf. 29. On the metaphor of the seraglio or harem, see p. 38.
60  Humphreys 1983: citation p. 16. See also Humphreys 1991.
61  Wagner–Hasel 1982: 5. See also her extensive discussion of public and private spheres, their relationship to the social and economic structure of the *polis* overall, and women's roles, in ibid.: section b, 67–272.
62  In a talk presented on 3 April 1981 at Wesleyan University to the Department of History Faculty Seminar, 'Marx and History', under the title, 'Ideology and the "Status" of Women in Ancient Greece', one section of which was published as Arthur, 'Women and the Family' (1982b). For a fuller discussion, see D. Cohen 1991c: esp. 14–69.
63  Foley, 1981b: citation p. 156.
64  Zeitlin 1985. On the opposition between masculine and feminine in Greek culture, see also Schmitt-Pantel 1984: 101 and *passim*.
65  Sissa 1992.
66  Schmitt-Pantel 1992b: 464, 466.
67  For a review of recent work in these subfields, see Katz 1989.
68  For discussion, see Laqueur 1986 and 1990.

69  Hanson 1990: citation p. 315. For further discussion of this topic, see also Lloyd 1983b; and King 1989b.

70  On which see especially, in addition to the essays in, Halperin, Winkler, and Zeitlin 1990; Halperin 1992; and Winkler 1990b.

71  For some recent contributions to this debate, see D. Cohen 1991b and 1991d; Thorp 1992; Boswell 1990.

72  For some exceptions to this general pattern, see Carson 1990; Sissa 1990; and Rousselle 1988.

73  It is worth noting in this connection that, as my student Audrey Prins Patt pointed out to me recently, Scarborough 1992 omits the term clitoris (which is Greek, and which is discussed by the ancient medical writers and lexicographers) from his discussion of 'Sexual Anatomy: The "Parts" (female)'.

74  D. Cohen 1991a and e.

75  Zeitlin 1986; Scafuro 1990.

76  Richlin 1992.

77  Meiners 1788–1800; hereafter cited in the English translation by F. Shoberl, London, 1808, by volume and page number.

78  Said 1978, whose study is limited to 'the Anglo-French-American experience of the Arabs and Islam, which for almost a thousand years together stood for the Orient' (17).

79  For example, D. Cohen 1989.

80  For some preliminary discussion of these issues, see my remarks in the longer version of the present essay, Katz 1992: 86–92, and the references cited therein.

81  For example, Turner 1981.

82  Or relegated to footnotes: see, for example, the remarks on the part played by 'contemporary racial thinking' in Matthew Arnold's work, in Turner 1981: 20–21 n. 4.

83  Bernal 1987. I shall not comment on the extensive dispute to which this book has given rise, other than to say that I regard the general burden of the historiographic account as largely correct, notwithstanding the fact that Bernal has sometimes been careless with the evidence.

84  See, for example, the recent discussion by Koppelman 1992, which contrasts Susan Okin's and Allan Bloom's views on the implications of Rousseau's theory of the family to contemporary feminist debate on the place of women in the social order.

# Chapter 3

# Approaching women through myth: Vital tool or self-delusion?

*Ken Dowden*

Women in Greek mythology are of interest both to those studying the place of women, and to those studying the nature of mythology. In this paper I ask whether Greek mythology gives the former category good value: how much may we learn about Greek women on the basis of the mythological evidence? What follows is divided into three parts: in the first part I ask on what suppositions Greek mythology might be thought to tell us about women; in the second part I look at the instances of Helen and Clytaemnestra; and in the third I try to set in context the apparently more concrete data that can be assembled from mythology related to female initiation rites.

## USING GREEK MYTH

### Myth as useful tool?

Myth is not a medium of historical record for times beyond our grasp. Indeed, it is to mistake the language of myth to suppose that it directly reveals historical data, let alone events.[1] Though it is a tradition, it is predominantly fictional and ideological, not documentary. For instance, actual matriarchies are not necessitated by mythological narrations about Amazons. Their topsy-turvy society where women are warriors, situated 'outside the range of normal human experience' (Walcot 1984: 42), so far from evidencing the arbitrariness of male domination of society, expresses that domination *kat' enantion*, by opposites – like the myths of battles against Giants or Centaurs.[2] Greek society is not the only one where the myth of matriarchy belongs to 'a prior and chaotic era before the present social order was established'.[3] Nor should conclusions be drawn about 'Daily Life in the Bronze Age' from Homer's telling of the mythology (cf. Pomeroy 1975: ch. 2).

There is a special danger for the interpreter when myth presents an extreme, unthinkable in 'normal' Greek life (e.g. Amazons). This danger may even vitiate Vernant's discernment of a specific exogamous system in those myths where sets of sons are to marry sets of daughters, for instance in the case of the Danaids (and similarly other myths that seem to indicate an endogamous system).[4]

If myth is so unhelpful for history, one may understand the depressive view of myth altogether in Cameron and Kuhrt (1993: x): 'Greek historians are *forced to work* extensively with material drawn from literature and myth' (my italics). This makes it look as though myth (and literature, which, as we shall see, is sometimes nearly the same thing) is a second-rate tool used when historical information runs short. But are there other uses which make myth more than a source of last resort? Perhaps it can in some way be more useful than the documentary evidence that we don't have, if: 'Myths *illustrate common attitudes* more clearly and simply than history' (Lefkowitz 1993: 49; my italics). Why should this be so? History is unavoidably processed and ideologised – otherwise why recount it – but history is also constrained by fact and truth, where myth may tell what it wishes without such inhibitions, provided a narrative results.

Yet, however usefully myth may 'illustrate common attitudes', allegiance to it for this purpose is far from steadfast. In the new edition of their fine sourcebook, Mary Lefkowitz and Maureen Fant continue deliberately to exclude mythology (1992: xxiv). Why, if myth is so useful an illustrative tool? One problem is that myths cannot be assigned to 'specific historical contexts' (ibid.). Though myth should be useful, it is difficult to determine or exhibit its significance immediately and transparently. In any case, whose version of a myth would one set down – and would each version bear a different significance?

Nonetheless, the perception of a revelatory quality in myth can be deepened by a theoretical framework accommodating psychology and culture, as exemplified by Froma Zeitlin (1986: 124): 'Myths . . . often address those problematic areas of human experience that resist rational explanation, and they explore and express the complexity of cultural norms, values and preoccupations.' This type of statement, even if, *un petit peu*, an article of Parisian faith, does have a remarkable power to command assent. Yet there still remains a considerable difficulty. Is it possible for myths to deliver statements about women that could not have been made otherwise? Zeitlin, indeed, specifically avoids stating that myth can deliver cultural data. Myth addresses, explores, expresses the complexity of, such data, but is not claimed itself to be the source of that data.

## Variables and constants, texts and intertext

Another difficulty which emerges is that of indiscriminacy. Whose attitudes are myths held to reveal? It is surely not possible in a critical age to speak of anything so gross as 'The Role of Women in Greek Society'. Yet if Greek societies can be viewed as relatively constant and unchanging, there may even be some justification for collecting all material regardless of historical circumstances, like Lévi-Strauss, thereby composing a single portrait of the Greek mind and its ideologies. By this path, an indiscriminate collection of Greek myth would deliver an indiscriminate portrait of Greek society.

Greek myth tempts us to this view. Any material which looks so non-historical misleads us into thinking that it is somehow unaffected by exact historical circumstance, that it is supra-historical. And, true, its messages (as one might expect from a product of Greek antiquity) do consistently differ from those broadcast by our own cultures. Greek culture, despite its local variations, was perhaps more stable and homogeneous than modern North American and European society. It did after all subscribe to the epic, dramatic and artistic corpus of fictions less ambivalently than, say, Europe subscribes to American screen fiction or the values of Eurodisney. It is therefore possible to see in Greek mythology certain recurrent and characteristic social views. For instance, the categories of women visible in myth undergo a certain ideological distortion: females may be *parthenoi* (maidens) or *gynaikes* (matrons), but not unmarried women.[5] Widows, too, barely register, except maybe for the Graiai who confront Perseus – marginal, disabled, disgusting. So, elementary social data of broad application, the constants of Greek society, are embedded in myth – even if a study of the orators might deliver this information more reliably.

Yet Greek society changes over the centuries, and substantially enough to cause us hesitation. The world of New Comedy and of the unhappy loves of the Hellenistic poets (themselves intensive users of mythology) is not the world of Athenian tragedy. The women's world of classical Athens was restricted to an unusual extent. And 'democratic' Athens altogether is a different world from that of the symposia of the Archaic poets – which itself may have had a different cultural ambience from however we imagine the reception of the Epic.[6] Such variation might lead us ultimately to the secure, if slightly Pyrrhonic, position of Christiane Sourvinou-Inwood (1991: 17), that myths must first and foremost be studied through their individual realisations, through what I now describe as 'texts' whether literary or artistic:

> we must read each individual articulation of the myth as it stands; we must not import narrative elements and meanings from one mythological articulation to another, and assume that one part of a myth in a text necessarily evoked for the ancient reader . . . all the other variants.

On this view, Greek society, on a first pass, is only safely viewed as a set of variables – and clearly cases can be shown where constants fail (e.g. the anomalous Aphrodite of Locri). Myth-criticism thus becomes text-criticism and finds a corollary in the method of Mary Lefkowitz (1986: 13): 'I am not going to try to interpret myths that only survive in summary or quotation, where we cannot know or recover the emphasis in the original.' Where literary criticism is not possible, neither is myth interpretation.

Between constants and variables lies the view that Greek mythology is an intertext – an accumulated and accumulating system of narratives and perceptions which determine the interpretation of any individual text within, or added to, the collection (Dowden 1992: 7–9). This intertext and its implicit ideologies continually evolve, and every text will introduce, however minutely, a new perspective. New tellings may largely reinforce an existing ideology, but they may also contribute, like change in language, to a gradual shift in the system. This is a flexible model, even if it does contain insoluble difficulties – how to determine the rate of change, or how to know the extent to which other elements in the intertext were present for authentic ancient interpreters (= ideal readers). Sourvinou-Inwood may consider the latter difficulty too great to allow scientific treatment of myth, but she also envisages a final restoration of the concept of myth by assembling and comparing individual articulations, whose common features will then illuminate the society encompassing the variants.[7]

Without this intertextual view, a book on Amazons or on Centaurs and Amazons (as such) is not possible. For instance, although Page duBois refers to individual texts involving Centaurs, she nevertheless envisages a body of material: 'In many of the episodes *in the Centaur myth*, the horse/men sustained Ixion's hostility to legal marriage and to the forms of exchange typical to Greek civilization (1982: 28; my italics).'[8] Is this indiscriminate writing, or is this making fair use of an intertext, a constant in Greek civilisation?

This, then, is the danger of indiscriminacy: can we depart from interpretation of a particular text, with the idiosyncrasies of its time, locale and author, to something of broader and more systematic significance? Can we talk about 'the Greek Oedipus myth' – or only about Sophocles' *Oedipus Tyrannos*? About 'the Amazon myth', or only about the figure of Penthesilea in Arktinos? Or not even that, as the text of Arktinos is lost?

## Psychoanalysis – or what?

One constant that might attract our attention is that monsters are often, even usually, female (e.g. Skylla, Medusa, Echidna). We may speculate that in the construction of the fantastic, the mind reveals something of how it really works. It is one of the joys of Classics, and especially of myth, that one can range freely between disciplines: literature, history, sociology. But there is a price of shallowness and amateurism to be paid. How are we to look into 'The Greek Mind', if we do not understand as experts how to look into the modern, or any, mind? It is very easy to write about the sexual symbolism of Medusa's snaky hair and to declare that the power of turning to stone is a metaphor for the perceived power to cause impotence, but we should have more exact motives for subscribing to such ideas than that they are interesting, modern and sexual.

If we turn to psychoanalysis for our answers, we may be thinking along these lines:

1   myth gives us an insight into 'The Greek Mind';
2   psychoanalysis is the expertise, the τέχνη, of the mind;
3   Freud devised a reliable and objective science of psychoanalysis.

DuBois has questioned this way of thinking, observing that 'Freud seems to believe that antiquity recorded, undisguised, the simple unrepressed desires of mankind' (1988: 22). More precisely, Freud believed that myths, like dreams, allowed the realities of the subconscious to emerge more clearly than is possible in real life. In addition, in common with the prevailing culture of his times, he ascribed undue authority to classical material, over-privileging Greek myth in the process. Moreover, Freud's myth, as duBois (1988: chs 1–2) has rightly underlined, delivers an unchanging, absolute map of the human psyche, not Greek but universal. Simultaneously, this absolute map is constructed on the basis of the hierarchies (notably male) and complexes of 'Victorian' Vienna, superimposing an ideology above Greek myth rather than uncloaking the ideology below. The real problem with Freudian psychoanalysis is to explain why it has appeared to work clinically. As with the success of ancient oracles, one should perhaps speak of unsatisfied needs, visible authority and a product that meshed fruitfully with the fictions, ideologies and (in the broadest sense) the myths by which people live.[9]

But if we abandon a Freudian solution, what verifiable basis do we have for the analysis of the psychological presuppositions of myth? Or shall we adopt a sort of post-structuralist literary criticism of myth in which the critic perceives and the reader, if so disposed, nods in approbation? Unless there is a describable science of exposing the relationship between Greek myth (particular texts, or intertext) and local or general Greek ideologies, it is hard to know how social attitudes may be deduced from myth without circularity. It may even be that myth can *never* be the starting-point, as implied by Christiane Sourvinou–Inwood (1991: 16): 'in order to make sense of Greek myths, it is necessary to investigate a variety of questions pertaining to all aspects of the Greek world, through a variety of methodological tools and approaches'. The converse, to use myth as a tool to make sense of the Greek world, looks increasingly difficult.

Thus we reach the dilemma. Myth is a vital tool if it bears on social values more directly or more profoundly than history does; but the science of interpretation is unclear and there are serious methodological pitfalls, notably self-delusion – just getting back what you put in.

## HELEN AND CLYTAEMNESTRA

As a sample of these problems, I turn to the deductions we might make about Greek society from the figures of Helen and Clytaemnestra in Greek myth. So far as possible I consider them in their intertextual form as opposed to the individual realisations by individual authors.

### The *oikos* and the Trojan War

I start from the *oikos*, something central to Greek society, a constant. Paris removes Helen to Troy and is therefore an extreme case of an adulterer. Extreme cases are characteristic of myth. The abduction of Helen functions as the cause of the Trojan War, which is therefore in some measure about the destruction that results from the undoing of the *oikos*. Destroy the *oikos*, destroy the city? The intertext of archaic and classical Greek myth also mirrors, or recapitulates, this theme at the end of the story: Agamemnon returns home to find his *oikos* too disrupted by adultery. This adultery destroys the *kyrios*, Agamemnon. The adulteress is Helen's sister, Clytaemnestra, and their sisterhood seems innately meaningful, as in Aeschylus' *Agamemnon*.[10]

So far, a message about the destruction of the *oikos*. Yet how shall this message be phrased? Perhaps: the Greek fear (shall it be an 'obsessive' fear?) of the destruction of the *oikos*, that fundamental building-block of their society, finds expression in myths of the Trojan War and Agamemnon's *nostos*, myths which entail awful suffering, destruction of man and of city. Or is this to drive the myth too hard, to look for trouble in the Greek psyche? Perhaps in the *maggiore*: the Greek positive evaluation of their fundamental building-block, the *oikos*, is asserted by their fictions of what happens when it is destroyed.

## Clytaemnestra

What of the women in these myths? Clytaemnestra is consistently treated as faithless and faulted for embracing adultery, calling into question the view that women were viewed as passive victims of adultery.[11] This is a model of a woman who fails the requirement to support the *oikos*, as indeed some women will.

But this tells us little until we see a fuller portrait in an individual text. Perhaps we will turn to Homer's Agamemnon, who considers that there is nothing worse than a woman and that Clytaemnestra has brought disrepute upon future women, even good ones (*Odyssey* 11.427–34). Yet that is said from Agamemnon's point of view, obviously partial; even he will admit that there are good women and that Penelope is an instance of one (*Odyssey* 11.444–6). And the interest of the *Odyssey* as a whole is to talk about the *oikos* and the forces that hold society together (like *xenia*). Within the context of the *Odyssey* one of the social foundations we learn about is the value of a good woman – part of which is negative reminiscence of Clytaemnestra.

It is not an uncommon characteristic of tellings of Greek myths to highlight the distinction, plainly that made by Greek men, between good and bad women. However much the Odyssean Agamemnon might think so, the purpose of these myths is not to give the impression that women as a whole are unreliable – that is simply to repeat Aristophanes' joke in *Thesmophoriazusai* where women have it in for Euripides because of his depictions of them. Yet it is clear that this compartmentalisation of women into good and bad reflects a very limited, and to our eyes distinctive, view of their place. They are there to make an *oikos* work and the failure to do so may even be, as Aeschylus depicts it in the *Agamemnon*, to lose the claim to womanhood, to live in some sort of androgynous no-woman's land. Included among their duties is to look after the children, but there may be something derogatory about Aeschylus resting Clytaemnestra's defence on Agamemnon's slaughter of Iphigeneia: this is the instinctive bonding of the mother to the child (like a bitch with her pups),[12] and to the female child at that – without credit, because killing Iphigeneia, though a foul act, did not in itself (unlike the murder of Agamemnon) destroy the *oikos*. This is a revealing emphasis, but it is the emphasis of a text, not of the intertext, of the myth however told.

Hesiod too had distinguished between the good wife and the bad wife, dwelling rather more on the latter (*Works and Days* 702–6). But this text, like other Greek misogynistic writing, should be handled with care. Indeed it reinforces the social values of an archaic Greek male. But the work, or rather the narrator's persona, does have its own particular character which is a large part of what makes it distinctive and interesting as a literary product. The narrator is ferociously miserable, pessimistic, conservative, old-fashioned and over the top.[13] There is surely, even for archaic Greek culture, something splendidly 'blunt' about 'First of all get yourself a house, a woman, and a plough-ox' (*Works and Days* 405).

**Helen**

The intertext lays more stress on Helen's beauty than her guilt – a contrast with Clytaemnestra. But beauty was then, as now ('Samantha Fox stole my husband', an interesting comparand), a double-edged asset. Hesiod warns against the woman who talks smoothly, shows off her *derrière*, but is after your granary (*Works and Days* 373–4). Pandora too, in specially ruinous intertextuality with Helen, overflows with beauty given by Aphrodite.[14] What then are we to deduce? Greek men recognised that their judgement could be distorted by sexual attraction? But is there more? There seems to be force in the accumulating picture of Woman in Greek Myth. There are good women and bad women: good women maintain the *oikos*; attractive women are a danger (their fault as much as the man's). Add to this the known exclusion of women from discussion and planning, that they were often fifteen years younger than their husbands, and then the mythology can be seen to relegate women in a way consistent with our knowledge of society.

Though this may be the drift of treatments of Helen, in the hands of a great artist such as Homer the picture can be modified in unexpected ways.[15] Emerging at the wall of Troy to view the duel between Menelaos and Paris, she is, as Kakridis (1971: 34) recognised, like the bride at the contest for her hand. Yet for all her beauty – recognised by the Trojan elders (*Iliad* 3.158) – she is now regretful and responsible, even integrated into the new *oikos*, though admittedly the balance of the relationship between Paris and her is incorrect in comparison with that between Hektor and Andromache. 'She is no longer the pitiable passive creature, but the still beautiful yet now invisible woman, torn by remorse, and aware of her responsibility' (Kakridis 1971: 36). In the *Odyssey* too, she is – perhaps a little too much, perhaps over-compensating – a repository of social correctness.[16]

But in other authors of the archaic period matters are simpler: the daughters of Tyndareus exist to be bad examples. This can be seen from passages of Stesichoros and of the Pseudo–Hesiodic *Catalogue of Women* (both preserved in a scholion on Euripides, *Orestes* 249):

> Because Tyndareus once, when sacrificing to the gods, forgot Kypris (Aphrodite) of the gentle gifts, she was angry and made his daughters two-marriaged, three-marriaged and men-leavers.
>
> (Stesichoros, fr. 223 Page)

> . . . At them laughter-loving Aphrodite
> felt envy as she looked, and she inflicted evil reputation upon
>     them.
> Timandre then had abandoned Echemos and gone,
> and came to Phyleus,[17] him loved by the immortal gods;
> and, just so, Clytaemnestra, abandoning divine Agamemnon,
> lay beside Aigisthos and took a worse spouse;
> and, just so, Helen shamed the bed of blond Menelaos.
>
> (Hesiod, fr. 176 Merkelbach-West)

Whether it is the envy of Aphrodite, or Tyndareus' forgetfulness leading to her revenge, it is the power of sex that makes his daughters disruptive and destructive. Thus Helen is most naturally characterised without redeeming features: she is a power for destruction in Aeschylus' *Agamemnon* (a Trojan Horse all on her own) and in Euripides' *Troades* an inexcusable, unduly attractive, criminal. This aspect is what makes it misleading of Brelich to have presented her as perfection, marriage to whom would be the ultimate fulfilment for the hero.[18] She is not. She is an excess. If she was mere perfection, she would have a greater husband than (Homer's or tragedy's) Menelaos. The accumulated sense of the intertext is based upon, and illustrates, the views of a male society concerned at the difficulties in controlling female sexuality, in keeping it within the bounds that a Helen would defeat, in preserving the *oikos* against this danger to male hegemony. Even so, the mythology only stresses the tensions we already perceived in Greek society (just read Lysias on the dangers of allowing your wife to attend a funeral). This is of course why Walcot's 1984 article first states the prevailing social conditions and then finds them in myth – less a case of 'mythological evidence' than mythological exemplification. The greater interest seems to lie in the stance taken up relative to the mythic intertext by great artists and in the ways in which they reformulate that intertext.

## Mythic women: conclusions

So myth provides illustrations of what we already know, but does not particularly add to our knowledge. This is shown by myths of girls going mad and hanging themselves, connected by Helen King with statements in Hippokrates.[19] That mythology is locked, indecipherable, until we have the Hippocratic material (though of course there is the interesting counter-conclusion that Hippokrates is to some extent mythologising life).

More fundamentally, it is the individual texts which present more complex and more interesting views. This must be a concern to the mythologist, because to interpret an individual text is not to interpret mythology, only to state how that myth is 'interpreted' in the context of this author's value system. This is what I, for one, understand as literary criticism – the explication of the value-coding, conscious and unconscious, of the texts of authors. If this is what the interpretation of myth consists of, there is no separate science of myth-interpretation, unless it be a particular form of literary criticism encompassing the intertextuality implicit in the reuse of myths.

Because, without reuse, there are no myths, only one-off fictions. The myth must have an existence over and above the individual telling. So, for instance, if we discuss Pandora, fruitful though that may be, we are not discussing mythology, we are discussing Hesiod.[20]

In the case of Helen and Clytaemnestra, I may have chosen figures who are not specially revealing, though they seem remarkable enough to me. Would Perseus, Medusa and Andromeda have proved more capable of delivering deductions about society that we had not already planted there? Would the figure of Medea have delivered results independent of the particular realisations of Euripides and Apollonius? I think she might pose questions, but the answers would have to come from elsewhere: perhaps a Detienne-ish study of family, butchery, cooking and herbs?

## HYPOTHESISING PASSAGE RITES

So far I have denied that social data and views over and above what we already know can be extracted from myth. This is not inconsistent with the attempt to reconstruct maidens' passage rites from mythology (cf. my *Death and the Maiden*, 1989), because myths can help us posit rituals of a certain, already broadly understood, specification, even if they do not help reconstruct otherwise unevidenced ideologies.

Mythology can be validly approached in different ways. One is to examine it synchronically, for instance in the context of Athenian society, e.g. by privileging the evidence of tragedy. Diachronically, however, individual myths have a history and I have argued (the method goes back to K.O. Müller) that myths come from somewhere and the somewhere is often stated internally in the myth by its localisation.[21] If accepted, this approach then delivers a historical context for the myth, though at an early ('original') and uncertain date, before it becomes part of any inter-state repertoire. The second step in this argument is to relate some of these myths (I do not know what proportion of Greek Mythology as a whole) to local ritual. In some few cases we will know of the ritual, notably the Arkteia at Brauron associated with the passage from childhood to adulthood. In other cases the Brauronian example is used as a model and a ritual hypothesised at some other place in the light of the motifs present in a myth located there (e.g.: girl at puberty, animal metamorphosis, exclusion from the community). This is a historical hypothesis claiming that a locally sited ritual would have some explanatory force for a myth of a certain type.

What, then, has one discovered by these means about women in Greek society? Perhaps that the step taken by maidens into adulthood had been sufficiently prominent and interesting to society at large for it to generate a substantial and colourful mythology; perhaps too that such rituals had been a regular feature of Greek societies before the historic age. Such rituals, what rituals? The word that comes to the lips is 'passage rites', carrying with it its own ethnological baggage. Yet there is a danger of assimilating Greek conditions unduly to prevalent ethnological images. Unlike initiations in most societies, Greek rites are typically selective: singular adolescent priestess, mythical trios of daughters, seven girls and seven boys at Corinth, select maidens as Bears at Brauron, or combined with select boys at Patrai, at most a 50-strong dance group mirrored in the Danaids.[22] It is difficult to capture the social dynamics here, except by appeal to what we know in the supposedly faded condition of these rites in classical times: the pride, for instance, of an Aristophanic Lysistrata. The mythology at most reinforces – and deepens the antiquity of – this selective world.

On the other hand, the mythology does suggest a social fact very sparsely attested in real life: no gap between marriageability and marriage. Unless this is the convenience and economy of myth, when translated into reality it suggests group marriage at the end of initiation – whether only of the selective participants, or of the whole age-group of which they are members. And at the same time, the mythology does allow us some limited access to a world-view where girls' transitions are felt, and felt important. The drastic mythic mutations (death, metamorphosis and madness) of girls at this moment, confronted by an angry goddess, reflect both the definitive break from maidenhood that Greek societies required and the need to place such a critical moment under the protection of a goddess. These Greek societies view themselves as consisting of strongly marked categories of membership – something reflected for gender in mythology of Amazons, and for life-stages in this mythology of passage-rites.

However, it is not clear that a specific ideology of maidenhood can be constructed from the myths, other than in the most obvious outlines (girls are there to become child-bearing women, not warriors, and at an early age compared to girls in our society). In particular, the different animals employed in different myths of metamorphosis (deer, bear, cow) neither deliver a uniform imagery nor appear intended to contrast with each other; they belong to local systems and are not, so far as we can discern, constructed systematically in relation to each other. Thus whatever one may imagine the place of 'bear' to be in Greek imagery or psychology, it delivers only a local conclusion (Brauron, or Kallisto's southern Arcadia).

Some of the puzzlement of mythology may be resolved by this approach, because the supposition of a link with rites which satisfy certain conditions explains the shape and existence of myths such as those of Iphigeneia or the Proitids. But I am less sure that the conditions requisite for such rites are sufficient to advance greatly our understanding of Greek society, and anyone who looks for this sort of illumination in work of this type is, I fear, likely to be disappointed.

## CONCLUSIONS

So, from the perspective of the historical age, mythic material may enhance our picture of Greek ideas about society in general and women in particular. It may also provide a congenial space within which the artist can construct a dialogue of ideas and values. Myth shows the power of particular attitudes if they can achieve the prominence of being incorporated into common societal fiction, though it offers no completely new evidence. Similarly, from the perspective of bygone ages of Greek society, whose social remnants can be perceived through Greek mythology, there is little to surprise and the picture is more derived from the historical conditions of Greek societies than one might think: one is not uncloaking a wholly new society, with different structures and values. I doubt if one could do that on the basis of the mythology of any nation.

In reverse, however, it must be said that our knowledge of Greek, and Athenian, society has much to tell us about the shaping and concerns of Greek Mythology. I thus conclude that the subject of women in mythology offers better value to the student of mythology than to the student of women. Is this why there are no myths in Lefkowitz and Fant (1992)?

## NOTES

1    Dowden 1992: e.g. 60–73.
2    Zeitlin 1978: 151; Dowden 1992: ch. 9.2.
3    Dowden 1992: 153f., citing J. Bamberger, 'The myth of matriarchy: why men rule in primitive society', in M.Z. Rosaldo and L. Lamphere (eds.), *Women Culture and Society*, Stanford, Calif., 1974: 276.
4    Vernant 1980a: 59–60.

5   For a differently loaded analysis of the constrained role of women in Greek myth, see Lefkowitz 1981: ch. 5, 'Patterns of women's lives in myth'.

6   Cf. duBois 1982: 27; Dowden 1992: 161f.

7   Sourvinou-Inwood 1991: 19f.

8   Similarly, Zeitlin 1986: 132f.

9   Though I doubt her approach, I draw attention to Farber 1975, who categorises Helen and Clytaemnestra as 'erotic mature' segments of the mother, disguised so as to allow discourse.

10   And by implication at *Odyssey* 11.438–9; Hesiod *Catalogue* fr. 176M–W.

11   Contrast Cantarella 1987: 41.

12   Semonides fr. 7.34.

13   Lefkowitz 1993: 53f., draws attention to exaggeration inherent in misogynistic invective.

14   For the stress put on beauty, see also the discussion of Semonides by Lefkowitz 1986: 115.

15   I cannot accept Kakridis' view (1971: 28) that Homer is reconciling different versions of Helen's degree of responsibility in a still fluid tradition.

16   Cf Lefkowitz 1986: 135–6, who perhaps produces too uniform a picture of Helen across different authors. Sensitive analysis in Kakridis 1971: 42.

17   Phyleus (the son of Augeias) 'having committed adultery with Timandra, sister of Helen and Clytaemnestra, took her off to Doulichion', Eustathios on Homer *Iliad* 2.627. Adultery is the natural result in reconciling traditions where one wife-name is shared by two men.

18   A. Brelich, *Gli eroi greci: un problema storico-religioso*, Rome 1958: 302; of course Brelich is using a rather double-edged example to prove a good point, that of fulfilment of heroes by a good marriage.

19   King, 1993a: ch.8; Dowden 1989:89; Zeitlin 1982: 134f.

20   Cf. Walcot 1984: 40–1, Vernant 1980a: ch. 8; Zeitlin Chapter 4.

21   Dowden 1989: e.g. 4–5, 46–7; 1992: ch. 7, esp. 106.

22   Dowden 1989: 170–2, 202–3.

# Chapter 4

# Signifying difference: the myth of Pandora*

*Froma I. Zeitlin*

The myth of Pandora is a variant of well-known theme in myths of origins the world over. How and why woman came into the world accounts for the fact that there are not one, but two sexes. Logically, both male and female should come into existence at the same time as the human species is created. Each is the complement of the other, each indispensable to the other's identity. As a pair, they attest to the universal fact of gender in nature and assure reproduction of one's own kind.

The mythic imagination does not view matters this way. More often than not, woman is an afterthought, created as a secondary category following the prior emergence of man. Her ontological status is therefore not a self-evident or spontaneous fact. To account for her supplementary presence requires a motive, a reason, a purpose – in short, a myth. Two of the most well-known examples of this type are the story of Eve in the book of Genesis and the Greek myth of Pandora, as recounted by the archaic poet, Hesiod. Each, in its own way, conforms to this pattern: Eve is created from Adam's rib as a companion to ease his loneliness;[1] Pandora is fashioned at Zeus' orders in retaliation for the Titan Prometheus' theft of fire. Whether created by the supreme male deity out of compassion or anger, woman's entry onto the scene is only the beginning of the story; it provides the occasion for an aetiological narrative that tells how through her agency the world was transformed into its present state. Her secondary status operates as a signifier of difference and disruption that brings about the so-called 'human condition'. That is, she introduces death, woe, and evil into the world, along with the laborious toil of human existence.

Hesiod tells the myth of Pandora in two versions, the first in the *Theogony*, a cosmogonic poem, and the second in the *Works and Days*, a didactic work of wisdom literature. The details differ, but in each case, she figures as the outcome of a game of wits between Prometheus and Zeus that resolves around a series of deceptions and counter-deceptions in connection with the exchange of gifts. Zeus wins, of course, and in return for the theft of fire, he has Hephaistos, the artisan god, fabricate the first woman as a molded creature, who astounds men by her god-given beauty and ruins them by her thievish gluttony. This 'beautiful evil' (*kalon kakon*), this 'dangerous trap' (*dolos aipus*), this 'great plague for mortals' (*mega pêma thnêtoisi*) sits like a drone inside a man's house and, like a rapacious belly (*gastêr*), consumes his substance without giving anything in return (*Th.* 561–591). Man is faced with two equally unpleasant alternatives: either marry and expect the worst or avoid woman altogether, in which case there will be no one to tend him in his old age, and upon his death his distant heirs will divide his possessions. In the second version in the *Works and Days*, the newly created woman is sent to Epimetheus (Afterthought) along with her jar. Although warned by his brother Prometheus (Forethought) to accept no gifts from the gods, he foolishly disobeys and learns to regret it when Pandora opens the lid of the jar and releases the swarm of sorrows and diseases that now wander silent and invisible over all the earth. Only the uncertain quality of Hope (Elpis) is left within, a small and ambiguous recompense for the life of toil and woe that henceforth constitutes the lot of humankind (*WD* 56–104).[2]

It would be difficult to overstate the degree of negativity in the Greek version of woman's creation. The myth of Adam and Eve justifies both the social, even organic, dependency of wife upon husband and her subordination to his authority. In Hesiod, by contrast, woman remains a separate and alien being, whose presence in his household he both requires and resents. Even the good wife, one who most resembles him, may turn out to be a burden all the same. The biblical account stresses the union of male and female in joint sex and procreation, decreeing that husband and wife cleave together to become one flesh and assigning a parity of labor that balances man's agricultural toil with Eve's travail in child-birth. Hesiod's myth, on the other hand, insists on contrasting the extremes of man's patient industry with woman's useless idleness. It elides any mention of sexual contact and, except by veiled allusion, omits any reference to woman's reproductive functions. The image of Pandora's jar in the *Works and Days*, as I have argued elsewhere, is a substitute for, and analogy to, the woman's womb, according to which Elpis is the child (or the hope of a child) and Pandora's acts of removing and replacing the lid of the jar represent the breaching of her virginity and the subsequent closure that is necessary for pregnancy to occur.[3]

This manufactured object called woman, accompanied by yet another artisanal product (the jar), is separated at the outset from the natural processes of generation by which the entire universe came into being. Yet if the myth undermines woman's maternal functions, we note that man in his turn has neither directly affirmed his paternal role nor his virile potency. As Boyarin comments,

> If the opening of the jar represents the breaching of Pandora's virginity, then she is made wholly responsible, as it were, for this act as well. The text refuses to record the first sexual act between a man and a woman, because by doing so it would have to reveal that which it seems determined to suppress, the simple fact that men are also agents in the performance of sex and thus responsible, at least equally with women, for whatever baneful effects it is held to have.[4]

Adam and Eve both eat of the fruit of the tree; both become aware of their identity as genitalized beings; both cover their nakedness, and they leave together when expelled from the garden of Eden. Hesiod's reticence on the topic of human sexuality and reproduction is all the more noteworthy, considering the broader project of the *Theogony*, which is to recount the creation of the universe through the birth of the gods.

The creation of Pandora marks the definitive rupture between gods and mortals, forever separating them into different categories. Until now, we have focused on the import of this separation that determines the nature of relations between the sexes in the human realm, affecting men's lives for all time to come. But what of the other side? The creation of Pandora is only a single element in the larger creative project of the *Theogony* that constructs an extended evolutionary design in which gods play the central roles. Here the *Theogony* differs from Genesis in two striking respects: first, woman is created on her own without any parallel and preceding account of how the category of man came into existence; second, if Pandora is meant to stand for all humankind, as some critics have suggested, the text does not situate her creation as the final and culminating display of divine generative power. It occurs, rather, at a very different juncture during the unfolding of a cosmogonic drama in which, unlike Genesis, there are a multitude of gods – gods, who themselves come into being by various means and at different moments of time. In these struggles at the divine level for differentiation, self-definition, and superior power, the place reserved in the text for Pandora's creation deserves detailed consideration in assessing her roles and functions.

The essential aim of the *Theogony* is to establish Zeus' claims to supreme power over the universe and to chart the steps that lead to the eventual consolidation of his reign. These claims depend, in the first instance, on his gaining hegemony over the other gods, and in the second, on the decisive separation of gods from mortals. The two themes combine in the circumstances of Pandora's manufacture, since, with Prometheus as advocate of human interests, the quarrel between two generations of gods (Olympian and Titan) is also staged as a contest between gods and mortals.

Given the vast scope of this topic, I will focus on Zeus' rise to power in the frame of a succession myth that requires both the replacement of a father by a son (Ouranos by Kronos and Kronos by Zeus) and the eventual triumph of male over female, particularly with respect to rights over reproduction and in matters of engendering and parentage – even, we might say, over the creative principle itself. The struggle begins with the castration of Ouranos (Sky) by his youngest son, Kronos, at the instigation of Gaia (Earth), the first maternal principle. In the face of the primordial father's refusal to uncouple from Gaia, castration is the drastic means she devises to allow their children to emerge from the mother's depths and see the light of day. But in his defeat, Ouranos initiates the first challenge to female fecundity, since his castration results in the birth of Aphrodite from his semen and in the engendering of the female Erinyes from the drops of his blood that fell to the earth from his severed phallus (*Th.* 184–200). In the second stage, Kronos may be said to imitate pregnancy itself by swallowing his children once they are born, and, when forced to disgorge his progeny, by 'giving birth' to them through his mouth (*Th.* 453–500). In the last stage, Zeus absorbs the female into himself, swallowing the pregnant Metis, principle of resourceful intelligence, and producing a female offspring – his daughter, Athena – from his head (*Th.* 886–895). Only in this way can he ensure the permanence of his rule, putting an end to the generational evolution of the male gods and appropriating both the physical and mental creative capacities of the female in the interests of paternal – or, more accurately, patriarchal – power.[5]

Before the narrative reaches this momentous event (*Th* 886–900, 924–996), Zeus has already accomplished his first creative act in producing the first mortal female, Pandora. In so doing, he ratifies the definitive split between gods and men. Two questions therefore arise: why is the story of Pandora placed where it is, and what dilemmas is the mode of her creation designed to resolve? Logically, Zeus ought to have instituted his sovereignty over the universe before turning his attention to the condition of mortals. But the text takes a curious turn and situates the quarrel with Prometheus and the subsequent division between gods and men just *after* the narrative of Zeus' own birth but *before* the narrative of the mighty battle against the Titans. One last challenge follows in Zeus' solo combat with Typhoeus, Gaia's last child, a monstrous offspring of her mating with the primal depths of Tartaros. Only after this victory are we are told that the 'blessed gods finished their toil (*ponon*)' and in the wake of their struggle for honors (*timai*) with the Titans, 'urged Zeus to rule and be king over them, by the counsels of Gaia. And he divided their *timai* in turn among them' (*Th.* 881–885). The birth of Zeus and his rescue from his devouring father Kronos, is itself preceded by another apparent interlude, introducing a remarkable female goddess, Hekate, whose appearance constitutes another kind of *hysteron proteron*, in that she is especially honored by Zeus, even though Zeus has yet to be born and she presides over human activities in a world of men that is not yet constituted.[6]

Why should this be so? Why should the 'hymn' to Hekate *precede* the birth of Zeus, the centerpiece of the entire *Theogony*, and why should the story of Pandora *follow* directly after?[7] What is the logic that insists on framing the birth of Zeus with the accounts of two female personages, who, taken together, form a complementary pair sharply divided into positive and negative poles? Situated as two points on a continuum of feminine characters that leads from Gaia to Athena, including especially Aphrodite and Styx, the figures of Hekate and Pandora are distinguished from all the others, not least because each is defined in a significant relation both to mortals and to gods, particularly to Zeus.[8]

On the principle that the sequence of the narrative is itself a determining factor in the production of meaning, I propose in advance that Zeus' own ontological status is indeed predicated on this intersection between immortal and mortal realms, as he evolves from the first instantiation of a divine child to the figure of sovereign ruler under the title of 'father of gods and men'. Thus, while Hekate and Pandora have been rightly interpreted as important factors in defining the ambiguities of the 'human condition', they are also essential in constructing the definition of Zeus himself. Let us therefore take a closer look, starting with the often discussed passage about the goddess Hekate (long a puzzle to critics, both for its unusual length and content),[9] before turning to review the question of Pandora herself.

## THE GODDESS HEKATE

Hekate crosses the generational line that divides Titan from Olympian divinity. Zeus honors her above all the gods and she is honored in turn by both men and gods alike. She retains all the powers allotted as her share 'at the first time, from the beginning', and she retains these privileges on earth, in the heavens, and in the sea, wielding her influence over all domains. The prestige of these prerogatives is underlined by her receiving them twice, once at the outset and then again from Zeus (411–412, 421–427). Moreover, these are formidable powers, far less restricted than those of other divinities to whom Zeus apportions their respective *timai* after the consolidation of his rule.[10] In her allotted role as intercessor between men and gods, Hekate is highly responsive to petition, bestowing her favor as she wills.[11] She is called upon by all men in all their diversified pursuits. These include war, athletics, horsemanship, navigation, law courts, assemblies, as well as the work of tending herds and flocks. Her most important epithet is fittingly reserved for last; it is hers through the offices of Zeus, but it was so, it seems, from the beginning (450–452). This is her function as *kourotrophos*, nurse of the young, a role that assures the continuation and well-being of life from its inception. Hekate is dedicated to fosterage but creates no new genealogical line of her own, for she remains forever a virgin.

What is more, she is called a *mounogenês*, a single-born child. She has no other siblings, and, oddly enough, her father bears the name of Perses, which in the *Works and Days* is also the name of Hesiod's rival brother, whose lazy and thievish conduct occasions the admonitory tale of Pandora's creation.[12] Unlike that brother, she is a daughter, and unlike him, of course, she has no one with whom she must share. Quite the contrary. She gets more than her share; she gets it all – not once but twice.[13] Her social position in Zeus' family circle is unclear. As a *mounogenês* from her mother, Hekate seems to remain inside the maternal sphere. As a daughter without brothers, she is also like an *epiklêros* or heiress to her father's line, and hence under the special paternal protection of Zeus.[14] But however we

understand her status, she is unique, both because of the archaic plen-
itude of her power in a world to be defined by the distribution of
*timai*, and because Zeus reconfirms her power, thus in a sense, recre-
ating her. Pandora, as Zeus' own invention, represents a new mode
of creation through which a singular being can be made, not born,
and needs no generational antecedents. Hekate's status, too, is the
result of another kind of innovative act. This time, Zeus' creativity
consists in redoubling the nature of an already existing entity under
a second dispensation. If his renewal of her privileges does not exactly
count as a 'second birth', it does award her a twofold status and
thereby combines the categories of the old and the new, the first
and the last.

As an intermediary in human affairs between gods and men,
honored by all alike, Hekate may be said to neutralize or at least
mitigate in advance the negative effects for mortals of Prometheus'
guileful mediation that will motivate the anger of Zeus and the
creation of Pandora. Hekate also compensates in advance for
the negative presence of Pandora herself, who henceforth will become
an integral dimension of human existence and remain its perennial
burden. These two female figures may be viewed as an antithetical
pair: the first represents an economy of abundance, the second of
scarcity and both are drawn into the essential game of reciprocity
and exchange. Pandora is a baneful gift, who takes and does not give,
herself given in exchange for something else that was taken away.
Hekate, by contrast, is one from whom nothing is taken away, one
who in fact receives even *more* privileges than she had before. She
receives these honors as gifts from Zeus and continues his beneficence by bestowing honors on mortals in turn, if she so wishes.

Convincing parallels have been noted between Zeus and Hekate.
In the range and extent of her powers, she looks like a 'small-scale
reflection' of Zeus himself and, given his sponsorship, she prefigures
the beneficent nature of his own rule, albeit in feminine form.[15] This
is an important observation. Yet in highlighting her role as *kourotrophos*,
Zeus also inaugurates a new form of feminine activity that shifts the
emphasis from nature to culture – from fecundity and generative
power to a maternal nurturance that is independent of the act of
childbirth, placed now under the auspices of the major male deity.[16]
*Kourotrophia*, it is true, was mentioned once before in passing as an
attribute (and etymology) of the *Kourai* (daughters of Tethys and
Okeanos), 'who with Apollo and the Rivers, nurture (*kourizousi*) men
on earth, a portion they received from Zeus'. But Hekate's function

extends to both gods and mortals, and its import is further underlined by its placement in the text as the last named of her attributes
– enunciated not once but twice in the space of three lines
(*WD* 450–452). Naming is a creative act that brings a figure, epithet,
or concept into existence. It founds a reality that until then is not
available for use in the world. The new role of *kourotrophos* anticipates
the innovations of Zeus' birth story and also those of Pandora's
creation, which leads to several significant consequences in both
human and divine realms. The nurturant function is transferred from
the mother of human offspring to a kindly feminine deity (sponsored
by Zeus) in advance of the creation of women, to whom, as we
have seen, no such role is ever assigned. But the general principle of
detaching nurse from mother may equally apply to the realm of the
gods and especially to Zeus himself, whose emergence into the world
is beset with unusual difficulties. Let us examine this matter more
closely.

If progress and evolution are to end in the establishment of a
permanent world system, then the first imperative is to put an end
to the inevitable replacement of father by son in the sequence of
generations (which Zeus does by swallowing Metis and giving birth
to a daughter, Athena). Before this outcome is concluded, Zeus'
birth story introduces two new elements into the system of generation that also come into play. The first is the father's threat to reabsorb
his young once they are born; the second is the postponement of
Zeus' retaliation upon his father until he himself has grown to adulthood. Two potential difficulties attend this new dispensation. Zeus is
the first instance of an infant god. This means that, like any child,
he requires nurture until he comes of age. It means too that he must
likewise undergo a maturational process that brings him perilously
close to the realities of the mortal condition and the exigencies of
human development.[17] Second, although the last-born child enjoys a
symbolic advantage in that he closes a genealogical series and
embodies the concept of progress, there is also an undeniable value
in being first, already present 'from the beginning'. Zeus' claim to
hegemony over the cosmos resides in his status as the last and most
developed of the Olympian gods. Yet he must somehow attain the
prestige of origins that will connect him to the first foundations of
the world[18] – that is, to Gaia, from whom Zeus is genealogically twice
removed.

By reason of her special status and her functions, the figure of
Hekate is indispensable for resolving both predicaments. Having

received her honors twice, both from the beginning and now again from Zeus, she exemplifies in advance a solution to the ontological paradox of being both first and last. But in her role as *kourotrophos*, she offers yet another service to Zeus, since, as an infant separated at birth from his mother, he also requires nurturance from a surrogate female. This personage is none other than Gaia herself, to whose care he is entrusted in order to save him from his father's greedy appetite. The order of the narrative is revealing. The naming of Hekate as *kourotrophos* ends the 'hymn' to the goddess (452). It also furnishes the point of transition to the account of how Rhea, in sexual conjunction with Kronos, 'gave birth to glorious children' (453), the last named of whom is Zeus. No sooner is the category of *kourotrophos* 'invented' for general use[19] than it is is immediately represented in the divine sphere by Gaia's role as nurse to Zeus.[20]

The goddess's initial association with the infant Zeus is an essential step in the process that leads to his eventual triumph. Gaia is the primordial principle of earth, the locus of origin for the entire cosmos. The nurture she gives him in her function as foster mother thus establishes a primary and enduring bond between the first and the last. The fact of her dual identity as active agent (divinity) and receptive element (earth) has still further import: *Gaia* takes the child from Rhea to nurse and rear (τρέφεμεν ἀτιταλλέμεναί τε: 480); *gaia* is the place she puts him, 'taking him in her arms and hiding him in a remote cave beneath the secret places of the holy *earth*' (ζαθέης ὑπὸ κεύθεσι γαίης: 482–484). When Zeus emerges from her care, we might say that he too undergoes a 'second birth', this time as a kind of autochthon, a child of earth in his own right. In this way, he too, like mortal men, can circumvent or pass beyond the natural facts of maternity to claim the kind of engendering Greek males like best – born (or reborn) from the female principle of earth and not from the womb of a mother.[21]

If the question of maternal affiliation is settled in Zeus' separation from his true mother and his secondary status as a nursling of earth, he still remains in the circle of women, whose protection is needed to safeguard his right to exist despite his father's hostility. But what about the paternal principle? Is it thereby also put into question? Kronos presents a curious case. His actions, as we have seen, imitate feminine functions in respect to pregnancy and birth. Yet he also remains a male and a father, who strives to suppress the future generation in order to ensure the permanence of his kingship. When Zeus compels Kronos to disgorge his progeny, he in effect 'forces him to yield up his *timê*', since 'the right to rule is identified with control over procreation'.[22] But there is more. Born once from their mother, the other Olympians are replaced in their father's belly only to undergo a 'second birth', this time from the paternal source. Thus, if Zeus' triumph over Kronos represents the victory of the son over the father, it also signifies the triumph of the father over the mother as a higher form of reproduction. Whether on the female side (autochthony) or on the male side (disgorgement), both are strategies that promote the idea of a second birth as a way of eliding the obvious and natural fact that man is from woman born.[23]

A further consequence of Kronos' obstetrical adventure provides another way of establishing the requisite connection between first and last. For, as the text is careful to note, the stone representing Zeus that Kronos had ingested *last* is necessarily brought up *first* (πρῶτον δ' ἐξήμησε λίθον. πύματον καταπίνων: v. 497).[24] On the maternal side, the last generation was aligned with the first through the nurturing function of Gaia, who substitutes for the real mother. On the paternal side, another kind of substitution also plays a role in joining first to last, starting from Rhea's original substitution of the stone for the child and ending with the reversal of the birth order when Kronos disgorges his progeny.[25] Masculine and feminine tactics combine in the final disposition of the stone. Sign (*sêma*) of its birth from the father, it is fixed in place by Zeus himself 'in the broad-wayed *earth* in holy Pytho, under the hollows of Parnassus',[26] a prodigy from heaven (*sêma*) destined to be a *thauma* (marvel) for mortals (*Th.* 498–500).[27] Sky and earth, male and female, father and mother: Zeus' action of setting up the *sêma* in the world founds his sovereignty. It converts his birth story into a visible emblem and also ratifies the principle of substitution in the form of a material sign that will stand at Delphi alongside another *sêma* of birth, namely, the *omphalos* stone which marks the site as the navel or center of the earth.

## THE WOMAN PANDORA

Once the stone has fulfilled its function in the divine realm, it is destined for mortals, both a sign and a wonder. The stone also links human and divine realms, this time through verbal echoes and in the matter of procreation. The stone, disguised as a baby, was a substitute for Zeus, and he was left behind 'in place of the stone' (*anti lithou*: *Th.* 489). Now in power, Zeus introduces another substitute, Pandora (*anti puros*: *Th.* 570), 'in place of the stolen fire', and like the stone, she too is a *thauma* to behold (*Th.* 500). The two have been justly taken as evidence of a higher level of social relations in a context of exchange and reciprocity.[28] Both were duplicitous gifts, given in response to a prior offense of unlawful appropriation. In semiotic terms, both *sêmata* function as second-order signifiers. The first prepares for the second.

> Zeus sets up the stone to be a sign of his control of signification, to be a sign to all who come to learn the mind of the father through the oracle of his son, that Zeus's regime is built upon the knowledge necessary to disguise, imitate, substitute – knowledge now securely embodied by the father of men and gods.

This capacity is put to immediate use, first in the contest of wits with Prometheus, and then in the fashioning of the first woman, by his plan and his own devising.[29] Zeus also redeploys another element from the story of Kronos in the transfer of the belly from its value as a sign of his father's voracious appetite into the permanent and defining attribute of woman (her *gastêr*-belly) via the *gastêr*-paunch of the fraudulent division of the sacrificial ox that led to her creation.[30]

At one level, Pandora is only a byproduct of a contest between males. She is a secondary, even tertiary effect, in that she comes in the third stage of that contest, as a return for Prometheus' theft of the celestial fire that Zeus had just received from the Cyclopes. Zeus' control over this cosmic fire, in fact, will later determine his decisive victories in the cosmos, first over the Titans, and then over the fire-breathing Typhoeus, the last of Gaia's progeny. But following just after the narrative of Zeus' birth and his subsequent triumph over his father, the creation of the first mortal woman mediates between past and present by renewing the question of male control over procreation (to be finally resolved in Zeus' mating with Metis) and also by reflecting upon Zeus' own status in the cycle of divine generations.

As a creation of the ruling masculine god, Pandora can be linked to the figure of Aphrodite and even to that of Athena.[31] Yet she also stands as a unique product, not only in reference to man and his estate but also with regard to the biological principles of creation that regulate the *Theogony*, whether through parthenogenesis or sexual reproduction, she has no family line. She also does not participate, except in a secondary and self-conscious way, in the basic genealogical scheme by which the *Theogony* suggests the natural unity of the world as it evolves from the moment that Chaos comes into being

and Gaia, or Earth, emerges immediately afterwards. Genealogy is
an effective means by which myth can posit a coherent scheme of
relations and affinities. By tracing out family ties through successive
generations, the generational scheme may sort out like from unlike,
modify and distinguish categories and concepts, and establish
temporal priorities and hierarchies of value.[32] Zeus is Pandora's
author, not her natural sire, and she has no mother. By contrast,
Athena's birth follows a heterosexual union (with the goddess Metis)
and, in a sense, follows the laws of organic procreation, despite the
inversion of head for loins and father for mother. Pandora's nature,
on the other hand, is determined by the gods' seemingly arbitrary
bestowal of gifts, which makes her only an imitation of the 'real thing',
and, detached from natural modes of reproduction, she has no family
line from which she is descended.

The result is that the introduction of the female sex as a *genos
gunaikôn*, a race of women apart, does not coincide with the creation
of gender as it does in the parallel myth in Genesis. Once Gaia
emerges independently after the neuter Chaos, the female principle
is established once and for all, and indeed is the source of the male
principle (Ouranos) derived from it. From that time on, the idea of
biological (genealogical) reproduction had coincided with the gram-
matical distinctions between male and female, so that all the various
entities that came into being were automatically endowed with a
gendered identity, enhanced, of course, by a polytheistic system of
gods, who follow anthropomorphic lines in their relations with one
another and in their modes of begetting. Zeus' invention of Pandora
and her subsequent status as a gift indicate, therefore, that she is far
removed from femininity as an original category. This is a strategic
move, with two important implications for the separation of gods and
mortals.

First comes the rupture of continuity with the principles of
both genealogical relationship and natural procreation. However
these categories have been manipulated in the divine realm, the
actual workings of nature remain the same. With the manufacture of
Pandora, on the other hand, mortals and immortals are henceforth
divided between nature and culture, or perhaps between the natural
and the 'non-natural'.

The second implication pertains specifically to the split between
woman and goddess. This strategy displaces the undeniable powers
of the female upward to the gods, allows for the 'deification' of
the female and feminine attributes, while repressing any validating

alternatives to the mortal woman.[33] Zeus adopts and empowers femininity in the person of the goddess Hekate, who assists men in all their undertakings, and who supports generational survival among mortals by sponsoring the growth of children apart from actual maternity.

Thus, in the complex interplay between immortal and human realms in which the dilemma remains how to separate the two categories while retaining their underlying kinship, the role of Hekate works in two directions. Maternal concern has been continuously present in the *Theogony*, not only in the proliferation of children in the divine realm, but in the mother's insistence on securing her offsprings' right to exist and in her alliance with them against a hostile father, as in the case of Gaia (vs Ouranos) and Rhea (vs Kronos). But Hekate, above all, represents this principle in its most disinterested form. A virgin and not a wife, a virgin and not a mother, a goddess and not a woman, only distantly related to Zeus but of an older generation, Hekate attests to Zeus' patronage of a femininity among both mortals and gods just before he is about to negotiate his own birth, nurture, and subsequent validation of paternal procreative powers. In the creation of Pandora (and later, when she puts the lid back on the jar at his command), Zeus exercises this paternal power in a new dimension. Yet in so doing, he contributes a new and supplemental category, which is that of woman.

This woman is hardly represented as a 'bringer of fertility' and the 'principle of reproduction',[34] as most interpreters like to insist – or, put another way, to the extent that she does, the text suppresses these functions as much as possible. It avoids any direct mention of sexual congress and only grudgingly acknowledges the need for a child, who is never mentioned as such but must be deduced from the context. In this sense, woman is deprived of those feminine powers that only goddesses and nature possess. But by her unwelcome presence and the necessities she imposes upon man's existence, she is empowered in another way. Her creation implies, as we know, that man can never be independent of woman because he requires progeny to remedy the facts of both aging and mortality. But since he is burdened by these limitations, it also means that man, through woman, can never successfully challenge the rule of Zeus, who under the sign of an elevated masculinity and paternal hegemony, has now earned his title of 'father of gods and men'.

Yet a serious paradox remains. Whether in the divine or human realms, whether by nature or by artifice, whether man or god is the subject, whether an abstract opposition can be maintained between a principle of unlimited growth (female) vs the limits of order (male), an underlying theme of the entire *Theogony* concerns the anxiety of the male confronted with fear of a 'natural' female superiority, best expressed in the deployment of a series of reproductive strategies. These run the gamut from the realistic norm in the natural union of male and female to parthenogenesis, autochthony, fictions of nurture, second birth, and, in the case of mortals, the alienation of woman from the species of man.

If the world of the gods aims to establish the paternal principle through inventive (and mimetic) tactics that harness the forces of nature and kinship in both sex and procreation, the case of Pandora addresses the same problem from the other side by transmitting to man a negative force of sexuality in the fabricated figure of a woman, whose reproductive capacities are at best a necessary encroachment on the integrity and self-sufficiency of the male self. We call it mortality. Yet, if Pandora is made to signify the difference between mortal and immortal realms of existence, she also continues to blur the lines between them. Fashioned by the gods to resemble them in the beauty of her allure, she is both an imitation and an original production, both a copy and a model. How to tell the difference? Once she is invented, the story has just begun.

## NOTES

\*    This is a partial and readapted version of a longer essay, 'Hesiodic Economies', in F.I. Zeitlin, *Playing the Other: Gender and Society in Classical Greek Literature* (Chicago 1995).

1    I acknowledge, but do not discuss here, the problem of the two accounts in *Genesis* of human creation, the first of which suggests, that male and female came into being at virtually the same time: 'And God created man in his own image, in the image of God created he him; male and female created he them' (1.27).

2    For the most influential treatment of these two versions, see Vernant 1980: 168–85; 1979: 37–132. For important refinements and correctives, see Loraux 1978: 75–117; Arthur 1982a, 1983. See too Pucci 1977. See also Vernant 1989.

3    See Zeitlin (1995). I base this argument on gynecological and other evidence that equates the woman's uterus with a jar or container.

4    Boyarin 1993: 85, commenting on an earlier draft of this essay.

5    See Zeitlin 1978 for a preliminary outline of this progression, and for full discussion, Arthur (1982a). Bergren 1983 follows the same scheme.

6    Zeus' victory is, of course, forecast already in the proem, and is alluded

to at strategic intervals, including in the narrative of his birth, where it is mentioned just after Kronos swallows the stone (*Th.* 488–491).

7   Arthur 1982a emphasizes this triadic structure. See also Boedeker 1983 and Clay 1984.

8   See Arthur 1982a: 69.

9   On the role of Hekate in the *Theogony*, see Kraus 1960. More recently, see Marquardt 1981; Arthur 1982a; Boedeker 1983; Clay 1984; and Griffith 1983: 51–55.

10   Clay 1984 observes that Hekate acts in concert with other gods (such as Poseidon and Hermes), but the text stresses the universality, not the limitation, of her powers in all domains.

11   Note that Hekate's assistance is reserved exclusively for men, in marked contrast to her later cultic and mythic associations with the world of women.

12   Walcot 1958: 13–14 and Nagy 1982: 65 note this connection.

13   Others have speculated on this curious fact. See, for example, Marquardt 1981: 245 and Nagy 1982: 65.

14   See Arthur 1982a: 69. Arthur further equates Hekate's 'social isolation' with 'the universality of her powers', arguing that 'Zeus' overvaluation of this goddess' is 'a compensation for her undervaluation in the patriarchal social order, and as an indication that the beneficence as well as the honor of the female are conceived in inverse proportion to female autonomy'.

15   On these parallels, see Boedeker 1983: 90–91 who interprets them to suggest Hekate's Indo-European heritage as a transfunctional goddess.

16   As Arthur 1982a: 70, puts it: 'The . . . redefinition of Hekate includes a revaluation of female generative potency to mean, in a more abstract and generalized way, the willing sponsorship of activities of human life. Life-giving has become life-sustaining' (i.e., *kourotrophos*). She further argues that 'Hekate . . . is the first female whose pre-eminence derives from the patriarchal father. And she embodies female fecundity in a transmuted form . . . *in abstracto* – as nurturance, tendance, fosterage, and not as the direct expression of the child from her womb.'

17   His maturation is swift, of course, as befits a god, taking the space of only one year (*Th.* 492–493), but the principle remains.

18   For the general concept, see Eliade 1958.

19   The category of *kourotrophos* was not needed until this moment. All the previous recitations of divine genealogies and births stopped short with parturition and only incidentally mentioned the rearing or *trophê* of offspring (*Th.* 313, 323).

20   On a frieze of a late Hellenistic temple in Lagina, Hekate is depicted as presenting the stone to Kronos, in imitation of Gaia's role. Hekate's role of *kourotrophos* is the only Hesiodic trait that remains in actual cult. See Marquardt 1981: 244 n. 2; and Boedeker 1983: 83–84 n. 21–22. On the rupture of the relationship between mother and son (Zeus and Rhea) and the role of Gaia as *kourotrophos*, see Arthur 1982a: 71.

21   Gaia also takes a leading role (along with Ouranos) in the entire affair. Together, they both inform Kronos that his son is destined to overcome him (*Th.* 463–465), and also suggest the ruse to Rhea (*Th.* 467–473),

although Gaia acts alone in tricking Kronos to give up his offspring (*Th.* 494–495). Arthur 1982a: 70–71 argues that Rhea's 'diminished potency' is a further sign of 'the weakening of female primacy' in favor of 'the elevation of the male (Kronos and Zeus) into the role of *genitor*'.

22  Arthur 1982a: 72.

23  In the last stage of the succession myth, Zeus will finally complete the inversion of gender roles and ratify the primacy of the father, first by absorbing the mother (Metis) into himself and then giving the first, original birth to the daughter (Athena).

24  West 1966 *ad Th.* 454 mentions this point, adding that Zeus would have been the first to attain maturity, since the other offspring remained in their father's belly.

25  Bergren 1983: 74, offers a compelling interpretation of the stone from another viewpoint:

> Here is the primary *mêtis*, the first imitation, one that seems to symbolize a supposititious child. For Kronos is baffled by the disguise, as any man would be, when his wife presents him with what she says is his child, for who except his wife can vouch for his true child, the legitimate heir to his property and his proper name? Only the female has the knowledge necessary to tell the true from the false heir, but it is this very knowledge that also makes her able to substitute for the truth, a false thing that resembles it. Her knowledge gives her the power of falsification in the domain of sexual re-production, just as on the level of language the knowledge of the Muses makes it possible for them to utter either *alêtheia* or *pseudea homoia etumoisin*.

26  See also Mezzadri's analysis (1987), who adds that Hestia, the oldest of Kronos' children and hence the last to be born, also combines the principle that applies to the stone-Zeus (but in reverse). His further remarks on the correlation between temporal and spatial structures at Delphi (with respect to the stone and the *omphalos*) are also pertinent.

27  *Sêma* has the two meanings of 'sign' and 'distinctive mark' or 'prodigy' (cf. e.g. *Odyssey* 23. 110, 188, 205 on the *sêma* of the bed as both a special object and a sign of recognition).

28  Arthur 1982a: 72–73, sees the fixing of the stone as 'the symbolic resolution of the father/son struggle in the form of the *sêma*, and the introduction of a cycle of reciprocity in the form of gift exchange'. As phrased, the latter seems to me less clear.

29  Bergren 1983: 75.

30  In this division, Prometheus offered Zeus the choice between a portion consisting of a shining layer of fat that contained only bones within and an unappetizing *gastêr*-paunch filled with edible meat.

31  Schwabl 1966: 80, notes the parallels with Aphrodite. For fuller exposition, see Arthur 1982a: 75, although I cannot follow her conclusion that Pandora is also a kind of Gaia reborn.

32  See Philippson 1936.

33  Rudhardt 1986 also notes that femininity arises at the beginning with Gaia but does not observe the distinction between the two levels. For the value of a two-tiered system of goddesses and women, see Zeitlin on

the *Oresteia* (1978), where the problem of woman (Clytemnestra) is displaced upward to the level of the Erinyes. The resolution in the *Eumenides* is also organized according to a theogonic model of a struggle between chthonic and Olympian forces and the dilemma is solved by a new distribution of *timai*.

34  Loraux 1978: 88–89; 'Nothing indicates that the woman is expected to "imitate the earth" as the standard Greek representations of fertility suggest.'

# Chapter 5

# The cults of Demeter and Kore

*Lucia Nixon*

Greek religion is a bisexual polytheistic system, i.e. there are female and male gods, all of whom are powerful in some way. Such a system is probably more woman-friendly than unreconstructed male mono-theism. But there is no doubt about who is meant to be in charge. Though females, whether human or divine, are not without import-ance, it is clear that males are in control, in heaven (Zeus) as on earth (mortal men). Thus this is not an egalitarian version of polytheism; gender asymmetry is built into the system.[1]

Why then is Demeter such a powerful deity? How could Greek society with all its inbuilt misogyny tolerate, much less celebrate, a she-god with power over fertility? After all, fertility, both human and agricultural, was a seriously dominant area of Greek life. Under-graduate students of Greek religion and myth are always quick to ask such questions, and generally remain unconvinced by theories stating that the story of Demeter and Kore and the founding of the Eleusinian Mysteries represent the incorporation of an admittedly powerful female element in a new stable world under male dominion.[2] Why then did a women-only cult like the Thesmophoria need to exist?

In this paper I look at the cults of Demeter and Kore with refer-ence most often to the Eleusinian Mysteries and the Thesmophoria. These two cults are usually discussed and interpreted separately, and on the face of it they are very different. The Eleusinian Mysteries were held only in one location, though they were strongly linked with Athens. Women and slaves could participate, as well as men, after initiation. The culminating event took place inside a unique congreg-ational structure, the Telesterion. The significance of the Mysteries is usually thought to be the cycle of growth through death and rebirth, both agricultural and spiritual.[3] Though different in many ways from other festivals in Greek religion, the Eleusinian Mysteries are somehow seen as 'safe', if not actually 'normal'.

By contrast the Thesmophoria were held everywhere in the Greek world, making them, in Nilsson's classic dictum, 'the most widespread cult in Greek religion'. Only citizen women could participate, and the festival apparently took place outside. The Thesmophoria are conventionally construed as an essential *polis* ritual in which citizen women of child-bearing age helped to ensure the survival of the *polis* through the production of food and the reproduction of legitimate heirs. Yet both ancient and modern discussions of this crucial cult convey considerable anxiety about it, from Aristophanes' play to Detienne (contradictions between women as simultaneously marginal reproducers and central religious celebrants), Zeitlin (women correlate negatively with disorder) and Winkler (despite their central role in the Thesmophoria and other cults, women can express themselves only indirectly and covertly; there is at best 'the possibility of a different consciousness').[4]

Insofar as modern scholars have considered the Eleusinian Mysteries and the Thesmophoria together, they have described (to use the model first proposed by Edwin Ardener) the Eleusinian Mysteries as a dominant, male cult, unproblematic and neatly fitting in with various ideologies, while the Thesmophoria represent a muted, female one – strange, possibly obscene, uneasily aligned with *polis* priorities.[5] But these descriptions make inappropriate use of the model, precisely because the Thesmophoria was not an obscure cult, infrequently celebrated in some ancient backwater.

In fact, several important similarities link the Eleusinian Mysteries and the Thesmophoria. They constitute two of the most important and durable religious festivals in the ancient world, both lasting well into the imperial period. They both required secrecy and were therefore different from other mainstream cults. They were both connected with fertility. And finally, they are both part of the observance of the same deity, and should therefore be seen as two parts of the whole package of Demeter cults.[6] In the Greek bisexual, polytheistic system it is perfectly possible to have two 'dominant' festivals of the same female god, but it is always relevant that it is a goddess.

In this paper I first look briefly at the archaeological evidence for four sanctuaries, focusing on the pre-Roman period. The second section is botanical. I discuss four plants mentioned in ancient sources and their applications. In the third section I return to the story of Demeter and Kore as told in the *Homeric Hymn to Demeter* (*HHD*).

I will then suggest another perspective and interpretation. Throughout the paper I include both the Mysteries and the Thesmophoria as part of the Demeter 'package', and use all three kinds of evidence without privileging texts outside the *Hymn*. In so doing I hope to contribute to the discussion of the larger questions raised above.

## SANCTUARIES

Brumfield's evaluation of the epigraphic and textual evidence for Demeter cults in Attica has given us an idea of the cult calendar in this region and its close links with the agricultural year. On the basis of this evidence most Demeter and Kore cults fall into one of two categories: those that could be celebrated only in one particular sanctuary (notably Eleusis), and those that could be celebrated at many locations. The fourth-century BC Peiraieus decree makes it clear that a sanctuary could be used for more than one festival; in this case, the Thesmophoria. Plerosia, Kalamaia, Skira, and private occasions are mentioned, all of which were for women only.[7]

On the ground the distinction between unique and multiple locations still holds. Eleusis is obviously the best example of a unique Demeter sanctuary. Multiple Demeter sanctuaries are the focus of a study by Cole, who notes, like Rolley, that they are often to be identified on the basis of the finds, which usually reflect agricultural concerns: *hydriai* (for water) and *kernoi* (for grain); terracotta figurines of women carrying *hydriai*, plants, and animals (especially pigs); terracotta pigs; and pig bones. According to Cole, Demeter sanctuaries could be located within cities, just outside, and on the borders of the territory. Because of the need for secrecy, even sanctuaries within city walls could be relatively isolated. Proximity to a water source seems also to have been a factor in the location of Demeter sanctuaries.[8]

Cole notes on the basis of the evidence from Attica that most Demeter sanctuaries were probably not just for the Thesmophoria, though she does not discuss attaching different votives to different festivals. It would be difficult, because there are several cities with more than one Demeter sanctuary. Were individual sanctuaries used only for certain Demeter rituals, e.g. those for women? Or were they used for all Demeter cults by members of the same kin group or neighbourhood? Or was it some combination of these? It is thus inappropriate to describe a Demeter sanctuary simply as a Thesmophorion, or even the Thesmophorion, of city X without further evidence.

In a short article it was not possible for Cole to indicate the wide local variation in votives (and their deposition), nor – more seriously – to address architecture. The votives at Demeter sanctuaries may be partially predictable, but the architecture never is. Here I look briefly at Eleusis, and then at three multiple Demeter and Kore sanctuaries, at Bitalemi/Gela, Acrocorinth, and Priene, to demonstrate links between Eleusis and other Demeter sanctuaries, and to show how far Demeter and Kore sanctuaries differ from the perceived norm of a *temenos* with peripteral temple, cult statue, and altar.

The sanctuary of Demeter and Kore at Eleusis lies within the city wall, but was separated from the town by the acropolis (Figure 5.1). The first large-scale Telesterion was built in the sixth century BC, and the sanctuary continued in use until later antiquity. As mentioned earlier, the Telesterion is a large congregational structure. There was a well outside the north entrance to the sanctuary. The finds included *kernoi*; at least three terracotta figurines of women, and a marble pig dedicated in the sanctuary. A fourth-century marble relief found at Eleusis shows worshippers approaching Demeter (with phiale and sceptre) and Kore (with torches) with a piglet.[9]

The sanctuary at Bitalemi lies on a low hill across the river from the city (and its wall) (Figure 5.2). A graffito on a fifth-century Attic vase fragment, 'to the Thesmophoroi from the skanai of Dikaio', confirms that this was a sanctuary of Demeter and Kore. The sanctuary was in use from the mid-seventh century to the Carthaginian destruction of Gela in 405, but was not re-established when the city was rebuilt in the fourth century. No architecture from the earliest phase has been preserved; what survives is certainly not monumental, consisting of *naiskoi* or *sacelli*. The largest structure, G2, identified by the excavator as a *lesche* or meeting-place, measures only 4 by 11 metres. Deposits of ash, animal bones, especially pig, burnt cooking pots, and knives suggest that ritual meals were consumed in the sanctuary. One deposit includes a two-stone hearth with a pig mandible and some 20 pots, used in the ritual meal, placed on top.

Among the early offerings were agricultural tools (iron plough-shares, sickles, hoes, and axes, and querns), 'premonetary' bronzes (*aes signatum*), and bronze jewellery. Terracottas of women carrying piglets, poppy flowers, or children as well as female masks and *protomes* were common, especially in later phases. Lamps and loomweights were also found. Ninety per cent of all offerings, however, consisted of unpainted pots set upside down, either isolated or in groups; *kylikes* (drinking vessels), *oinochoai* (wine jugs), and small *hydriai* were the

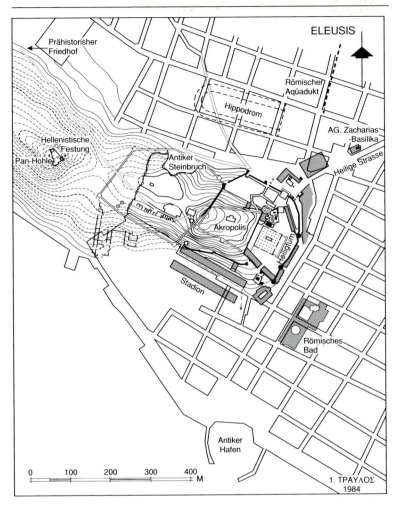

*Figure 5.1* Eleusis, plan of the sanctuary and city

*Source:* Travlos 1988: fig. 105

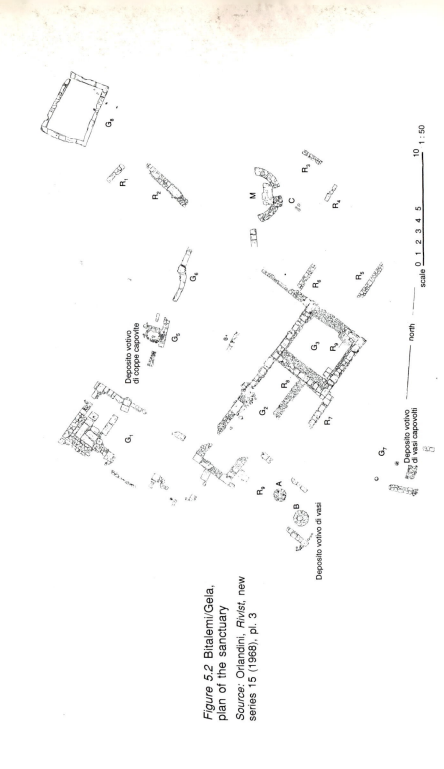

*Figure 5.2* Bitalemi/Gela, plan of the sanctuary

*Source*: Orlandini, *RivIst*, new series 15 (1968), pl. 3

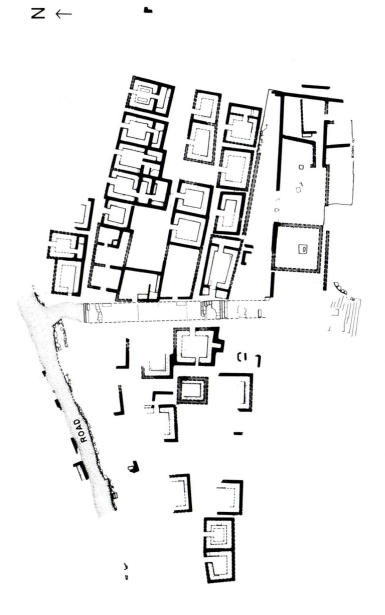

N ←

ROAD

*Figure 5.3* Corinth, plan of the sanctuary of Demeter and Kore, *c.* 400 BC    *Source:* With thanks to Nancy Bookidis; also published in Bookidis 1993: 46

predominant shapes. In one instance, 100 fifth-century unpainted cups were placed upside down, more or less in a semi-circle, near an earlier structure. In one corner there was a terracotta figurine with a piglet and poppy flowers. Within the semi-circle stood an *oinochoe* and a cup, right side up.[10]

The Demeter and Kore sanctuary at Corinth lies within the city walls, about 15–20 minutes' walk south of the city centre, on the lower slopes of Acrocorinth (Figure 5.3). Cult activity began in the seventh century, reached its peak in the sixth to fourth centuries, and continued in the Hellenistic period until 146 BC. After 100 years of abandonment the cult was revived, and remained active until the fourth century AD. The identification of the sanctuary is confirmed by *graffiti* and *dipinti*.

The sanctuary is arranged on three terraces with three different functions. The lowest terrace, at the northern end, was used for dining. By the late fifth century, there were 30 dining-rooms with couches for 200 people (more than at any other Greek sanctuary), most with additional facilities for sitting, washing, and cooking. Very few bones were found in the dining-rooms, but one fifth-century example (Figure 5.3: N: 21–2) has pig and other bones on the floor. The number of querns found in the sanctuary suggests that grain may have been an important item on the menu.

The middle terrace was used for sacrifice and offerings. Seven miniature *kalathoi* (baskets) were set upright at the bottom of one stone-lined pit. At the eastern end of the terrace another, larger stone-lined pit dated to the Hellenistic period was full of ash and charred pig bones. Elsewhere on this terrace, some 50 pots, mostly classical *kalathoi*, were piled up in a 'pottery pocket' against one wall of a room.

On the upper terrace at the southern end of the sanctuary there were two rock-cut theatral areas with room for 85–90 spectators. Near the western theatral area was a rock-cut well.

Besides finds already mentioned there were some 23,000 terracotta figurines, including standing females with *polos* (archaic), jointed female figures, described as dolls (classical), standing females, often with *polos*, with a piglet and sometimes a torch as well (Hellenistic). Other terracotta dedications included miniature offering trays, some perhaps related to *kernoi*, others in the shape of *likna* (winnowing fans), containing small cakes, loaves, and fruit. Miniature vases – *kalathoi*, and later *hydriai* – were found in abundance, as were lamps and loomweights. Among the more expensive dedications were a scarab and a silver ring. Table, cooking, and storage vessels were also

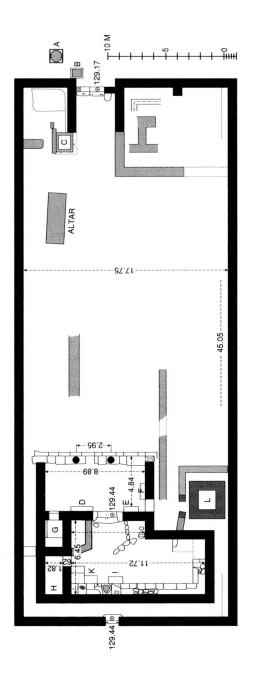

*Figure 5.4* Priene, plan of the sanctuary of Demeter and Kore

*Source:* Wiegand and Schrader 1904: 148

present; the only tools discovered were knives, probably used for sacrifice/butchery, rather than as votives.[11]

The sanctuary of Demeter and Kore at Priene is again within the city wall, but on the west end of a terrace above the city centre, on the way to the acropolis (Figure 5.4). It was built in the mid-fourth century at the time of the relocation or expansion of the city, and remained in use at least until the first century BC. It was eventually destroyed by Christians. The identification of the sanctuary is confirmed by two inscribed bases of statues representing priestesses of Demeter and Kore just outside the entrance to the *temenos*, on the east. Just inside the entrance there was a water basin, and there may have been a spring near the *temenos*.

Within the *temenos* was a structure with its entrance – a porch with two Doric columns in antis – on the eastern side, but with its long axis oriented north-south. The walls were constructed of earth and rubble, faced in and out with marble plaster, incised to imply socle and orthostate blocks. The structure had three rooms, one large (11.7 by 6.5 metres) and two small, on the north side. The large room had a bench running along its back (west) wall which continued around the two corners; it (and the two marble tables set along it) may have provided space for offerings. In the north-east corner of the large room were found two marble heads of female statues. Outside the structure on the south-east was a stone-lined pit, empty except for rubbish and fallen stones. Between the structure and the later wall enclosing the pit was an accumulation of miniature *hydriai* and 212 terracotta figurines (third to first centuries). They include dancing and standing girls and women, female *hydrophoroi*, pigs, and the unique Baubo figurines (the oldest dated to the early second century): a female body without head or breasts, with the face represented on the stomach, carrying a *kithara*, a torch, or an offering tray with small cakes or fruit.[12]

I hope I have shown that there is good reason to consider all sanctuaries of Demeter and Kore as part of the 'package' of cults associated with them. Like other Demeter sanctuaries, the Telesterion at Eleusis has an isolated location (even within the city wall) with provision for water. Two of the four sanctuaries discussed have space for communal viewing (Eleusis, Acrocorinth); we cannot say what the two large rooms at Bitalemi and Priene were used for (though it is interesting that they are of comparable size). There are special deposits of offerings at Bitalemi and Acrocorinth; we cannot be certain that the votive 'accumulation' at Priene was actually placed, and not enough information has been published about votives at Eleusis. Piglets link all four sanctuaries; women with torches connect three (Eleusis, Acrocorinth, Priene), as do miniature *hydriai* (as far as we know none were found at Eleusis).

Not enough work has been done on votives and the way they were deposited in sanctuaries to say whether the deposits in these sanctuaries are as unusual as they seem. But their architecture alone should serve to put all of them in a different category from that of sanctuaries with the conventional arrangement of temple with cult statue inside and altar outside. The two Doric columns and incised marble plaster at Priene serve only to remind us how unusual this and the other three sanctuaries actually were.

## PLANTS

The symbolic significance of plants in texts is frequently acknowledged; their pragmatic importance is not always full explored. Here I look at four plants linked with Demeter and Kore: pennyroyal and pomegranate (from the *Homeric Hymn to Demeter* (*HHD*)),[13] whose story is connected with the Eleusinian Mysteries; and pine and vitex (the chaste-tree) from later texts concerning the Thesmophoria. All four had a number of different medical applications; I focus on those connected with human reproduction.

In the *HHD*, Demeter requests a drink, *kykeon*, made of barley meal, water, and tender pennyroyal, *Mentha pulegium L.* The text is clear as to the species, and translators do no service by rendering it simply as mint. Aristophanes makes it clear that he and his audience knew of its use as an anti-fertility drug. In the Hippocratic Corpus, pennyroyal is recommended for opening the uterus for various reasons: preconceptual purgation, hysteria, emmenagogue, expulsion (of foetus/afterbirth), and stimulation of lochia. Dioscorides, Pliny, and Galen also recommend it as emmenagogue and abortifacient. Soranus mentions it as one of several aromatic restoratives in labour. Pennyroyal and its extract, the ketone pulegone, work by stimulating contractions of the uterus, hence its use in preventing or ending a pregnancy. It can also be used to strengthen contractions in labour, to help expel the placenta, and to assist the involution of the uterus after birth, though these uses are not specifically mentioned in ancient sources.[14]

Immediately after the *kykeon* episode in the *HHD*, Metaneira offers Demeter the job of looking after her baby son and Demeter accepts, making it clear that she is a skilled practitioner of herbal medicine: she knows the right antidote (literally 'anti-cutting' of plant or root) for dangerous medicine, as well as a strong safeguard against bad magic. Demeter's positive connection with plant lore is in striking contrast with the more common, negative associations of women and 'root-cutting' represented by Medea and Circe.[15]

Towards the end of the poem Persephone tells Demeter that Hades tricked her and forced her to eat a pomegranate seed. In so doing, Hades compelled Persephone to spend part of the year with him in the underworld, but he may also, presumably unwittingly, have caused Persephone to be sterile. In medical texts the value of pomegranate, *Punica granatum* L., as an anti-fertility drug is only gradually realised. In the Hippocratic Corpus it is an astringent cleanser, mostly for conditions affecting the uterus and female genitals, such as abnormal uterine discharge, thrush, prolapse, and hysteria. Like pennyroyal, pomegranate is used for expulsion (of foetus/afterbirth). Pomegranate seems not to be recommended as part of any treatment to promote fertility in the Hippocratic Corpus. Pliny says that it is 'useful for doctors'; Dioscorides apparently makes an oblique reference to pomegranate as an abortifacient. But Soranus is very clear on the main use of pomegranate: he lists no fewer than five different prescriptions for contraceptive pessaries. Clement of Alexandria says that women at the Thesmophoria were not allowed to eat pomegranate seeds that had fallen on the ground. It is now known that the pomegranate contains female sex hormones, hence its effectiveness as a contraceptive.[16]

Two other plants are later connected with the cults of Demeter. The scholiast on Lucian, who gives the most complete account of the Thesmophoria, says that during the festival Greek women threw pine branches (*konou thallous*) into chasms along with piglets, and that both are symbolic of the *genesis* of crops and men and therefore a suitable offering to Demeter. Stephanos of Byzantium says in connection with Miletos that at the Thesmophoria there, pine branches (*pituos kladon*) were used in the temporary shelters, and that pine cones (*konon pituos*) were used as offerings, again because of their connection with *genesis*.

According to the Hippocratic Corpus, pine resin (from *Pinus brutia, laricio, halepensis, pinea*) is one of several emollient *pharmaka* that bring on strong *katharsin* (usually meaning cleaning of the uterus through menstruation); it could be used as an extract or as the resin which is present in branches. Most of its applications are gynaecological:

abnormal uterine discharge, thrush, prolapse, hysteria, amenorrhoea, preconceptual softening, cleansing, and opening of the womb, emmenagogue, expulsion of afterbirth, and stimulation of lochia. Pine bark was recommended for some of these applications and for fumigation in a difficult labour. Dioscorides says that pine products are abortifacient; Pliny names the ground pine (*Ajuga chia Schreb.* or *A. chamaepitys Schreb.*) as an emmenagogue. Soranus says that pine bark can prevent pregnancy and that it can improve breast milk. Recent research suggests that the Scotch pine (*Pinus sylvestris* L.), like pomegranate, contains female sex hormones (and therefore can have contraceptive effects), and that pine needles can inhibit implantation and early pregnancy in rats.[17]

The earliest associations of vitex with the Thesmophoria, usually in Athens/Attica, occur in Dioscorides and Pliny, and are therefore relatively late: women are said to sit or lie on branches of vitex during the second day of the festival. In the Hippocratic Corpus vitex has various uses, mostly gynaecological: for abnormal uterine discharge, hysteria, conception, expulsion of afterbirth/foetus, speeding up labour, galactagogue. Its applications partially overlap with those of pennyroyal, pomegranate, and pine, but it is clearly not regarded as an opener or cleanser of the uterus. Dioscorides says that it brings on menstruation, birth, and milk, and that it was considered a purifier because of its association with the Thesmophoria; Pliny that vitex promotes menstruation, purges the uterus, encourages abundant milk, and preserves chastity by inhibiting sexual desire; he seems to be the first to mention vitex as an anaphrodisiac.

Modern research has produced ambivalent results on vitex as an anti-fertility drug – one study says that it has no contraceptive effect, others suggest that it is an abortifacient. Other recent studies have established, more plausibly, that vitex is not itself hormonal (unlike pomegranate and pine) but instead acts on the pituitary gland so that hormones are produced in the right order and in the right quantities. Thus vitex can be used for any gynaecological problem connected with hormonal imbalance, e.g. regulation of menstrual cycles; encouragement of conception, labour, and lactation; treatment of fibroids, ovarian cists, and endometriosis; management of symptoms of menopause.[18]

The three plants identifiable by species (pennyroyal, pomegranate, vitex) are all easily recognisable and extremely common; nor were pines of various species difficult to find. The processes of making the various medicines were not complicated. The references to pennyroyal in Aristophanes suggest that plant lore and the preparation were familiar subjects to ordinary women as well as to the male authors who wrote about them. The positive association between Demeter and herbal medicine has already been mentioned. Also important is the general agreement by ancient medical writers on the uses of these plants, nearly always confirmed by modern scientific research.

It is all the more striking, then, that both ancient and modern commentators on the cults of Demeter and Kore have assumed that known anti-fertility agents could have nothing to do with cults associated by them with fertility. Thus the use of pennyroyal as an abortifacient has often been considered irrelevant to cults at Eleusis; and the non-anaphrodisiac effects of vitex have been thought 'contradictory' for the Thesmophoria.[19] Similarly, ancient and modern commentators have clung to the symbolic fertility of pomegranates and pine cones, and have screened out their attested medical uses as anti-fertility drugs.

There is at least one other way of assessing the significance of these plants, which avoids all contradictions. Of course the cultic functions of (for example) pennyroyal and vitex were not transferable between the Eleusinian Mysteries and the Thesmophoria. The point is that together the plants could provide an easily accessible way for women to regulate every stage of their reproductive lives (menstruation, conception, abortion, delivery, lactation, and possibly menopause). The conventional assumption in most interpretations of the cults is that fertility, human as well as agricultural, was always to be promoted. The connection of the plants with the cults of Demeter and Kore suggests that control of human fertility – both promotion and suppression – might well have been in the hands of women. Kalligeneia, the third day of the Thesmophoria, may refer to births that were beautiful because they were chosen. It then becomes possible to suggest a truly polyvalent interpretation of the cults, as male and female desire for controlled fertility can have at least two meanings: men may have wanted to ensure legitimate heirs, but women knew that fertility was a matter of choice, and that they were only as fertile as they wanted to be.

## THE STORY OF DEMETER AND KORE

The *HHD* is a surprising poem. It tells an unusual kind of story and it has an unusual focus. In this section I discuss its departure from, and subversion of, the usual Greek story told about girls. I then go on to look at the *HHD*'s focus, which is not on the father-son relationships that preoccupy much of Greek mythology, but instead on the relationship between a mother and a daughter.

In my introduction I noted that Greek religion could be described as a bisexual polytheistic system, in which males were nonetheless in charge, in heaven as on earth. In this asymmetrically gendered system, Greek gods and humans did come in both sexes, no matter how much this was deplored at the human level.[20] But there is one category in Greek religion that did not come in both sexes, namely heroes (epic rather than local). Epic heroes are always male, and their life-stories follow a general pattern elucidated by scholars such as Lord Raglan and Propp.[21] While heroes always manage to complete their heroic tasks, they are not always successfully fertile. Even if heroes do have sons, their offspring may not survive them, as in the case of Jason.

If females cannot be heroes, there can be no direct equivalent of the hero story for women. The only female story pattern to have emerged is Burkert's interestingly named 'girl's tragedy', with its sequence of departure, seclusion, rape, tribulation, and rescue after the birth of a male child, usually destined to be a hero; Danaë is a good example.[22] In this type of narrative, the girl's story usually ends as the boy's begins; indeed the whole point of the girl's 'tragedy' is the birth of a baby boy.

The story of Demeter and Kore in the *HHD* more or less follows this pattern to begin with, but there are some obvious differences: first, the rescue takes place not after birth, but after contraception (through Hades' administration of the pomegranate seeds; cf. discussion on p. 86), and there is no suggestion in the *HHD* that Kore will have children of either sex; and, second, the rescue is performed by the girl's own mother who also happens to be a god.[23]

The *HHD*, then, is the story of a mother using her own power on behalf of her daughter, in order to change the terms of a contract put together by the daughter's father and uncle, so that the daughter can have a different marriage and therefore a better future. Like the multiple girls' 'tragedies' and boys' heroic lives, the story is part of mainstream Greek mythology; unlike them, it seems to be unique. Indeed, for a time I wondered if the story were not unique, full stop, until I realised that it occurs, and more than once, in a more recent narrative tradition, the European fairy tale.

There are several fairy tales in which a mother, often transformed or acting through an intermediary, helps her daughter to negotiate a better future, in the form of a good marriage, by rescuing her from an ordeal of some kind, often involving a drop in social status. For example, in the German versions of Cinderella, it was the tree growing on Cinderella's mother's grave (and the bird living in it) that worked the magic; in French versions it is the fairy godmother who waves a wand and rescues Cinderella from kitchen work so that she can marry the prince.[24] In fairy tales the daughter generally has centre stage (Kore does not speak until the end of the *HHD*, whose main character is really Demeter), but rescuing a daughter from tribulation and negotiating a better future through marriage are still crucial parts of the story.

Even more recently, the rescue of a female child has emerged as a theme in feminist science fiction in English. In these stories, outsiders, usually female and often multiple, but still recognisably maternal, intervene to rescue a girl from an oppressive society and therefore to provide her with a future that is both active and free; marriage is irrelevant.[25]

The Demeter and Kore story was both unique and important in its own time, no doubt because of its connection with contemporary cults. By contrast, both fairy tales and science fiction have produced more than one example of the story, but the connection of the female children to their biological mothers is progressively diluted as the ending of the story becomes increasingly radical, ultimately requiring the removal of the child from her natal society, while the link with mainstream religion was severed long before the time of the Brothers Grimm. Similarly, the circulation of these later stories has probably decreased over time – everyone presumably knew the story of Demeter and Kore, most people knew the stories of Cinderella and the Goose Girl, but relatively few people read science fiction.

The story of a daughter's rescue by a maternal figure is therefore an unusual but durable one in European culture. The *HHD* provides a unique and surprising Greek example, in that it subverts the more common stories of 'tragic' girls. It is now time to move from girls' stories to a discussion of the *HHD*'s equally unusual focus on mother-daughter relationships.

The connection between father and son is one of the most important relationships in Greek myth, as in Greek culture.[26] As stated earlier, the *HHD* is unusual in focusing on a mother-daughter relationship. This focus, moreover, is not simply a difference in gender, but also a difference in the kind of relationship between parent and child. Fathers want sons, even though the succession from father to

son may not be an orderly handing over of power from one generation to the next, but a source of conflict, often violent. The struggles
of Ouranos, Kronos, and Zeus come to an end because of Kronos'
defeat, followed by Zeus' marriage to Metis whom he swallowed
rather than let her bear a second, male, powerful child.[27] The story
of Laios and Oidipous provides an example at the human level; the
story comes to an end because Polyneices and Eteocles kill each other
over the succession. As for heroes, they are sometimes responsible for
the death of a father or father-figure, as with Jason who killed his
wicked uncle Pelias. The violence associated with the Greek father-
son relationship may explain the ambivalence towards reproduction
expressed as heroic infertility. Father-son violence does of course occur
in other cultures, for example, in the Judaeo-Christian tradition where
the stories of Abraham and Isaac, and God and Jesus are usually
classified as 'sacrifice', with Mary as a 'tragic girl' *à la* Burkert.[28] The
case of Demeter and Kore is therefore strikingly different from these
stories, as the mother rescues the daughter without resorting to
violence, and the daughter seems glad of the continuing link with her
mother.

Any focus on parent-child relationships necessarily embodies a view
of human fertility and can be used to explore ideas about it. The
father-son relationship, though often difficult, was nonetheless
extremely important in Greek culture. Thus the dominant Greek
scientific theory of conception, that of Aristotle, is ideologically linked
with non-scientific views in earlier texts, and is vehemently male
monogenetic, i.e., humans are stuck with bisexual reproduction, but
there is only one true creative principle involved and it is male; fathers
therefore are primarily responsible for engendering sons.[29] Delaney
has noticed a link between male monogenesis and male monotheism:
'the theory of conception and the conception of the deity are . . . two
aspects of the same system'.[30] Her link is relevant to this discussion.
The privileging of the father-son relationship in Greek culture and
the Greek male monogenetic view of conception have already been
mentioned. Zeus is only one of a number of gods, but he is definitely
in charge; while not the sole creator of the world, he is frequently
described as 'father'.[31]

Theories of male monogenesis and a latent male monotheism might
well suggest that Greek women had no active role in any aspect of
fertility. But the references to pennyroyal and pomegranate in the
*HHD* (and to pine and vitex in allusions to the Thesmophoria) imply
that any woman with knowledge of these plants could regulate her

own reproductive life as she chose. Demeter's control of agricultural fertility is made very clear in the *HHD*, and is all the more surprising for being couched in male monogenetic terms – the all-important (male) seed will not grow because Demeter hides it and the earth cannot send it back up (*aniemi*): there is no question of an equal, creative female contribution from Demeter or the earth.[32]

To conclude this section, the story of Demeter and Kore is unusual in several respects: it subverts the usual Greek girl's story, and it focuses on a harmonious mother-daughter relationship rather than a violent father-son dyad. Finally, it suggests that despite a male monogenetic view of conception and a male god-in-charge sort of polytheism, both human and agricultural fertility were subject to some degree of female control. Agricultural fertility is overtly restored when Demeter sends the hidden seed back up; human fertility is covertly prevented when ignorant Hades administered a known contraceptive to his wife, who might otherwise have borne him a child.[33]

## CONCLUSION

I hope I have shown the usefulness of considering the cults of Demeter and Kore as constituent parts of one system. The sanctuaries of Demeter and Kore have a number of shared peculiarities with respect to their location, architecture, and finds, making them unusual compared with most other sanctuaries. The Eleusinian Mysteries and the Thesmophoria, are further linked by the four plants mentioned in connection with them, all of which have to do with the control of human fertility. The *HHD* has an unusual focus on a mother-daughter relationship nearly destroyed by a marriage arranged by others.

I conclude that there are at least two views of fertility in the cults of Demeter and Kore, depending, so to speak, on whom you might have talked to about them.[34]

The dominant male view would be the conventional view of ancient and modern male commentators, mentioned at the beginning of this paper – fathers want sons, women are necessary to produce legitimate heirs in order to perpetuate the *polis*, so let the women have their separate fertility cults as well as participating in the Mysteries. The not-so-muted female view could well have been different – women knew ways of controlling their own fertility and in remembering the anger and power of Demeter negotiating on behalf of her daughter, they helped their own daughters manage their married lives by passing on that knowledge. If Demeter

Thesmophoros was the bringer of order then perhaps it was an order in which women had some say.

## ACKNOWLEDGEMENTS

Earlier versions of this article were given at the Women in Antiquity Seminar, Oxford (1991) and in classes (1991, 1993) at the University of New Brunswick at Saint John (as well as at the Women in Antiquity Conference, 1993). I thank the members of these audiences for their comments, as well as the editors of this volume. Special thanks to Jennifer Moody and Oliver Rackham who taught me to take plants seriously, and to Anne McIntyre, MNIMH for help with references on plant remedies. Thanks also to Simon Price, Robert Parker, and Christiane Sourvinou-Inwood who read the draught; and to Elizabeth and Miranda Nixon for providing support during the final writing-up. I am most grateful to librarians in Saint John (Science Fiction and Fantasy Collection) and Oxford (Ashmolean and Taylorian Libraries) for their help, and to Nancy Bookidis for providing a plan for the sanctuary at Corinth. I am, of course, responsible for the faults that remain.

## NOTES

1 Arthur 1982a on three stages in Hesiod, for a view of the building of that system.
2 Arthur 1994: 241.
3 Foley 1994: 65–71.
4 Nilsson 1906: 313; Detienne 1989; Zeitlin 1982: 129–47; Winkler 1990a; Foley 1994: 71–4; cf. now Osborne 1993. For the timing of these and other Demeter cults, see Brumfield 1981; and Foxhall, Chapter 6.
5 E. Ardener 1975a and b.
6 Clinton's proposal that in Eleusis the Thesmophoria were held in the forecourt of the Telesterion suggests an important physical link between the two cults; Clinton 1988: 72–3, 76, 79, and 1993: 113.
7 Brumfield 1981; Foxhall, Chapter 6. Peiraieus decree *IG* II$^2$ 1177 = *LSCG* 36. In addition there are the Eleusinion at Athens and a possible Eleusinion at Paiania (the latter's function is not known); and lesser mysteries not only at Agrai but also at Phlya and Phrearrhioi; Brumfield 1981: 162, 177 n. 21, 142.
8 Cole 1994; Rolley 1965. Cities with more than one sanctuary of Demeter mentioned by Cole: Megara, Hermione, Gela, Selinous. Thasos may have had two Demeter sanctuaries: the excavated extramural sanctuary identified as a Thesmophorion (part of which was used for a local phratry cult); and a sanctuary of Demeter Eleusinia attested by an inscription mentioning its priestess, found in the agora; see also Rolley 1965.

9  Eleusis: Mylonas 1961; Travlos 1988 (both with plans); Clinton 1992 (who rightly remarks that it is wrong to think of Eleusis only in connection with the Eleusinian Mysteries, which may postdate the Thesmophoria, Clinton 1992: 6–7, and cf. 28–37; cf. also Parker 1991. There is, alas, no complete publication of the site and its finds. Three archaic female terracottas, two seated and one standing, Mylonas and Kourouniotes *AJA* 37, 1933: 282 and fig. 15. Marble relief, *LIMC* IV, s.v. Demeter no. 234.

10 Bitalemi/Gela: Kron 1992 (with plan) usefully summarises the results of excavations by Orsi (1901) and Orlandini (1960s), with references. The combination of agricultural tools and *kourotrophos* figurines (though in different periods) underlines the significance of agricultural and human fertility: Sfameni Gasparro 1986: 279–80. Some finds are not obviously connected with Demeter, e.g. the terracotta silenus figure, Orlandini, *Kokalos* 12, 1966: 20 and plate X.1.

11 Corinth: Bookidis 1993; Bookidis and Stroud 1987, both with plans. 'Pottery pocket', Stroud, *Hesp.* 37, 1968: 304–5, plate 88a. Some of the finds were connected with Dionysos: Bookidis and Stroud 1987: 27. Male names as dedicators suggest that men were somehow involved in the cult; cf. also the 40 large terracotta statues of youths: Bookidis 1993: 50; Bookidis and Stroud 1987: 14, fig. 12.

12 Priene: (re)location of city, Demand 1986. Inscriptions naming Demeter and Kore, or Kore: von Gaertringen 1906: nos 171–3; note number 196 mentions Philios' dream of the *thesmophorous . . . potnias*, not a Thesmophorion. Sanctuary and finds: Wiegand and Schrader 1904: 147–63, with plan; Raeder 1983: 26, 28, 38–9. Terracottas, Töpperwein-Hoffmann 1971. Once again, not all the terracottas have an obvious link with Demeter; e.g. Eros leaning on Hermes. Baubo figurines, *LIMC* III, s.v. Baubo, no. 1 and cf. esp. no. 2; S. Ardener 1987; Olender 1990; the Baubo figurines leave out the one part of a woman's body generally thought of as good, i.e., the breasts, crucial for the nourishment and survival of babies. Cf. also Golden 1988 on piglets and obscenity.

13 I have focused on pennyroyal and pomegranate because they were actually consumed, but other plants are mentioned in the *HHD*, notably the flowers in the meadow (6–8, 425–9; cf. Richardson 1974). Two of these, narcissus and crocus, may have had some special connection with Demeter and Kore; cf. Soph. *OC* 681–5. Both are recommended as emmenagogues as well as for other treatments, mostly gynaecological, e.g. Hippocr. *Mul.* I.74 (Littré: 8.154.15, 16; 156.16). I present here a selection of references to Hippocr. as in notes 14, 16–18 below. Cf. other uses in Soranus, summarised in Temkin 1956, Materia Medica, s.v. narcissus and saffron, with references; Riddle 1992: 105 (crocus).

14 Pennyroyal: *HHD* 208–10. Aristoph. *Peace* 706–12, *Lys.* 87–9. Hippocr. *Mul.* I.37 (Littré: 8.92.7), I.74 (8.156.2), I.78 (8.178.18, 190.17, 194.5); *Mul.* II.134 (8.304.13); II.157 (8.334.12); *Nat. Mul.* 32 (7.364.2), 53 (7.396.6). Diosc. *MM* 3.31 (1.2). Pliny *NH* LIV.154, Galen, XI.867. Soranus II.2 (Temkin 1956). Discussion: Scarborough 1991: 144–5; Riddle 1992: 53–4, 59. Additional uses: McIntyre 1988: 100–1, 107, 108; cf. Potterton 1983: 142.

15  *HHD* 225–30. Richardson (1974) at I. 230 notes that another meaning for erusmon, safeguard, is 'the name of a vegetable whose seed is said to relieve pain in childbirth', Paus. Gr. fr. 182. Root-cutters, Scarborough 1991: 144.

16  Pomegranate: *HHD* 412. Hippocr. *Mul.* II.192 (Littré: 8.372.6, 15, 20); *Nat. Mul.* 60 (7.398.16), 5 (7.318.4); *Mul.* I.90 (8.216.5); *Nat. Mul.* 32 (7.356.12). Pliny *NH* XII.23.113. Soranus I.62, cf. III.44. Clem. *Protr.* II.19.3. Riddle 1992: 26, 33, 51–2 (Diosc.). Cf. Potterton 1983: 148. In depictions of Demeter and Kore, the main emblem of fertility seems to be the grain stalk, *LIMC* IV.2, s.v. Demeter; and Peschlow–Bindokat 1994. Pomegranates do occur at Kore's sanctuary at Locri but may not be emblems only of fertility: Sourvinou–Inwood 1978:107–9 (1991: 157–60); and *Notizie degli Scavi* 1911, 73.

17  Pine: Schol. Lucian, *Dialogues of the Courtesans* (Rabe 1906: 275–6); Steph. Byz. s.v. Miletos. Hippocr. *Superf.* 33 (Littré: 8.502.2); *Mul.* II.119 (8.260.3), 192 (8.372.3); *Mat. Mul.* 60 (7.398.17), 5 (7.318.6), 87 (7.408.8); *Mul.* 13 (8.22.11); *Steril.* 217 (8.420.7); *Mul.* 1.74 (8.516.4), 78 (8.180.19); *Steril.* 234 (8.448.9); *Mul.* 1.34 (8.80.19). Diosc. *MM* I. 69; Pliny *NH* XXIV. 29–30; Soranus 1.62, III.44. Riddle 1992: 51–2, 81, 83–4, 94. No research seems to have been done on the other effects noted by ancient authors.

18  Vitex: Hippocr. *Mul.* II.198 (Littré: 8.382.3), 201 (8.386.5); *Mul.* 1.75 (8.162.16), 78 (8.184.4), 77 (8.172.9), 44 (8.102.18). Diosc. (Thesmophoria generally; conusion of agnos, vitex and *hagnos*, pure), *MM* I.103. Pliny (Thesmophoria in Athens) *NH* XXIV. 59–64; Cf. Galen (Athens) XI.807, 809; Aelian (Attica) *NA* IX.26. Contraceptive: Hippocr., Diosc. *MM* 1.103: Pliny *NH* 24.59–63. Anti-fertility effects: Riddle 1992: 35. General regulation of female reproductive system: McIntyre 1988: 57; Mabey 1988: 124–5 and 282 (with references); Böhnert and Hahn 1990; Mills 1992. Vitex in the cults of Artemis: King 1993: 122–3; of Hera at Samos: Kron 1988: 138–41.

19  Detienne 1972: 153–58, 1979: 105–6, 1989: 147.

20  Loraux 1978.

21  Summarised in Dowden 1992: 146–8.

22  Burkert 1979: 6–7. The stories associated with local cult heroines like Iphigeneia are different from the hero story and girl's tragedy discussed here.

23  The Greek story was influenced but not definitively shaped by Mesopotamian precedents: Penglase 1994: 145–6, 157–8. In later myths Persephone was said to have had a child: Foley 1994: 110–1; cf. also Le Guin 1992.

24  Cinderella: Zipes 1987: 86–92 (German); Opie and Opie 1974 (French); Bottigheimer 1987: 44–5; cf. the role of Falada in *The Goose Girl*: Zipes 1987: 322–7; and that of the good fairy at Sleeping Beauty's christening, who commutes the death sentence to sleep: Opie and Opie 1974. For the reappearance of the fairy godmother in two recent works of popular fiction, see McCullough 1987; and Stewart 1988.

25  Russ 1981: 79–80; to her list of examples should be added Le Guin 1990. The work of Brown and Gilligan 1992 suggests that girls still face

difficulties ('the wall') as they approach sexual maturity.

26 Strauss 1993.

27 Hesiod, *Theog.* 886–93, 924–6; cf. Zeus' refusal to marry Thetis because of a similar prophecy: Aesch., *Prometheus Bound* 755–74, 907–15; Pindar, *Isthm.* 8.27–37.

28 Cf. Delaney 1986: 6–8, 298–303, who links the stories of Laios and Abraham with the Islamic Festival of Sacrifices.

29 Dean–Jones 1994: esp. ch. 3; cf. Lloyd 1983a: 87–94 for 'alternative theories of the female seed'.

30 Delaney 1991: 11; Delaney 1986 for basic exposition.

31 Zeus in charge in *HHD*: decision to marry Kore to Hades (1. 9); decision to bring Kore back from Hades and approve the one-third down/two-thirds up arrangement (ll. 441–8); Zeus as father (ll. 321, 347, 364).

32 *Aniemi* and hiding in *HHD*: ll. 306–7, 332, 353, 451–2, 471. The plants (pennyroyal, etc.) were perhaps thought to operate in a similar fashion, helping or rejecting the seed, rather than stimulating or preventing female contribution. It is beyond the scope of this paper to discuss the possibility of some earlier stage in Greek religion when goddesses were perhaps more powerful and there might also have been a less male monogenetic view of human fertility. But cf. again Arthur's analysis of the *Theogony* (1982a); cf. the inverse relationship between Christian elements and powerful heroines like the Goose Girl in fairy tales: Bottigheimer 1987: 46–7; and note in particular the effects of Christianity on matrilineal mythology in New Mexico: Gutiérrez 1991: 162.

33 Certainly marriage and children go together in the *HHD*; Kore was to have been a *thaleren* ... *akoitin*, l. 79; Demeter as nurse wishes for husbands and children for Keleos' daughters, l. 136.

34 Cf. Taggart 1990: esp. 219–24, where he suggests that versions of the same story will vary according to the gender of the story-teller.

# Chapter 6

# Women's ritual and men's work in ancient Athens[1]

## Lin Foxhall

## THE BACKGROUND

From the early days of the study of Greek religion the connection between agriculture, seasonality, fertility and females has been a favourite theme of scholarship. Though these elements may constitute a significant matrix, their integration, and hence the precise meaning of that matrix, is seriously problematic. For this reason it is difficult to say anything sensible about what the significance of the relationships between these elements might be.[2] Moreover, we all suffer now from a legacy of over-the-top Frazerian and other nineteenth- and early twentieth-century approaches to religion. These studies, set in an evolutionary framework and drawing on the social science of the period, perceived Greek religion, especially early Greek cult, as located towards the lower end of the developmental scale. The religion of classical Greece could therefore be 'mined' for the archaic customs which were held to be vestiges of an earlier and more primitive era (as, for example, in Nilsson's[3] and, more recently, Burkert's[4] work). Hence a concern with origins, roots and beginnings characterised this mode of scholarship. And so the cosmological ties between the cycles of farming and females, 'obvious' as they are to those of us steeped in that heritage of scholarly tradition, were (and often still are) eagerly held up as an explanation, indeed, as *the* explanation, for many Greek rites.[5]

Subsequent generations of scholars have coped with this groundwork in rather different ways. A surprising number[6] still focus on the primordial – the elements of classical religion which were supposed to be especially meaningful because they survived from the dim and distant past. Others have found it rather off-putting and dismissed the whole line of argument as irrelevant. Even a dyed-in-the-wool

*Table* 6.1  Agricultural jobs and festivals in Attica

| Modern month Attic month | Sept.–Oct. Boedromion | Oct.–Nov. Pyanopsion | Nov.–Dec. Malmakterion | Dec.–Jan. Poseideion | Jan.–Feb. Camelion |
|---|---|---|---|---|---|
| **Agricultural jobs** | | | | | |
| | manuring and field clearing | | | | fallow p |
| | | ploughing and sowing cereals and legumes | | | vine |
| | vintage and pressing | trenching, manuring, pruning vines | | | |
| | | trenching, manuring, pruning other fruit trees: planting new trees | | | |
| | fig harvest | | | | |
| | | olive picking and pressing (every other year) trenching, manuring, pruning olive trees | | | |
| | watering | | | | lambing an |
| | | | lambing and kidding | | |
| | | | | | sheep and goa |
| **Festivals and rituals** | | | | | |
| | Greater Mysteries 13–24 or so | 5 – Proerosia announced at Eleusis | only 1 known Attic festival this month (Pompaia) | 25–26 – Haloa (Rural Dionysia) | (C 12–15 – Lenaio L M (mi |
| | | 9–13 Thesmophoria 9 Stenia 10 T. at Halimous 11 T. Athens (1) 12 Nestaia (2) 13 Kalligeneia (3) Apalouria 19–21 or 26–28 | | | |

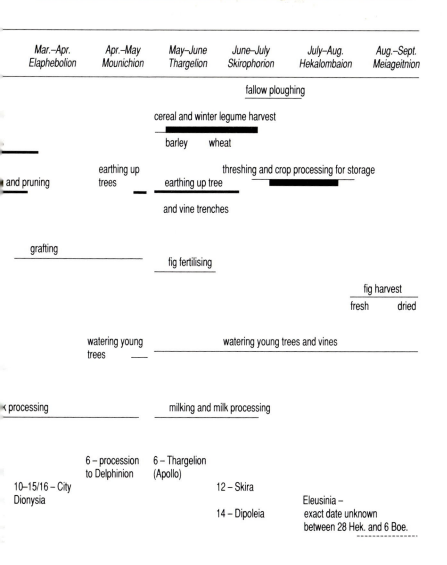

| Mar.–Apr.<br>Elaphebolion | Apr.–May<br>Mounichion | May–June<br>Thargelion | June–July<br>Skirophorion | July–Aug.<br>Hekalombaion | Aug.–Sept.<br>Meiageitnion |
|---|---|---|---|---|---|
| | | | fallow ploughing | | |
| | | cereal and winter legume harvest | | | |
| | | barley     wheat | | | |
| and pruning | earthing up trees | earthing up tree | threshing and crop processing for storage | | |
| | | and vine trenches | | | |
| grafting | | fig fertilising | | | |
| | | | | fig harvest | |
| | | | | fresh     dried | |
| | watering young trees | watering young trees and vines | | | |
| processing | | milking and milk processing | | | |
| 10–15/16 – City Dionysia | 6 – procession to Delphinion | 6 – Thargelion (Apollo) | | Eleusinia – exact date unknown between 28 Hek. and 6 Boe. | |
| | | | 12 – Skira | | |
| | | | 14 – Dipoleia | | |
| | | | | 28 – Panathenaia | |

evolutionist such as Burkert (who frequently uses ancient roots and beginnings as explanation)[7] is prepared to state that there is little correspondence between the festival calendar of Athens and the agricultural year.[8]

The most interesting insights have emanated from and been inspired by the work of French structuralists, such as Detienne's[9] work on the Thesmophoria and the Adoneia, Zeitlin's[10] incisive analysis and Winkler's[11] re-evaluation. This school of thought locates the many and varied practices of women's ritual firmly in the contemporary present of classical Athens, and there is much in it that is persuasive. But Detienne's structuralist patterns of oppositions are so carefully arranged that they are rendered inflexible, and Detienne is thus unable to accommodate 'discrepancies' in the data which do not fit his scheme.

Zeitlin's subtle study, full of important insights, has been much inspired by structuralist thought in this same tradition combined with American cultural anthropology. Again her interpretations focus on symbolic oppositions that are conceived as largely fixed and relatively inflexible, especially in relation to the meanings of space.

Winkler has convincingly modified Detienne's approach in a way which allows more malleable understandings by the participants. But he has construed women's rites entirely as a political expression of and reaction to oppressed femininity, not (as I would argue) as an on-going discourse which regularly reasserts and readjusts men's and women's cosmic and social places in relation to each other.

Discussion of women's cult practices in Greek religion has in some senses painted itself into a corner. The frustration with the present state of intellectual immobility is nicely summed up by Sally Humphreys:[12]

> we must be particularly careful, in studying the symbolic discourses of another culture to suppress our own intuitive assumptions about the real. It should not be taken as self-evident that if a ritual refers to political organisation, social categories and agricultural processes, its 'original' concern must have been agricultural. This assumption has given us a very unsatisfactory account of the Thesmophoria, which leaves a lot of questions unanswered.

Any attempt to relate religious festivals closely in date to agricultural activities rapidly becomes problematic, both being subject to considerable local variation, but the Thesmophoria certainly came at a time when farmers were busy.

Undoubtedly Humphreys[13] is right that the presence of agriculture and its cycles in ritual belong to quotidian reality rather than primordial vestiges. But where do we go from here? It is precisely because farming was such a significant part of daily reality that there is a need to look carefully again at its relationship to ritual as a formulator of meanings. It seems to me that the relationships of the matrix with which we started, farming, females and their cycles of reproduction, need to be considerably fine-tuned if we are to get beyond the level of the simplistic and the blatant. Few discussions which specifically focus on this matrix have got much beyond the Frazerian level – Allaire Brumfield's *The Attic Festivals of Demeter* (1981) is a notable exception. Far from having a simple or obvious relationship to the sequence of farming tasks, I will attempt to show that the rhythms of the festival year and the agricultural/working year weave in and out of the social and political structures of family and civic life. Though functionalist, it has avoided many of the inter-pretative pitfalls and wilder speculations of earlier works. She attaches Demeter festivals to critical points in the farming year – times of crisis and uncertainty. Generally her arguments are convincing, though she runs into trouble in trying to explain the timing of all festivals, for example, why there are sowing festivals but not harvest festivals dedicated to Demeter. Sensibly she does not try to fit every-thing to that single paradigm.

The central project of this paper is to reconsider the relationships between women's rites to Demeter (including 'women's mysteries' which are part of festivals celebrated more generally by both sexes) and the seasonal cycle of farming and gendered work patterns in ancient Attica. I shall attempt to examine them in the broader ritual setting of other gendered rites and celebrations in the official Athenian festival calendar. This means I shall concentrate on three state festi-vals which wholly or partially exclude men: the Thesmophoria, the Haloa and the Skira. Far from being a simple or obvious relation-ship, I will attempt to show that the rhythms of the festival year and the agricultural/working year weave in and out of the social and political structures of family and civic life. The arguments which follow refer to the calendars in Table 6.1.

## THE FESTIVALS AND THE CALENDAR

The fact that there was an official state calendar in Athens (as in other Greek *poleis*) which included some, but not all of the celebrated religious occasions is itself significant. The Athenian state used its religious calendar to construe itself as both a cosmic and a political order. At this point it is a truism that religious festivals were polysemic and no self-respecting scholar would talk about *the* meaning of a festival or ritual. Further, meanings obviously changed over time (though exactly how is generally not clear from our scattered and fragmentary sources). And religious ritual plainly held different meanings for different groups and individuals. Winkler[14] is surely correct that male and female insights, perspectives and experiences of women's rites were different. But it is surely also significant that the existence of these separated and distinct perspectives was state-sanctioned.

Why the state appropriates some but not other rites is sometimes obvious, but sometimes it is not. Given that the position of women *vis-à-vis* the state is often portrayed as marginal (both by the ancients themselves as well as by modern academics)[15] it is interesting and significant that 'women's mysteries' celebrating Demeter are fully included in the state calendar, and thus fully sanctioned by, and incorporated as part of, the *polis*.[16] Other women's celebrations, such as Detienne's 'opposite' to the Thesmophoria, the Adoneia, are not. Indeed though we have considerable evidence that these Demeter rites excluded men, we have little evidence to suggest that most religious festivals excluded either men or women.[17] Hence the state festival calendar constitutes an official version of the dynamics of gender on many levels, in terms of cosmology, work and social relations. This resides at the heart of the state, along with the continual discourse of gender relations which is constantly manipulated and modified by the participants.

It has long been recognised that the Thesmophoria is one of several festivals attached to (among other things) the autumn sowing of cereals. The other significant ones were the Eleusinian Mysteries and the Proerosia, which did not exclude men, indeed they were run by them.[18] The latter may have been celebrated in several locations in Attica,[19] but the best documented Proerosia is the Eleusinian sacred ploughing of the Rarian field. It seems most likely that this was a 'moveable feast', which occurred sometime in Pyanopsion. In the Eleusinian calendar (*IG* II$^2$ 1363) the announcement of the Proerosia is recorded, but not the festival itself, presumably because it depended on the inception of the rains in any particular year.[20] The Eleusinian Mysteries, celebrated in Boedromion, had a complex symbolic paradigm of their own in the classical period, in which the relationship to the agricultural year and the growth cycle of cereals was significant but not pre-eminent. Its emphasis was more on the general *fact* of the cultivation of cereals and the civilising effect on humanity of that gift of Demeter, than on the particularities of the cycle of farming.

The Thesmophoria consisted of three days proper plus two days of related festivals. This festival was celebrated with many local variations throughout Greece at both city-state and village level – conceptually a bit like the local and national variations on Christmas – but everywhere it was restricted to women.[21] In Athens the women took over the city, held their own sacrifices and performed a series of confusingly described rituals involving piglets and things that were composted into a 'sacred goop' (to pinch Winkler's[22] wonderful term) which was then mixed with the seed-corn. The timing of local and city Thesmophoriae varied from place to place, but they all fall in our months October and early November – the official Athenian celebration fell 9–13 Pyanopsion, which would be late October in most years.

Virtually all commentators have described the Thesmophoria as a sowing festival.[23] In fact, it occurs before the main period of the cereal sowing in November,[24] which coincides with the busiest time of year for farmers (November-mid December). In the most usual Attic farming systems, vines and fruit trees were also pruned and trenched at this time of year – the latter was particularly arduous and time-consuming work. In the years when the olives fruited, it was also the period of the olive harvest and pressing. So the group of autumn Demetrian festivals, and the women's Thesmophoria in particular, coincided with the period just before the busiest, most frantic and most critical period of the farming year for men. Significantly, during this busy time, more or less coinciding with the month Maimakterion, there are no major religious festivals and not a single recorded instance of a meeting of the assembly.[25] Though Mikalson[26] attributes this to the inclement weather it is much more likely to be sheer pressure of agrarian work.

It is also interesting to note the proximity of the Thesmophoria to the Apatouria,[27] dedicated to Apollo and celebrating male descent groups via phratries, a point to which I shall return later (p. 107).

The Haloa took place at the end of Poseidon. Despite the resemblance of the name to *halos*, threshing floor, the festival has nothing to do with threshing or threshing floors. Whether the name is derived from the word for threshing floor[28] or has something to do with another word, *aloai*, which means vineyards or orchards or even fields,[29] is irrelevant for my argument. Although not all the festivities excluded men, there seem to have been raucous, all-female bonfire parties, held at night, as well as a special, all-female meal. The deities on whom the celebrations centred were Demeter and Dionysos. Rites were held at Eleusis ([Demosthenes] 59.116). In the Eleusinian accounts of 329 BC (*IG* II² 1672) there were substantial purchases of wood and vine prunings at the time of the Haloa. This backs up the confused literary evidence for bonfires. The specific mention of vine prunings perhaps emphasises both the preceeding autumn season's work, as well as the connection with Dionysos.

A joint celebration of Demeter and Dionysos was particularly appropriate for the time of year since the most fraught work on the vineyards and the cereal sowing would have just finished, for at the time when the Haloa generally fell, late December-early January, the weather would be too cold and wet in most years for work in the fields to be feasible. In balance with the group of festivals before the sowing (and generally busy farming period) earlier in the autumn, the Haloa provides a ritual termination point celebrated by women when this busy and critical season of men's work has come to an end.

It has frequently puzzled northern European commentators that there is no harvest festival dedicated to Demeter in the Athenian festival calendar. The one excuse for a harvest festival (which frequently has been identified as such, though it is much more compli- cated than a simple 'harvest home') is the Thargelia, which occurs in late May-early June in most years. In fact, as Brumfield[30] has noted, the cereal harvest in most of southern Greece is drawn out over a period of two months or so, depending on the variety of cereal and the specific micro-climate of the plot where it is planted.[31] The Thargelia in fact does not really coincide with the cereal harvest (despite the dedication of *panspermia*, a kind of ancient *kollyva* or frumenty), since the festival really falls too early in most years. If there were any genuine overtones of harvest celebration attached to this festival in classical Athens (and I am rather dubious about that), it would bear the same relationship to the 'real' harvest that the Thesmophoria, etc., bore to the sowing – that is, taking place before the event. Again, if there is any relationship to the cereal harvest, it is perhaps significant that it has been appropriated by Apollo, the ultimately masculine deity.[32]

The Skira has sometimes been interpreted as a harvest festival,[33] though never convincingly, since it falls at an inappropriate time in June, usually mid-June.[34] Even Brumfield[35] has considerable difficulty making it fit the cycle of cereal growth.[36] Like the Thesmophoria, it was celebrated in individual demes as well as by the City.[37] In fact it can be shown to fit the pattern of 'boundary marking' festivals or groups of festivals already observed. After the long period of harvest, when the sheaves are stacked up to await threshing, there is a short lull before the threshing begins in earnest in mid-July or so. This lull nicely corresponds with the Skira.

Moreover, the word *skiron* has as one of its basic meanings what the Greeks rather imprecisely called 'white earth', *ge leuke*.[38] This term generally seems to refer to various calcium compounds such as gypsum (calcium sulphate) that frequently occur as natural deposits. Toponyms which include this root (such as Skiras in Attica or the island of Skyros) frequently have deposits of such compounds. Indeed those which occur on the island of Skyros are today used for plastering flat roofs.

There is evidence of another activity for which gypsum (*vel sim.*) (and other similar calcium compounds) was used (and the best evidence for it comes from a ritual context): sealing and repairing threshing floors. In Attica both earth and stone threshing floors were used. Most Attic limestone, and even some of the schist, is rather lumpy, while the surface of earth threshing floors was not particularly durable. A coat of gypsum would give a smooth, hard, strong finish, though it would need regular renewal since on a threshing floor it would be exposed to the weather.

The Eleusinian accounts for 329/8 BC (*IG* II² 1672) contain an entry for the tenth prytany (which should have fallen in the month Skirophorion) for the cleaning of the sacred threshing floor (232–4), followed by the cost of hiring a roller(?) (*trochilea*) and labour costs (234–7). Lines 238–43 contains a contract for *enkausis*, 'burning' – gypsum has to be heated before it is used as plaster/cement – and *koniasis*, plastering. I suggest this is in preparation for the celebration of the Skira.[39]

So one major symbolic element of the procession of women and the sacred objects (*skira*) they carried in the Skira festival must have been the ritual (and probably practical) plastering of threshing floors in preparation for crop processing. Again work on the threshing floors and the threshing itself was men's work for which women were ritually responsible.[40]

## CONCLUSIONS

A detailed consideration of the timing of the three best documented (most important?) 'women's mysteries', celebrated as part of state festivals to Demeter, in relation to both the festive and the farming calendars is helpful in understanding how these rites were performed and interpreted, in both symbolic and practical terms. It is clearly inappropriate to talk about 'sowing' or 'harvest' festivals as if these celebrations happened simultaneously with the seasonal task in hand. In fact these festivals serve as markers before and after periods of intensive and critical work. They are moments in which the community ritually takes a deep breath before the rush hits, or lets out a sigh of relief when it has finished. There are both symbolic and practical reasons for this. In fact, during the busiest periods of agricultural work ritual and political activity is at a low ebb. Further, the intensive and critical work which women's festivals of Demeter bound and celebrate is stereotypically men's work.[41] It is as if men's practical activities are ineffectual without the partnership of women's ritual activities.

But as well as acting out a ritual partnership with men, these festivals of Demeter simultaneously provide arenas in which women may constitute themselves as a distinct social and political group. However much men may have wanted to believe that women were under control within the limited space allowed them in women's ritual activities, the general unease in the sources about what the girls got up to strongly suggests that women did not necessarily passively accept men's ideas about how they ought to behave.[42] Moreover, though women celebrate these festivals as a community of women, it is clear that within the larger gathering they attended and celebrated in smaller groups of their own choosing.

Sometimes these are not always what one might expect, as, for example, the wife of Euphiletos who in Lysias 1.20 is alleged to have gone to the Thesmophoria with her adulterous lover's mother! Younger married women must often have arrived with mothers-in-law, while younger unmarried women must have gone with their mothers and other older female relatives.[43] But particularly at the Thesmophoria, and to a certain extent also at the Haloa and the Skira, women gathered together from all over the city – indeed from all over Attica. This must have provided an opportunity for women to socialise and maintain the links with their natal families, especially their mothers and probably also their sisters.[44] Under Athenian law and social practice girls were never fully detached from their natal families on marriage and might expect to return there if the marriage dissolved.[45] Regular meetings in these religious contexts, even for girls who had married into households located some distance away from their natal families, reinforced these legal and social precepts.

These social practices also have cosmological significance. Like most societies, the Athenians construed kinship in several different ways simultaneously (depending on the context) and manipulated and played off these different notions of kinship with each other (again depending on context). The myth of Demeter and Kore celebrates and elevates to cosmological pre-eminence the ties between mother and daughter. Brumfield[46] has argued that Kore's abuction/marriage reflects the severing of that mother-daughter relationship by marriage and conjugal sex. I disagree. Even in the myth though Kore's relationship with Demeter is changed forever, it is only modified, not broken – hence the significance of the reunion of Kore and Demeter which might well parallel the 'real' reunions of mothers and daughters at the women's festivals of the Two Goddesses.[47] Lines of mothers and daughters always remained one way of construing kinship, even if most of the time in everyday reality (and in our sources) that relationship was suppressed by patriarchal and patrilineal constructions of kin. Though men might understand women's role in the bilateral kindred as linking man with man, the ties of mothers and daughters could not be completely obliterated.

Hence it is interesting to note the proximity in the official state calendar of 'masculine' festivals to the female celebrations which made men uncomfortable. I am sure it is not accidental that the Apatouria, dedicated to Apollo and celebrating the patrilateral clans (phratries) in which only men actively participated is just a week or two after the Thesmophoria.[48] The Skira is followed two days later by the Dipoleia, in honour of Zeus Polieus, the male tutelary deity of the city. The victim offered to him at this unusual sacrifice was man's best friend, the plough ox that had tilled the land for Demeter's corn, and whose hooves had trodden the seeds from the ears. It is as if there is a need to reassert male constructions of kinship and community after the celebration of lines of mothers and daughters and the community of women in the Thesmophoria and the Skira. The 'appropriation', if that is what it is, of the Thargelion by Apollo might be similarly construed.

Finally, the cycle of festivals of Demeter and Kore that include 'women's mysteries' in the Athenian state calendar reflect one major aspect of the cosmological construction of the state as based on a farming community. That it probably was not altogether economic reality in the fifth and fourth centuries BC was irrelevant. Cereals were not only the most important food staple in practical terms[49] but also the most important agricultural signifier of civilisation.[50] And cereal cultivation was held to have been a gift of the Two Goddesses, the Mother and the Daughter, the human relationship with whom was largely mediated by the women of the Athenian community.

Robertson's perhaps unconscious portrayal of the Athenian state's self-image constructed on male rituals in male festivals[51] must be erroneous. Women were actively constituted as part of the state, cosmologically, socially and politically, and they did not always allow themselves to be passively constituted. There was a complex symbolic relationship between the state, the women who constituted it alongside men and the goddesses who carry the *thesmoi*, which, whether they are customs or corn[52] or both, provided the foundations for the civilised *polis*.

## NOTES

1   This paper owes a great deal to helpful discussions with Michael Jameson, Sally Humphreys and Hamish Forbes, who are, of course, neither responsible for any errors nor bound to agree with any of the views expressed. Thanks are also due to Helen Forbes for constructing the bibliography.

2   Cf. Lowe 1995.

3   Nilsson 1932, 1964.

4   Burkert 1985.

5   Even in Zeitlin 1982: 140.

6   Robertson 1992; Clinton 1988, 1992; Simon 1983.

7   Burkert 1985: 61.

8   Burkert 1985: 226.

9   Detienne 1977, 1989.

10   Zeitlin 1982.

11   Winkler 1990b.

12   Humphreys 1993: xxiv-xxv, her new introduction to *The Family, Women and Death*; xxxviii, n. 61.

13   Humphreys: personal communication

14   Winkler 1990b: 188–9, 206.

15   For example, Zeitlin 1982: 139, 142.

16   Farnell 1896–1909: vol. I: 45–6, 75–112; Zeitlin 1982: 139. On the celebration of the Thesmophoria and other Demeter rites in the demes see Parker 1987.

17   Despite Detienne's (1989) assertion that women were excluded from the act of sacrificing most of the time, it certainly does not follow that

they were excluded from participating in civic festivals (and that some festivals like the Panathenaia, construing communality, were mixed is positively documented).

18  Dow and Healey 1965; Clinton 1992.

19  See Dow and Healey 1965: 14–20; Parker 1987: 141.

20  Dow and Healey 1965: 15; Brumfield 1981: 58–9.

21  For the references to celebrating the Thesmophoria in the Attic demes see Parker 1987: 142.

22  Winkler 1990b: 196 n.

23  For example, Johansen 1975: 80; Zeitlin 1982: 138.

24  As Winkler 1990b: 193 realised.

25  Mikalson 1975.

26  Mikalson 1975: 86.

27  As Zeitlin 1986: 140–2 also has, though her interpretation heads off in a different direction.

28  Simon 1983: 35.

29  Brumfield 1981: 104–5.

30  1981: 152, 232–3.

31  Forbes 1982: 268–70.

32  In fact there is another agrarian side to the Thargelia that I find much more convincing than an association with the cereal harvest. This relates to the custom of bedecking the two ugly old men who served as *pharmakoi* with necklaces of black (for men) and white (for women) figs (Simon 1983: 77–8; Hesychios s.v. *pharmakos*). Nowadays in late May-early June necklaces of 'wild', male figs, inhabited by the fig wasps which fertilise domestic figs, are flung by farmers on to their fig trees (Forbes 1982: 267–8). Aristotle (*History of Animals* 5.32 [557b 25–31]) and Theophrastos (*Causes of Plants* 2.9.5–15; *History of Plants* 2.8.1–3) document similar practices for antiquity. The black and white figs of the Thargelia necklaces worn by the *pharmakoi* were the two main classes of domestic fig varieties – 'white' figs (green to us) tend to ripen early in the season, while the dark reddish-purple, 'black' figs tend to ripen late. For a similar association with figs in sixth-century BC Kolophon, see Hipponax fr. 5–11 West.

33  Simon 1983: 22.

34  Brumfield (1981: 168) argued that it was too late for the harvest. Depending on the year, the crop and the location, however, some harvesting may still have been going on in some years. Unlike the sowing season, where the beginning is firmly marked by the inception of the autumn rains and the end is fairly clear because the weather becomes too wet and cold to continue any longer, the harvest has less marked starting and finishing points.

35  Brumfield 1981: ch. 9.

36  She interpreted it as relating to the storage of cereals in plaster-lined pits, a practice for which there is in fact no positive evidence in Greek sources (Brumfield 1981: 172–4).

37  Dow and Healey 1965: 39; Parker 1987: 142.

38  Brumfield 1981: 157–8, 169–72.

39  *IG* II$^2$ 1672.232–9:

for cleaning the sacred ? at Eleusis [. . . [34] . . .]
and the sacred threshing floor to Aristokrates
and Archi(ades?) 23 dr. [. . . [36] . . .]
for the 16 [m]en, 3 per day, for 12 days 96 dr.
[. . . [34] . . . to the public]
235   slave 2 dr. to Pamphilos Otryneus, the
contract(or) for the rolle[r(?) . . . [34] . . .]
in the towers 100; four bronze cauldrons
for the[. . .[35] . . .]
minas, to(tal) 40; from Kallikrates out of the
Thesio[n . . .[34] . . .]
and the burning to Leukon from Skambonidai 40
dr. 1.25 ob.; for carrying off to El[eusis
. . .[24] . . . to the con-]
tractor for plastering, the leftover 100, for
the iron roll[er? or pulley? . . .[28] . . .]

40  This is in contrast to the cereal harvest itself in which both men and women, ideally and really, took part.
41  Winkler 1990b: 205.
42  Cf. Winkler 1990: 188–9 and *passim*; Zeitlin 1982: 146–8.
43  I would guess (though as far as I know there is no positive evidence one way or the other) that only post-menarcheal daughters attended the 'women's mysteries', which might have served almost as a kind of informal female initiation, remotely analogous to the women's secret societies and initiation groups found in Africa and the Pacific. It is clear from Sourvinou-Inwood's (1987) work that the Brauronian festival was not really 'female initiation' in any sense, and that most of the participants were between 5 and 10, and thus pre-pubescent.
44  Other large official festivals, not exclusively female but which women regularly attended, such as the Eleusinian Mysteries and the Panathenaia, must also have served as meeting-places for female relatives on occasions. And 'private' religious celebrations, whether family sacrifices or the Adoneia, must have been facilitated gatherings of female relatives if they lived close enough (cf. Winkler 1990b: 200).
45  Foxhall 1989.
46  Brumfield 1981: 225–7.
47  Significantly, in some versions, this reunion was brought about by Demeter's mother, Rhea, and is depicted on some fifth-century BC Athenian vases (Simon 1983: 26–7, plates 8.2, 9).
48  Pyanopsion 19–21 or 26–8 are the most likely dates (Mikalson 1975: 79). See also Zeitlin 1982: 140–2.
49  Foxhall and Forbes 1982.
50  Cf. Johansen 1975: 86–7.
51  He barely mentions female festivals at all, and only then to marginalise them (Robertson 1992: 25–6).
52  Perhaps seed-corn?

# Chapter 7

# Women's identity and the family in the classical *polis*

*Sarah B. Pomeroy*

Knowledge of the family and kin groups is fundamental to understanding the development of the political and legal framework of the *polis*, and the study of the family as an institution has always been part of the mainstream of Athenian history.[1] Since W.K. Lacey (1968), and other scholars including myself, first published our views on women and the family in Athens, a different scenario for the creation of the *polis* has been envisioned. Many historians have abandoned the evolutionary view which had posited that social structures such as phratry and *genos* were vestiges of an early tribal society whose members were linked by descent from male ancestors.[2] According to the revisionist view, phratry and *genos*, like deme, are part of the political fabric of the mature *polis* traceable back to the Cleisthenic reorganization. Using the old evolutionary framework based on actual family relationships, scholars were obliged to carve out a place for women. This framework was made able to accommodate women by importing ideas about early Roman history. Roman historians have now discarded most of these ideas, but the Greek version persists. The new historical model not only provides a better explanation of the development of the Athenian *polis*, but is more consistent with what is known about women. The revised view also sheds light on the subject of the identity of individual Athenian women and on the difficulties facing the historian of women. In this paper I will discuss some of the important implications of the paradigm shift for women's history and historiography.

## FAMILY IDENTITY AT FUNERALS

It was not unusual for the *polis* to dictate the parameters of funerals to be conducted by private families. Our most detailed legal information comes from Athens and from cities that adopted Athenian laws. The legislation, which was attributed to Solon, included these provisions:[3]

> the *prothesis* must be held indoors;
> the *ekphora* must be held before sunrise on the succeeding day with men walking in front of the cart; and women behind;
> only women over the age of 60 or related to the deceased within the degree of second cousin are permitted to participate, with the latter also permitted to return to the house after the burial;
> women must not wear more than three *himatia*, nor must the dead be interred in more than three;
> food and drink brought in the procession must not be worth more than one obol;
> the offering basket must not be longer than one cubit;
> laceration of the flesh, singing of prepared dirges, or bewailing anyone except the person whose funeral is being held is forbidden;
> visiting the tombs of non-relatives except at their funerals is forbidden.

Previous discussions have emphasized the negative aspects of the legislation governing funerals.[4] A hypothesis behind these interpretations is that Solon's laws were designed not merely to record, publicize, or normalize existing practices, but rather to alter them substantially. The assumption here is that the prohibitions are a negative image of actual behaviour. For example, we could suppose that previously the *prothesis* could be held out of doors and last longer than one day; the *ekphora* could take place in the daytime with women walking in front; non-related women of all ages and women whose relationship to the deceased was more distant than that of second cousin participated, and so on. Such deductions from ancient lawcodes, however, are naive. Without further information, we can have no confidence about the relationship, if any, between law and historical reality. The problem is increased by the fact that laws attributed to Solon present specific questions concerning authenticity and dating.

A second hypothesis of those who emphasize the restrictive element in the funerary legislation is that aristocratic *gene* controlled political and religious affairs in archaic Athens, and that Solon's legislation was intended to curb their dominance. Accordingly the funerary laws limited opportunities for powerful clans to advertise their importance by parading in a huge, noisy cortege and thereby to intimidate less fortunate citizens. Lavish expenditures for grave offerings, used by the wealthy *gene* to flaunt their prosperity, were proscribed. The family was defined as a smaller unit than the *genos* as far as the number of members directly affected by the death were concerned. The notion of the *genos* had led to the hypothesis that numerous women who were distant relatives of the deceased would gather at funerals to participate in deliberations over the fate of widow, orphans, and property. To historians of Athenian women it seemed to be a golden age in comparison to the post-Solonian *polis* whose restrictions are well known.[5] There is, however, at least one flaw in this line of reasoning. Since the number of male participants was not restricted, and since they marched in front of the hearse, it was still possible for the bereaved to display their potential to use force in attaining objectives that may have been divisive in terms of the public good. Such a group of men parading through the city had to be of more concern to the legislator than women's lamentations and conversations.

The major problem with the interpretations just outlined above is that they rest on a foundation that historians are currently questioning, if not actively dismantling. Fustel de Coulanges (1980), and other historians based their ideas about aristocratic clans in control of political and religious life and engaged in competition and strife largely on analogies with archaic Rome. From this construct followed the notion that Solon destroyed the social structure resting on the *gene*. Similar reasoning attributed to Cleisthenes a change in the composition of phratries from blood kin to pseudo-kin. Felix Bourriot has reviewed the so-called textual evidence for an Athenian social structure based on huge archaic clans and found it unconvincing.[6] There were some large and powerful groups of kin, but the premise that clans based on blood relationship were fundamental to social organization is questionable. Bourriot found few references to any kin group larger than the *anchisteia* ('all descendants of a common great-grandfather'), and he argues that in the time of Solon the *gene* were being created, not destroyed.[7] Archaeological evidence indicates that Athenians were buried in small groups or as individuals. *Prothesis* and *ekphora* scenes on geometric and archaic vases and funerary plaques likewise portray small groups of mourners.

Considered together with the limitation on trousseaux attributed to Solon, the funerary legislation affecting women appears to be principally sumptuary in nature. Cicero and Plutarch understood them as sumptuary.[8] Like the laws affecting trousseaux, those concerning funerals affected individual families, not huge clans. The legislation was definitely effective, at least for a while. Large decorated gravestones went out of fashion during the first three-quarters of the fifth century BC when the democracy flourished. Although we know of no specific legislation curbing the use of such monuments until the enactments of Demetrius of Phaleron, their avoidance is consistent with the intention of the Solonian sumptuary laws. In compliance with this legislation, the *prothesis* (in which women were prominent) was brief and private. Moreover, in the *ekphora* (the public stage of the funeral) the family would be represented chiefly by its male members.

## IDENTITY AS DAUGHTER AND WIFE

Membership in the family group precedes the identity supplied by an individual name. Admission to the cult of the hearth signified membership. The head of the household was the chief priest for his family and determined who was to be admitted to its cults. Worshipping the same gods as their father established infants as members of the family, and inclusion in a cult that excluded others confirmed such affiliation. In the *Laws* (729c) Plato refers to all the members who share the worship of the family gods and who have the same natural blood. It is important to keep Plato's second point in mind when considering the family affiliation of a married woman.

When the father decided to rear the infant it was carried around the hearth at the Amphidromia. Friends and relatives attended and sent gifts, and thus became witnesses to the existence of the baby and to its family membership. The various words for 'baby' that appear in the sources do not differentiate between girls and boys. Therefore we deduce that the Amphidromia was the same for a daughter as for a son.

Unless they were adopted, children were lifelong members of their father's family, and even upon marriage the daughter did not relinquish her membership. For example, after a woman was married and living in her husband's house, she was polluted by the death of her blood relatives. It is often asserted that when they entered a new household, brides and slaves were regularly introduced to the family cults, but I have not found any evidence for this. Fustel de Coulanges was probably influenced by the Roman law of marriage with *manus* when he wrote erroneously of the bride:[9]

She must abandon the paternal fire, and henceforth invoke that of the husband. . . . She must give up the god of her infancy, and put herself under the protection of a god whom she knows not. Let her not hope to remain faithful to the one while honouring the other; for in this religion it is an immutable principle that the same person cannot invoke two sacred fires or two series of ancestors.

The idea that an Athenian could have ties to only one family is based on the male model. The woman's situation is more ambivalent.

Inasmuch as a wife's sojourn in her husband's house was more tentative than that of a child born in the house, the incorporation ceremonies were less elaborate than those for infants, and we know less about them. Although antiquarians record many diverse customs, no complete description of a classical wedding is extant. We are told that a shower of dates, sweets, and nuts marked the entrance of the bridegroom and bride when they came home after the wedding procession. Such a shower also marked the admission of a new slave. As I have mentioned, the hearth and the family cults, like the rest of the household, belonged to the husband, but he might invite his wife or slaves or other persons to participate. For example, in Xenophon's *Oeconomicus* (7.8) a husband and wife offer sacrifices together at home, but he initiates these, though she is often the leader in other activities. The Pseudo–Aristotelian *Oeconomica* notes that the Pythagoreans stated and common custom directed that the husband was not to harm his wife, but to treat her as if she were a suppliant raised from the hearth.[10] Literary references to the hearth are found, as in descriptions of the Amphidromia, but archaeological evidence for a fixed hearth in private homes is virtually nil. Practical considerations, however, make it likely that it was situated on the ground floor or even in the courtyard. Despite symbolic associations of women with the hearth,[11] in Athens it was not upstairs in the women's quarters. (Hestia, goddess of the hearth, was not married.)

Names were an indication of family membership. Children were identified by their own name and patronymic. Matronymics were not normally used, except in derogatory contexts such as accusations and curses. Because rules of etiquette required the suppression of respectable women's names, at least while they were living, the quantity of evidence available for the study of their names is far less than that for men of the same social class. Moreover, because a married woman was often buried alone, or with her husband's family, it is sometimes impossible to detect links between her name and those in her natal family. Available evidence indicates that, like a boy, a girl was given a name that was derived from those in the patriline, skipping a generation. Thus the oldest daughter would be named after her paternal grandmother. Few families had more than one daughter, and rarely are the names of more than one known. Nevertheless we do find the same names, or names constructed on the same stem, repeated in families through generations. For example, women in the family that supplied priestesses of Athena Polias often bore a name beginning with 'Lys-.' Agariste was a common name for an Alcmaeonid woman, and the name Coisyra was also used.

Naming patterns sometimes reflect the more tentative quality of girls' ties to their natal family, and when this occurs it becomes more difficult for the historian to identify them. A cursory examination of some 448 Athenian epitaphs yielded eighty-one in which the name of a father and his daughter were clearly identifiable.[12] In only eleven of these, or 14 per cent, was there any correlation,[13] for example, Cleo, daughter of Cleon[14] and Chairestrate, daughter of Chairephanes.[15] These epitaphs do not record the mother's name, so it is not possible to determine how often a woman's name reflected her matrilineage. In the same group of epitaphs there were 153 in which the name of a father and son could be identified. In this sample the names of forty men, or 26 per cent, correlated with that of their father,[16] for example, Eubius, son of Eubius[17] and Euxitheus, son of Euxithius.[18] In brief, naming patterns linked 26 per cent of men and 14 per cent of women with the patriline.

## POLITICAL IDENTITY

Membership in phratry and deme was inherited from the father. The father enrolled his baby in his phratry as being legitimate and his own, and presented him at the festival of the Apaturia held annually by the deme. Some Byzantine lexica mention the introduction and enrolment of both boys and girls: perhaps this occurred in the Hellenistic period or in cities other than Athens. Classical sources, which must be considered more reliable inasmuch as they are contemporaneous, refer to the enrolment of males.[19] The name 'phratry' ('brotherhood') implies that women are peripheral. Only one text indicates that a father had the option of letting his phratry know that he had a daughter, but even she was not enrolled. The speaker in Isaeus 3.73 alludes to the possibility of introducing (*eisagonti*) a daughter to a phratry if she was destined to be an *epikleros* and eventually to produce a son who was to be enrolled in the phratry as the adopted son of his grandfather. The speaker in Isaeus 3 is describing an event which did not occur, contentiously asking why a certain father did not introduce his daughter into his phratry, and the case is special inasmuch as the girl was potentially an *epikleros*.[20] The decree of the Demotionid phratry, the only extant complete decree describing admission, describes the introduction of a son and does not mention daughters.[21] In his edition of the Scholia to Aristophanes, *Acharn.* 146 Dindorf[22] had cited the Suda s.v. *meiagogein* and expanded the Greek text so as to give the impression that both girls and boys were inscribed in the phratry lists. This emendation, which became a crucial bit of evidence for the registration of girls,[23] is now properly omitted in Wilson's edition.[24] Plato (*Laws* 785a) mentions the enrolment of women in phratries. He is not describing Athens, however, but rather an idealized state where women do participate to a limited extent in politics. Inasmuch as a phratry was a 'brotherhood' with political responsibilities it is difficult to conceptualize why a girl would be admitted or even how membership might be exercised. For boys, in contrast, admission to the phratry was the principal route to full membership in the *polis*. Age, birth, and sex criteria for membership in the phratry were the same as those for deme membership. In Pseudo-Demosthenes 59.122 the speaker distinguishes between male and female progeny: 'This is what marriage is: when a man engenders children and presents his sons to the phrateres and demesmen and gives his daughters as being his own in marriage to husbands.'

Some scholars have assumed, without justification, that a girl belonged to her father's phratry, and have debated whether she remained in it throughout her lifetime as a boy did, or whether she was transferred to her husband's upon marriage.[25] Yet if the father did not introduce his baby daughter to his phratry, it is even less likely that the bridegroom introduced his wife. The notion that a wife was introduced to her husband's phratry at the *gamelia* is not supported by the most trustworthy ancient sources.[26] Harpocration (s.v. *gamelia* Dindorf) declares that Didymus stated that Phanedemus' definition of *gamelia* was erroneous (*FGrH* 325 F 17). Although Didymus reported that Phanedemus had said that wives were introduced to the phratry at the *gamelia*, in fact he said no such thing. Furthermore Didymus had not been able to cite any evidence from the orators. In fact Isaeus (3.79.8) and Demosthenes (57.43) speak of presenting the marriage feast to the phratry (*gamelia*) on behalf of (*huper*) a wife.[27] In other words, the *gamelia* served as an occasion at which a marriage was made public and created witnesses to the legitimacy of the children born as a result of it. In view of the obscurity of respectable women that we have mentioned briefly on p.115, it is extremely unlikely that a bride was introduced at the *gamelia* which was apparently a festive party of the 'brotherhood.'[28] According to the most reasonable estimates, the average phratry consisted of several hundred members.[29] If an entire phratry knew a woman, such familiarity would be prima facie evidence of her lack of respectability, and if she were introduced to a series of phratries (her father's, then each husband's at subsequent marriages),[30] she would be quite notorious. It is more likely that the bridegroom announced that he was marrying the daughter of so and so, and did not specify the woman's name but gave the name and demotic of his bride's father, as in the decree of the Demotionid phratry concerning the introduction of sons (*IG* II[2] 1237 lines 119–20): 'let a deposition be made to the phratriarch . . . of his name, patronymic, demotic, and the name and demotic of his mother's father'. Moreover, the consequence of the view that the phrateres were not relatives at all, but only pseudo-kin is that it is even more unlikely that a husband would introduce his bride to them. In two speeches where it would have been useful to call as witnesses a woman's phrateres (had such existed), this step is not taken. A man whose citizen status had been challenged partially on the allegation that his mother was not a citizen did not call his mother's phrateres as witnesses, but he did call phrateres of his mother's male kin (Ps.-Demos. 57.20–3, 40, 67). Another man who had to verify the identity of his mother and prove that she was married to his father argued that his father had offered the *gamelia* to his phratry upon the marriage, and had subsequently introduced the speaker and his brother as his sons to his phratry (Isaeus 8.18–20).

Women are not identified by their own demotic until post-classical times, and even then such identification is not common. I have found only eight examples.[31] Because the phratry system became extinct, the women with demotics were not also members of phratries. Instead, in the classical and Hellenistic periods their family roles are recorded as essential features of their identity, but the repertoire is strictly limited. In the index of 'Significant Greek Words', in the most recent catalogue of funerary monuments in the Athenian agora, there are more entries for *gune* (ninety-nine) and *thugater* (eighty-eight) than for any other word.[32] In contrast, no man is commemorated as a husband, and the word *huios* appears only twice. There are no citations for the actual word *pater*, for fathers are referred to by the patronymic. In view of the importance of women's reproductive role, it is interesting to find only two appearances of *meter* (cf. p. 119). To have identified a dead woman as a mother of a daughter would have compromised the reputation of a daughter (if she were still living, as was likely), whereas to refer to her as the mother of a son would perhaps have suggested that she wielded authority over him. The fantasy of descent from male to male found its way into a wide range of documents.

The girl's membership in her natal family is declared only at the Amphidromia in the presence of close friends and relatives, whereas a series of ceremonies at the phratry level make the boy's family membership indelible in the minds of a large group of men. It has also been noted that naming patterns are more likely to tie boys than girls to their ancestors. Indeed, it is precisely the lack of explicit identity in her natal family that permits a bride to leave it and join another. Nevertheless, she does not become a permanent member of her husband's family, for if she is divorced or widowed she may join the family of another husband, or return to her family of birth.

## IDENTIFYING WOMEN

The lack of enrolment of daughters and wives in phratry and deme has important implications for historiography, for it contributes to the obscurity of women. One of the most useful books on the Greek family is J.K. Davies, *Athenian Propertied Families*.[33] Davies provides elaborate genealogical charts frequently showing descent directly through males. Sometimes male kin on the mother's side are known, and the woman is referred to in a primary source. She is not, however, identified by name, but only as a daughter, wife, and mother. Davies includes such a woman on his charts as *hede* ('that female'). The charts also reflect the Athenian practice of regarding the married woman as an invisible link between two families of men. Such genealogical charts are a reflection of the primary sources. We know more about the elite whom Davies studied than about less fortunate members of Greek society, but upper-class women are those who can best afford to avoid the public eye.

The Athenian family has several versions. One, as we saw in the discussion of the phratry, is a pseudo-kinship group restricted to male citizens. Families comprised of both women and men manifest themselves in two versions, one oriented toward the public, the other more intimate and private. As we have seen in the discussion of the funeral, though the first of these admits some women, men predominate. Only the private version accommodates women, though men are not necessarily excluded. The several versions of the Athenian family that have been discussed make it clear that although women were identified with the family and identified by their family roles, the family's identity depended on men.

## NOTES

 1  For further documentation and discussion of the material in this paper see Pomeroy forthcoming.
 2  Following Bourriot 1976 and Roussel 1976.
 3  The following list is assembled from the testimony in Ps.-Demos. 43.62 = Ruschenbusch 1966 F 109; Cic. *de Leg.* 2.63–4 = Ruschenbusch F 72a; from Demetrius of Phaleron, F 135 (Wehrli) = Jacoby *FGrH* 228 F 9; Plut. *Solon* 21.5 = Ruschenbusch F 72c.
 4  Thus, e.g. Alexiou 1974: 6–7, 14–18.
 5  See further Pomeroy 1975: 43–5, 80.
 6  Bourriot 1976.
 7  Bourriot 1976: 325–6, 338–9, and *passim.*
 8  See note 3, above.
 9  Fustel de Coulanges 1980 (1864): bk 2, ch. 2, 35.
10  Ps.-Arist. *Oec.* 1344a10–12, Iambl. *Vit. Pyth.* 84.
11  For these see Vernant 1955.
12  Bradeen 1974: 35–90, nos 31, 36, 54, 56, 59, 79, 80, 82, 88, 103, 112, 120, 121, 128, 132, 139, 141, 142, 145, 150, 153, 155, 157, 158, 162, 164, 166, 168, 172, 186, 192, 200, 213, 224, 231, 243, 258, 285, 304, 320, 329, 332, 333, 342; Osborne 1988: nos 4, 6, 7, 8, 11, 25, 26, 30, 32, 37, 38, 39, 41, 44, 46, 51, 56, 57, 60, 62, 66, 67, 69, 79, 82; and see note 13.
13  Bradeen 1974: nos 69, 81, 135, 140, 151, 191, 194(?), 346, 357; and Osborne 1988: nos 35, 59.
14  Osborne 1988: 13, no. 35.
15  Bradeen 1974: no. 81.
16  Bradeen 1974: 35–90, correlation: nos 28, 35, 48, 51, 53, 65, 138, 147, 152, 159, 170, 179, 188, 189, 216, 218, 237, 252, 264, 289, 312, 324, 350; and see notes 17 and 18; no correlation: nos 27, 29, 30, 34, 46, 52, 55, 59, 66, 72, 77, 81, 83, 84, 89, 91, 96, 101, 106, 113, 114, 125, 129, 133, 136, 148, 149, 160, 163, 164, 165, 167, 178, 183, 185, 187, 188, 197–9, 202, 205, 212, 225, 231, 233, 240, 241, 259–61, 263, 275, 277, 279, 284, 290–6, 298, 302, 303, 306–9, 314, 321, 323, 327, 341, 344, 345, 347, 353–5, 363, 364. Osborne 1988: correlation: nos 2, 9, 10, 15–17, 19, 23, 47, 59, 63, 68, 70, 80, 85; no correlation: nos 1, 3, 12, 14, 20–2, 24, 27, 29, 33, 42, 45, 48, 49, 52–4, 58, 65, 71–9, 86.
17  Third to second century: Bradeen 1974: no. 47.
18  Fourth century: Bradeen 1974: no. 174. Naming for the father became

more common in the Roman period, in imitation of the Roman practice.

19   Pollux 8.107 s.v. *phratores* and the *Suda* s.v. *Apatouria* (Adler) mention both
boys and girls. See also note 24 below.

20   On Isaeus 3, see Ledl 1907: 173–96. Ledl argues that women were not
registered.

21   *IG* II² 1237, line 10 = *SIG*³ 921 = *LSCG* 19. Women are not named in
other extant phratry lists: *IG* II–III.2.2, 2344–5.

22   Dindorf, Scholia: 346, lines 5–7.

23   Cited most recently by Kearns 1985.

24   Wilson 1975: 29, 146b.

25   On the debate Collignon 1904: ii, pt 2, 1642, 1644. Collignon decides
that the wife remains in her original phratry.

26   Mikalson 1983: 85; Burkert 1984: 255; and Golden 1985 retain the
notion that the bridegroom introduced the bride to his phratry, contra
Collignon 1904: 1642, 1644–5, and most recently Davies 1988: 380.
Stengel 1910: cols 691–2, asserts incorrectly that the *gamelia* was an
offering at the Apaturia when a son was introduced to his phratry. The
latter notion is based on *Anek. Gr.* 1.228.5 and *Etym. Magn.* s.v., among
the least reliable of all the sources on the *gamelia*.

27   Sim. Pollux 8.107 s.v. *phratores*.

28   According to Pollux 3.42 the *gamelia* was a sacrifice; according to Hesych.
s.v. a banquet; according to Harp. s.v., *Anek. Gr.* 1, p. 233.31, and the
*Suda* s.v., a donation (probably for a banquet).

29   Roussel 1976: 143, suggests that the size varied from several dozens to
several hundred. Flower 1985: 234, gives an average of 133. The statement of Aristotle, *Ath. Pol.* F 3, that there were twelve phratries would
indicate far larger memberships, but Aristotle must be incorrect: see
Rhodes 1981: 69.

30   So Golden 1985: 13, n. 26.

31   In inscriptions that are undated or dated to the Roman period a few
women have demotics: *IG* II² 5276, 5428, 6255, 6780, 6781, 6810, 7764;
Bradeen 1974: 47, no. 107. I would see these as further evidence of the
increase of women's political role in the Hellenistic world. Previously the
father's demotic is given, or, more rarely, the deme name with the suffix
*-then* ('from').

32   Bradeen 1974: 238–4, index 11. Vestergaard *et al.* 1985: 181, found 121
examples of women named with uxorial status, and almost 500 with filial
status.

33   Davies 1971.

# Chapter 8

# Some Pythagorean female virtues*

*Voula Lambropoulou*

As is known from the sources, Pythagorean societies included both men and women in perfect equality. Admittance to the community was after strict examination and under the condition of years of silence.[1] The requirements for initiation into the Pythagorean philosophy, and the subsequent duties, were common to both men and women without exception. Women, however, were further assigned some extra duties, which, according to the Pythagoreans, were proper to their sex. Thus, although we treat Pythagorean morals as a whole, without distinction between men and women, we cannot ignore some, perhaps later, peculiarities concerning the morals of women.

Apart from scientific differences, it is certain that the Pythagorean school was distinguished from similar ones by its moral direction. According to several scholars, the Pythagorean school, as its way of life, morals, beliefs and political pursuits showed, undoubtedly originated from moral and religious motives.[2] But a real picture of its moral tendencies and orientations cannot be accurately drawn from later descriptions. Pythagoras undoubtedly had the intention of establishing a seed-plot for the cultivation of piety and strict principles of temperance, order, obedience to rulers and to the law, bravery, loyal friendship and, generally, all those virtues which, according to the Greek and especially the Dorian perspective, characterize the brave man, and which are particularly stressed in the Pythagorean apophthegms on morals.

It has been claimed that the Pythagorean doctrines remained carefully confined to the limits of the school and that any transgression was followed by a severe reprimand. It is unlikely, regardless of their symbolic religious meaning, that the philosophical doctrines and the mathematical theorems were kept secret. Besides, the distinction between internal and external students in the Pythagorean organization was due to other reasons than secrecy.[3] Pythagoras was interested in spreading his doctrines on virtue, and contradictory evidence either reflects popular beliefs or dates from much later.

The Pythagoreans exacted above all worship of gods and demons, and a genuine respect for parents and for the laws and traditions of one's native town, which should not be frivolously replaced by foreign ones. They considered anarchy as a major vice, for they believed that it is not possible for the human race to live and thrive without some kind of authority. Rulers and ruled ought to be bound together by mutual friendship: ἄρχοντας ἔφασκον οὐ μόνον ἐπιστήμονας ἀλλὰ καὶ φιλανθρώπους δεῖν εἶναι καὶ τους ἀρχομένους οὐ μόνον πειθηνίους ἀλλὰ καὶ φιλάρχοντας[4]. Each citizen must subordinate himself to the whole. The young and the adolescent must be educated for the state; the men of mature years and the old must act for it. The Pythagorean philosophy also recommends loyalty, trust and tolerance in friendship; obedience of the young to the older; gratitude towards parents and benefactors. He who possesses a true love for the beautiful will not turn to external luxury, but to moral activity and to internal self-sufficiency. Science flourishes only where it is practised with zeal and love. In fact, this Pythagorean belief may account for several prohibitions, symbolisms[5] and regulations (διατάξεις). In some cases, man is dependent upon luck, but in most he is the master of his own destiny.

From the same spirit derive the moral 'regulations' of the Golden Verses, which are addressed to both men and women: respect towards gods and parents, loyalty towards friends, justice and tolerance towards everyone, temperance, propriety, modesty, self-discipline, prudence, chastity, wisdom, submission to destiny, regular self-control, prayer, attendance at holy ceremonies, abstinence from impure fare, approaching temples in clean attire and with a clear mind, avoidance of extravagant desires, keeping secrets and sworn oaths. If all these duties are fulfilled, there is hope for a blissful lot after death.[6] Faith in a posthumous recompense enjoined an absolute acceptance of the moral order in the family, the state and social contact in general.

Originally, ἀρετή (the Latin *virtus*) did not have an ethical meaning for the Presocratic philosophers. It had meant the group of qualities that make man extraordinary and perfect, so that he excels among others. Some scholars argue that, no matter how unquestionable the religious and moral nature of Pythagoreanism, it is not possible to claim that Pythagoreanism established an ethical system. Ethos, for the Pythagoreans, is confused with religion, and religion has two aspects: one is purely theoretical, where natural science is reduced to the science of numbers; the other is purely practical, and reduced to deeds and rituals. Ethical life has the purpose of liberating the soul from passions, which keep it a slave to the body, and of giving it absolute freedom; for the soul knows no other law or bonds other than those of reason and action.[7]

Pythagorean philosophy and its followers' way of life helped them to achieve divine perfection. Philosophy is an arduous task indeed, and a philosopher is one who seeks to conceive the universe as cosmos (a word which etymologically means ornament), as a harmonious order of beauty, and to achieve this beauty of harmony in his personal life. Pythagoreanism teaches the virtues of devotion, faith, piety and measure through harmony as a dominating principle.[8] Human life is an effort, a trial, and death is not its end but only a transition towards regeneration according to the laws of just recompense.

We know that the primary concern of Pythagoreanism was the study of order, propriety or κοσμιότης (notice the etymological connection with 'cosmos') rather than the material essence of the universe or natural changes: that is why they tried to comply with 'cosmic' laws. The concept of propriety and harmony in moral life was expounded by Perictione in her work, *On Woman's Harmony*:[9]

τὴν ἁρμονίην γυναῖκα γνῶσασθαί δεῖ φρονησέως καὶ σωφροσύνης πλείην· κάρτα γὰρ ψυχὴν πειθνῦσθαι δεῖ ἐς ἀρετήν, ὥστ' ἔσται καὶ δικαίη καὶ ἀνδρηίη καὶ φρονέουσα καὶ αὐταρκείη καλλυνομένη καὶ κενὴν δόξαν μισέουσα.

One must deem the harmonious woman to be full of wisdom and self-control; a soul must be exceedingly conscious of goodness to be just and courageous and wise, embellished with self-sufficiency and hating empty opinion.

(trans. V.L. Harper)

For woman, harmony is prudence and temperance. These virtues are also found recommended by Pythagoras in his 'speech' to women. A woman's soul, says Pythagoras, must seek virtue in order to become just, brave, reasonable, self-sufficient, by qualities adapted to her nature, and disliking vain glory. The harmonious nature of woman must not be disturbed by lack of wealth, noble descent, glory or other things that are often more harmful than useful and cause envy and hate:

ἀναγκαῖα δὲ μὴ ἡγεέσθω εὐγενίην καὶ πλοῦτον καὶ . . . μεγάλης πόλιος . . . καὶ δόξαν καὶ φιλίην ἐνδόξων καὶ βασιληίων ἀνδρῶν· ἢν μὲν ἔῃ, οὐ λυπέει· ἢν δὲ μὴ ἔῃ, ἐπιζητέειν οὐ ποιέει· τούτων γὰρ δίκα φρονίμη γυνὴ ζῆν οὐ κωλύεται. κἢν ἔῃ δὲ ταῦτα ἅπερ λελάκαται, τὰ μεγάλα καὶ θαυμαζόμενα μή ποτε διζέσθω ψυχή . . . βλάπτει γὰρ μᾶλλον ἐς ἀτυκίην ἕλκοντα ἢ ὠφελέει. τούτοισι γὰρ ἐπιβουλή τε καὶ φθόνος, καὶ βασκανίη προσκέειται, ὥστε ἐν ἀταραξίῃ οὐκ ἂν γένοιτο ἡ τοίηδε.[10]

But let her not think that nobility of birth, and wealth, and coming from a great city altogether are necessities, nor the good opinion and friendship of eminent and kingly men. If these should be the case, it does not hurt. But, if not, wishing does not make them so. Even if these should be allotted to her, let her soul not pursue the grand and wonderful. Let her walk also apart from them. They harm more than they help, dragging one into misfortune. Treachery and envy and malice abide with them; such a woman would not be serene.

The prudent woman, without refusing any material goods she happens to own, should not pursue 'the grand and the wonderful'. A woman's conduct does not concern herself alone, but is reflected upon the whole family. Woman is the most basic foundation of an *oikos* (household), as perceived and hallowed by the Pythagoreans.

We know that there was a connection between ethics and politics in Pythagorean society. Ethics becomes prominent in politics. Perictione, inspired by these Pythagorean doctrines, presents this most clearly:

πολλάκις δὲ καὶ πόλει, εἴ γε πόλιας ἢ ἔθνεα ἢ τοίη γε κρατύνοι, ὡς ἐπὶ βασιληίης ὀρέομεν[11]

If, at any rate, such a woman should govern cities and tribes, as we see in the case of a royal city.

She might have had in mind the great queens Semiramis, Tomyris and Artemisia, who excited great admiration in antiquity. It is therefore obvious that Perictione does not exclude Pythagorean women from participating in politics. What is of importance here is that the distinction between *oikos* (household) for females and *polis* (city) for males does not hold.

In the following passage, Perictione is deeply animated by the moral principles of earlier Pythagoreans:[12]

κρατέουσα ὧν ἐπιθυμίας καὶ θυμοῦ, ὁσίη καὶ ἁρμονίη γίγνεται·
ὥστε οὐδὲ ἔρωτες αὐτὴν ἄνομοι διώξουσιν, ἀλλ' ἐς ἄνδρα τε
καὶ τέκεα καὶ τὸν οἶκον ξύμπαντα φιλίην ἕξει. ὁκόσαι γὰρ
ἐραάστριαι τελέθουσιν ἀλλοτρίων λεχέων, αὗται δὲ πολέμιαι
γίγνονται πάντων τῶν ἐν τῇ οἰκέῃ ἐλευθέρων τε καὶ οἰκετέων·
καὶ συντιθῇ ψύθη καὶ δόλους ἀνδρὶ καὶ ψεύδεα καὶ πάντων
μυθίζεται πρὸς τοῦτον, ἵνα μούνη δοκέῃ διαφθέρειν εὐνοίῃ καὶ
τῆς οἰκίης κρατῇ ἀργίην φιλέουσα. ἐκ τούτων γὰρ φθορὴ
γίγνεται ξυμπάντων ὁκόσα αὐτῇ τε καὶ τῷ ἀνδρὶ ξυνά ἐστι.

Having mastery over appetite and high feeling, she will be righteous and harmonious; no lawless desires will impel her. She will
preserve a loving disposition towards her husband and children
and entire household. As many women as become lovers of alien
beds become enemies of all at home, gentry and servants alike.
Such a woman continually contrives lies and deceits for her
husband and fabricates falsehoods about everything to him, in
order that she may seem to excel in good will and, though she
loves idleness, may seem to govern the house to such an extent,
let these things be said.

The Pythagorean beliefs about illegitimate liaisons were the
strictest of all those expressed by other ancient philosophers.
They were the only ones to judge illegitimate relationships that
were tolerated by common law. That is, not only did they prohibit
what was condemned by the law, namely the wife's unfaithfulness to
her husband, but they also regarded the husband's unfaithfulness
to the wife as equally unjust despite the prevailing local custom;
for the Pythagoreans professed complete equality between men and
women. Moreover, they did not distinguish between social classes
in the discharge of social duties. Both free men and slaves were on
an equal footing.

Pythagoras urges a life lived 'chastely and piously', and Perictione
talks about temperance of desires. A woman must be 'righteous'
(ὁσίη) and 'harmonious' (ἁρμονίη). The conduct of a law-breaking,
deceiving or lying woman is both pitiable and improper and,
furthermore, it disturbs the harmony of her soul. This is why
Perictione recommends harmony and love for one's family, husband, children and domestics. Virtue is harmony, and so is every
other good quality. All these are in agreement with the Pythagorean
beliefs about women, as derived from the Master's speech to the
women of Croton:

παραγγεῖλαι δὲ καὶ κατὰ πάντα τὸν βίον αὐτάς τε εὐφημεῖν
καὶ τοὺς ἄλλους ὁρᾶν ὅποσα ὑπὲρ αὐτῶν εὐφημήσουσιν,
ἵνα τὴν δόξαν τὴν διαδεδομένην μὴ καταλύσωσι μηδὲ τοὺς
μυθογράφους ἐξελέγξωσιν, οἱ θεωποῦντες τὴν τῶν γυναικῶν
δικαιοσύνην ἐκ τοῦ προίεσθαι μὲν ἀμάρτυρον τὸν ἱματισμὸν καὶ
τὸν κόσμον, ὅταν τινι ἄλλῳ δέῃ χρῆσαι, μὴ γίγνεσθαι δὲ ἐκ τῆς
πίστεως δίκας μηδ' ἀντλογίας, ἐμυθοποίησαν τρεῖς γυναῖκας ἑνὶ
κοινῷ πάσας ὀφθαλμῷ χρωμένας διὰ τὴν κοινωίαν.

(Iambl. *V.P.* 55)[13]

He also exhorted the women to use words of good omen through
the whole of life, and to endeavour that others may predict good
things of them. He likewise admonished them not to destroy
popular renown, nor to blame the writers of fables, who surveying
the justice of women, from their accommodating others with
garments and ornaments, without a witness, when it is necessary
for some other person to use them, and that neither litigation nor
contradiction are produced from this confidence, – have feigned
that three women used but one eye in common, an account of the
facility of the communion with each other.

(trans. T. Taylor)

The order εὐφημεῖν (to use words of good omen), as addressed to
women, is fully adapted to the ancient Greek conception of women's
position in society, which hardly differs from modern Greek reality.
Εὐφημία, or good reputation for a woman, was absolute silence about
her name, as is similarly reported by Thucydides.[14]

Pythagoras, according to Iamblichus, characterizes women as 'just'
(δικαίας) because they are willing to share their possessions with
others and do this with great generosity. Perictione repeats this, as
we saw on p. 124 (δικαίη καὶ ἀνδρηίη). This is brave behaviour on
the part of women and is never observed among men. Trust without
witnesses or oaths is another Pythagorean female virtue.

The virtue of female simplicity, as professed by Pythagoras, is also
repeated by Perictione: αὐταρκείη καλλυνομένη καὶ κενὴν δόξαν
μισέουσα ('embellished with self-sufficiency and hating all empty
opinion'). As is known, the great philosopher influenced women and
children through his personal prestige towards temperance and
frugality, and recommended the avoidance of luxury; and in this
almost all our sources are in agreement.

Next Pythagoras treats the subject of 'temperance':

ἐφεξῆς δὲ ἔλεγε περὶ σωφροσύνης . . . εἶτα προετρέπετο θεωρεῖν
ὅτι μόνης τῶν ἀρετῶν ταύτης καὶ παιδὶ καὶ παρθένῳ καὶ γυναικὶ
καὶ τῇ τῶν πρεσβυτέρων τάξει ἀντιποιεῖσθαι προσήκει,
καὶ μάλιστα τοῖς νεωτέροις ἐτὶ δὲ μόνην αὐτὴν ἀπέφαινε
περιειληφέναι καὶ τὰ τοῦ σώματος ἀγαθά . . . τῶν γὰρ βαρβάρων
καὶ τῶν Ἑλλήνων περὶ τὴν Τροίαν ἀντιταξαμένων ἑκατέρους δι᾽
ἑνὸς ἀκρασίαν ταῖς δεινοτάτας περιπεσεῖν συμφοραῖς.

(Iambl. *V.P.* 41–2)

In the next place, he spoke concerning temperance . . . afterwards
he exhorted them to consider that this alone among the virtues
was adapted to a boy and a virgin, to a woman, and to the order
of those of a more advanced age; and that it was especially accommodated to the younger part of the community. He also added
that this virtue alone comprehended the goods both of body and
soul . . . for when the barbarians and the Greeks warred against
one another about Troy, each of them fell into the most dreadful
calamities, through the incontinence of one man.

Besides frugality, temperance is presented as a fundamental virtue for
everyone and as one of primary importance both for the mind and
for the soul. In the passage, the 'virgin' is distinct from the 'woman',
and the word ἀκρασία (incontinence) is used instead of ἀκράτεια
(intemperance). At any rate, it is the opposite of the virtue of
ἐγκράτεια (temperance).

The fact that measure, order and harmony were held by the early
Pythagoreans to be the foundations of moral and social life is also
known from Plato's *Gorgias*.[15] There Plato says that the Pythagorean
'wise men' profess social contact, friendship, propriety and justice as
cosmic principles. The same holds good for the terms φιλία (friendship) and φιλανθρωπία (philanthropy) in the passage. Next he urges
us to notice the 'geometric equality' and the 'concord' among them.

A continuity of Pythagorean 'prudence', in the narrow sense of
women's prudence, is found in Phintys' *On Woman's Prudence*.[16] The
virtues are now determined and distinguished among the sexes:

τὸ μὲν ὅλον ἀγαθὰν δεῖ ἦμεν καὶ κοσμίαν· ἄνευ γὰρ ἀρετᾶς
οὐδέποκα γένοιτό τις τοιαύτα. ἑκάστα γὰρ ἀρετὰ περὶ ἕκαστον
γιγνόμενα τὸ αὐτᾶς δεκτικὸν ἀποδίδωσι σπουδαῖον.

A woman must be altogether good and orderly; without excellence
she would never become so. The excellence appropriate to each
thing makes superior that which is receptive of it.

According to Phintys, a woman should become good and decent, and without virtue she cannot become such. The female virtue *par excellence* is prudence, which is suitable for women, as eye virtue is for eyes, ear virtue for ears and so on:[17]

ἁ μὲν ὀπτίλων τὼς ὀπτίως, ἁ δὲ τᾶς ἀκοᾶς τὰν ἀκοάν, καὶ ἁ μὲν ἵππω τὸν ἵππον, ἁ δ᾿ ἀνδρὸς τὸν ἄνδρα· οὕτω δὲ καὶ <ἁ> γυναικὸς τὰν γυναῖκα. γυναικὸς δὲ μάλιστα ἀρετὰ σωφροσύνα.

The excellence appropriate to the eyes makes the eyes so, that appropriate to hearing, the faculty of hearing, that appropriate to a horse, a horse, that appropriate to a man, a man. So too the excellence appropriate to a woman makes a woman excellent. The excellence most appropriate to a woman is moderation.

The main female virtue, therefore, is moderation. According to this Pythagorean, there are occupations which are suitable for men and others which are suitable for women. There are also virtues which are common to both men and women:[18]

ἴδια μὲν ἀνδρὸς τὸ στρατηγὲν καὶ πολιτεύεσθαι καὶ δαμαγορέν, ἴδια δὲ γυναικὸς τὸ οἰκουρὲν καὶ ἔνδον μένεν καὶ ἐκδέχεσθαι καὶ θεραπεύεν τὸν ἄνδρα. κοινὰ δὲ φαμὶ ἀνδρείαν καὶ δικαιοσύναν καὶ φρόνασιν.

I agree that men should be generals and city officials and politicians, and women should keep house and stay inside and receive and take care of their husbands. But I believe that courage, justice and intelligence are qualities that men and women have in common.

(trans. M.R. Lefkowitz)

This passage reveals clearly: first, a deviation from Pythagorean beliefs, as we know them from speeches attributed to Pythagoras; second, the much later language of the text; third, that these words would fit better in a fourth- or third-century BC Ionian or Athenian setting, if they had been written in the Attic dialect. Therefore, Phintys cannot have been Lacedaimonian, particularly as her words are contrary to the ethos of Lacedaimonian state.

With the virtues common to men and women, we come back to the Pythagorean positions without excluding Platonic. One of these common virtues is the health of both body and soul:[19] καὶ ὡς ὑγιαίεν τῷ σώματι ἀμφοτέροις, ὠφέλιμον. οὕτως ὑγιαίνεν τᾷ ψυχᾷ. ('And just as it is beneficial for the body of each to be healthy, so too, it is beneficial for the soul to be healthy.') The virtues of the body are health, strength, sensitivity and beauty. There are virtues which are suitable for men, as there are virtues more appropriate for women. Courage and quick resolution are more suitable for man because of the constitution of his body and the strength of his soul. Modest reticence is more appropriate for woman: σωφροσύναν δὲ γυναικί.[20]

Without condemning learned women or women philosophers, Phintys recommended, besides intelligence and study, the virtue of prudence, the fruits of which are propriety, modesty and reticence. These virtues give grace to women. With the virtue of prudence, woman τὸν ἴδιον ἄνδρα καὶ τιμὴν καὶ ἀγαπὴν δυνασεῖται ('will be able to honour and love her husband'). Conjugal faith is considered to be the first necessary condition for female prudence.

Similarly, another Pythagorean, Melissa, characterizes conjugal faith as 'beautiful': εὔμορφον γὰρ τὰν ἐλευθέραν ἰδέσθαι τῷ αὐτᾶς ἀνδρί, ἀλλ' οὐ τοῖς πλάσιον ('a free woman should appear beautiful to her husband, not to outsiders').[21] According to Melissa, a basic condition for a woman seeking 'prudence' (here she uses a strong verb, γλίχομαι, used by epic and tragic poets, which means 'to desire ardently, to fight for something') is not luxury of attire but, first, the correct management of her home; and, second, her endeavour to be liked by her husband only.

The learned women of that period must have been taking private lessons and must have been familiar with the theories of Xenophon and Aristotle, and this can be concluded from the similarities of their texts.

The following passage by Phintys again can be considered as a sample of the private and public life in ancient Greece, as far as the position of women is concerned:[22]

τὰς δὲ ἐξόδους ἐκ τᾶς οἰκίας ποιεῖσθαι τὰς γυναῖκας τὰς δαμοτελέας θυηπολούσας τῷ ἀρχαγέτᾳ θεῷ τᾶς πόλιος ὑπὲρ αὐτᾶς καὶ τῷ ἀνδρὸς καὶ τῷ παντὸς οἴκῳ· ἔπειτα μήτε ὄρφνας ἀνισταμένας μήτε ἑσπέρας ἀλλὰ πλαθυούσας ἀγορᾶς καταφανέα γιγνομέναν τὰν ἔξοδον ποιεῖσθαι θεωρίας ἕνεκα τινος ἢ ἀγορασμῶ οἰκήῳ μετὰ θεραπαίνας μίας ἢ καττὸ πλεῖστον δύο εὐκόσμως χειραγωγουμέναν. τὰς δὲ θυσίας λιτὰς παριστάμεν τοῖς θεοῖς καὶ καττὰν δύναμιν, ὀργιασμῶν δὲ καὶ μητρῳασμῶν τῶν κατ' οἶκον ἀπέχεσθαι.

Women of importance leave the house to sacrifice to the leading divinity on behalf of themselves and their husbands and their households. They do not leave home at night nor in the evening and they make their departures from the market-place openly, to attend a festival or to make some purchase, accompanied by a single female servant or at most leading two servants by the hand. They offer prayers at sacrifice to the gods also to the best of their abilities. They keep away from secret cults and Cybeline orgies in their homes.

The time when the market-place was crowded was the most appropriate for a woman to come out of the women's quarters of the house. Except for the phrase τὰς θυσίας λιτάς, nothing else here is reminiscent of the Pythagorean tradition.

Man outside the home and woman inside it[23] epitomizes, as is well known, the grandeur of ancient Athenian society. Silence was recommended for women, as well as staying at home. Endless silence. This kind of silence is different from the one that Pythagoras recommended and exacted from his male and female students in order to be certain of their secrecy. He did not accept chatty or ambitious women. Temperance of speech was held to be most difficult to achieve. This silence was called ἐχεμυθία (discretion) or ἐχερρημοσύνη.

Another Pythagorean, Lysis, praises the courage of Damo, Pythagoras' daughter, who followed the Pythagorean tradition and, although she had fallen into extreme poverty, kept Pythagoras' 'memoranda', that is his written works, and refused to hand them over even for big material offers:

λέγοντι δὲ πολλοὶ τὺ καὶ δαμοσίᾳ φιλοσοφὲν, τόπερ ἀπαξίωσε Πυθαγόρας, ὅς γε Δαμοῖ τᾷ ἑαυτοῦ θυγατρὶ τὰ ὑπομνάματα παρακαταθέμνος ἐπέκαψε μηδενὶ τῶν ἐκτὸς τᾶς οἰκίας παραδίδομεν. ἁ δὲ δυναμένα πολλῶν χραμάτων ἀποδόσθαι τὼς λόγως οὐκ ἐβουλάθη, πενίαν δὲ καὶ τὰς τῶ πατρὸς ἐπισκαψίας ἐνόμισε χρυσῶ τιμιοτέρας ἦμεν. φαντὶ δὲ ὅτι καὶ Δαμὼ θνάσκουσα Βιστάλᾳ τᾷ ἑαυτᾶς θυγατρὶ τὰν αὐτὰν ἐπιτολὰν ἐπέτειλεν.[24]

Many say you should philosophize in public, which Pythagoras forbade. He carefully set aside his notes, giving them to his daughter, Damo, with the instruction that she was to surrender them to no one outside the household. And she, although she was able to sell his works for much money, declined, thinking poverty and her father's instructions more valuable than gold. They say indeed that when Damo died, she gave the same instruction to her daughter, Bistala.

(trans. R. Hawley)

Lysis complains that even male students of Pythagoras did not manage to reach the heights of Damo and of her daughter Bistala.

Another Pythagorean woman who is mentioned as silent and brave is Timycha,[25] wife of Myllios Crotoniates, who cut her own tongue out so as not to give away secrets about Pythagorean beliefs.

Therefore, women fulfilled the requirements asked from them in order to be initiated into Pythagorean philosophy: piety towards the gods, obedience towards parents, absolute devotion to one man (their husband), secrecy, prudence, bravery, harmony, avoidance of luxury, frugality in attire and food and genuine shyness.

One might be surprised at the strictness of the moral principles laid down by female Pythagorean students, and not by Pythagoras himself, in order to keep women inside their homes, occupying themselves with only their duties as wives and overseeing children and maidservants. Woman, as an active member of the household, not in the least inferior to man, in order to become initiated into philosophy, should be even more devoted than he and should strictly keep the moral precepts of the Pythagoreans, which were very strict for both sexes. This strictness may have been aimed at protecting women, and this is related to the great Pythagorean belief that 'people are bad'.

The aim of Pythagoras' 'preaching' was to create a cultural aristocracy and a religion based upon moral principles. No woman can have remained indifferent to the demands of Pythagorean philosophy, which propagated so noble a cause. The Pythagoreans believed in man's natural weakness. They professed that human beings were created to be happy, and the whole organization of private life and the political community was aimed, for them, at creating lasting happiness and making it accessible to everyone.

Philosophy purges. It purges human life by delivering it from the disorder of matter and the corrupting passions of the body. But this has been difficult for man to achieve because our souls, slaves to our bodies, have always been vulnerable to material passions; they have often moved away from god, abstained from concord and order, and gone deeper into the dark labyrinth of impropriety. The Pythagoreans believed that they would prevent so great a danger through hard and strict exercise, which would keep them in continuous touch with the dominating unity of the divine word and the harmonious balance of the hierarchical order of the world. God, being the essence of happiness and thus the only reason for the creation of beings, created for each being a situation that is best suited to it. Therefore, the continuous submission to order, harmony and the beauty of the universe meant union with this common link that combined everything with the Whole and was nothing else but the will and the thought of god himself.

Finally, there is a point not directly relevant to my paper that I should like to make. I do not accept scholars' recent distinction of the works written by alleged Pythagorean women as I, II, or even III, e.g. Theano I, Theano II, etc. It is useless and pointless. Men may also lie behind these female names, and women may lie behind male. Even if there is a difference in the language, these works may have been written at different stages of the same author's life. This is true especially for the letters: they are all written under pseudonyms, and it would be better if this were made clear first and the name and the content followed: in any case these letters are not characteristic of Pythagorean principles and beliefs.

## NOTES

\* I am grateful to the editors for help with the English version of this paper, and especially to Richard Hawley for the word-processing, checking of references in Thesleff 1965 and some translations.

1 Iambl. *VP* 72, cf. 94, 71. Porph. *VP* 19 (= Dicaearchus 33 Wehrli). Diog. Laert. 8.10. Gellius *Noct. Att.* 1, 9. Apul. *Floril.* 2, 15. Clem. Alex. *Strom.* 5, 11, p. 371 Staehlin. Hippolyt. *Haer.*, pp. 555–8. Diels. Lucian *Vit. Auct.* 3.1. Philopon. *In Aristot. De Anima Comment.* 1, 2 p. 69 Hayduck (cf. 5.3, p. 122, 30 Verbeke).

2 Iambl. *VP* 54; cf. 37–8. Diog. Laert. 3.21–3. Pseudo–Pythagoras *Carm. Aur.* 30–1 (= Thesleff 1965: 144, cf. 95–6).

3 Aristox. in Diog. Laert. 8.15; cf. 42, 52. Iambl. *VP* 31, 75, 144. Plut. *Num.* 22. Aristocl. in Eusebius *Praep. Ev.* 11.3.1. *Patr. Graec.* 21, 848a. Clem. Alex. *Strom.* 5.9, p 364 Staehlin. Porph. *VP* 58. Plat. *Epist.* 3.314a.

4 Pyth. 58D, p 469.20 Diels–Kranz (= Stob. *Ecl.* 4.25, 45 Hense). Iambl. *VP* 38. Diog. Laert. 8.23.

5 Pyth. 58C, pp. 462–6 Diels–Kranz. Porph. *VP* 41, 42. Diog. Laert. 8.34, 17. Aristot. *Frag. Pyth.* 5, 6, 7 Ross. Iambl. *VP* 82–6. Aelian *Var. Hist.* 4.17. Suda s.v. 'Anaximandros'. Plut. *De lib. educ.* 17 = 12de; *Quaest. Conv.* 7.10 = 727b.

6 Pseudo–Pythagoras *Carm. Aur.*, Thesleff 1965: 159–62. Jerome *Contr. Ruf.* 3.39. Diod. Sic. 10.7–11. Plut. *Quaest. Conv.* 3.6.3 = 654b. Porph. *VP* 22, 38, 39. Iambl. *VP* 34, 55, 132, 171; cf. Cic. *Cato* 2.38; Shakespeare *Twelfth Night* 4.2.50–6, *As You Like It* 2.1.15–17, *Merchant of Venice* 5.1.83–5.

7 Aristot. *Eth. Mag.* 1.1.1182a10–22. Diog. Laert. 8.31.

8 Thesleff 1965: 168, cf. 183–4. Pomp. Trog. 20.4.3, 6–12.

9 Thesleff 1965: 142, 17. See Lambropoulou 1976.

10 Thesleff 1965: 143, 28ff.

11 Thesleff 1965: 142, 23ff.

12  Thesleff 1965: 143, 1ff.
13  Cf. Iambl. *VP* 149; cf. 39, 46; Aristoph. *Eccl.* 446–51.
14  Thuc. 2.45. Cf. Plut. *Mul. Virt.* 1 = 242ef. Hes. *Theog.* 270. Aesch. *PV* 795.
15  Plat. *Gorg.* 508a; cf. Archyt. 47B.2, 3 Diels–Kranz.
16  Thesleff 1965: 151, 20ff.
17  Thesleff 1965: 152, 1ff.
18  Thesleff 1965: 152, 9ff. Cf. Musonius in Stob. *Ecl.* 2.123, p. 236 Wachsmuth.
19  Thesleff 1965: 152, 13ff.
20  Thesleff 1965: 152, 17–18. On 'Moderation': see Waithe 1987: 26–9; 'Chastity': see Lefkowitz and Fant 1992: 84; see also Taylor 1965.
21  Thesleff 1965: 116, 6–7.
22  Thesleff 1965: 154, 1ff.
23  Cf. Plut. *Coniug. Praec.* 30 = 142c, 32 = 142d. Lucian *Amores* 42. Juvenal *Sat.* 6. Diod. Sic. 12.21.1
24  Thesleff 1965: 114, 4ff.
25  Iambl. *VP* 189–94. Cf. St Ambros. *De Virg.* 1.4, *Patrol Lat.* 16, 203b–205b David, *Proleg.* 11.10 (= p. 33 Busse). Procl. *Comment in Plat. Rep.* p. 420 Basil; cf. vol. I. 248 Kroll. Aristot. *Pol.* 1.13.1260a30. Soph. *Ajax* 293.

# Chapter 9

# Self-help, self-knowledge: in search of the patient in Hippocratic gynaecology

*Helen King*

In medical history recently, there has been a trend towards looking at medicine 'from the patient's point of view'.[1] Instead of taking at face value the claims of medical practitioners, one looks at the full range of types of medicine available to a patient, the factors influencing the choice of healer and the patient's construction of what is happening to him or her – why me? why this illness? how is this therapy supposed to help me?

This type of history is far from simple. Sometimes records exist giving the patient's point of view – for example, diaries showing the progress of an illness and the reasons for choices of healers[2] – but, more often than not, the historian of the ancient and medieval worlds in particular has to work obliquely, reusing the canonical texts but addressing new questions to them.

In this paper I want to examine the extent to which such a history may be possible for the Hippocratic gynaecological texts, and perhaps for other ancient texts on women and medicine. These seem most unpromising sources for history from the patient's point of view; the Hippocratic texts, for example, were written by anonymous men from the fifth century BC onwards, and include advice on medical etiquette, aphorisms to guide medical practice, case histories and lists of recipes, as well as theoretical discussions of health and disease. The patient is clearly object, not subject, here. I will be arguing, however, that, even within the work of male practitioners who construct women's bodies, create a language for women's experiences and order the patient how to behave if she wishes to recover, opportunities are imagined to exist for the woman patient to become an active agent. These opportunities centre on the woman patient's assumed 'knowledge' of her own body – a knowledge which is not merely permitted in, but taken as central to, male constructs.

I would set this inquiry in a wider context of changing focus within studies of women in ancient societies. It seems to me that we have moved on from 'weren't women treated abysmally?', to 'finding women's voices in otherwise unpromising sources' and on to 'strategies women used within the system'. I am of course aware that these labels are, to a greater or lesser extent, caricatures, but I use them for convenience and because they clarify what has been happening. This paper falls into three parts, around these shifts of focus.

In the 'weren't women treated abysmally?' period, studies placed most emphasis on the Hippocratic texts as male constructs. Paola Manuli, for example, powerfully presented Hippocratic gynaecology as a set of male theories taking the male experience as the norm and setting out to demonstrate that woman is a structurally sick being.[3] Her wet and spongy flesh accumulates excess blood and must evacuate this to restore some sort of balance. But, precisely because of the nature of her flesh, further blood will eventually accumulate. The dominant image of the women patient here was of a silent, passive recipient of whatever the doctor provided. This image can be reinforced by the commonplace of classical (and later) medicine that women do not talk about their own bodies, because of 'youth, inexperience and embarrassment';[4] it can be used to add a further dimension to Galen's comments on the woman sick from infatuation with the dancer Pylades:

> She replied hesitantly or not at all, as if to show the folly of such questions, and finally turned over, buried herself completely deep in the blankets, covered her head with a small wrap and lay there as if wanting to sleep.[5]

Confronted with the battery of Hippocratic and Galenic treatments for women's diseases – beetle pessaries, uterine clysters, fumigations, animal excrement,[6] shaking and drenching with cold water – one can perhaps understand why the sensible response may be to refuse to answer questions and to put one's head deep under the blankets.

This image of the silent patient – silent because of her ignorance of her own body, or silent because she does not wish to be involved in the medical encounter – may however be better understood simply as the corollary of the talkative doctor. The whole point of the Hippocratic assertion of the norm of female ignorance and silence is to make it obvious why the Hippocratic doctor is so necessary: the whole point of Galen's emphasis on the absolute silence of the patient is to demonstrate his own brilliance in deducing what is wrong with her from observing her erratic pulse, which reveals the embarrassing secret of her love-sickness by speeding up at the mention of the name of the beloved. Her mouth is closed, but her body is an open book for the man who knows how to read it.

From an uncritical acceptance of this image of the silent woman patient, Hippocratic studies – with other areas of women's studies[7] – moved on to 'finding women's voices in otherwise unpromising sources'. There are no named women medical practitioners in the Hippocratic texts – only an isolated cord-cutter or *iatreousa*[8] – so the type of history that recovers lost 'famous women' has not been possible here, in contrast to later classical medicine in which one can find women named in inscriptions as *maia* or even as *iatros*.[9] Instead, the emphasis has been on finding traces of women's traditional medicine beneath the male-authored texts, using in particular the collections of recipes which feature throughout the Hippocratic *Diseases of Women* but which are focused on what Littré saw as the 'appendice necessaire' of the closing chapters, 74–109, of the first book.[10] For those trying to hear women's voices, the recipes become the product of centuries of women's experience. One may cite here Aline Rousselle's view that they pass on traditional women's remedies, based on detailed observations of their bodies made over many years, transmitted from mother to daughter.[11] The role of the male doctors is to appropriate them, expressed in the act of writing them down.[12] This requires a dramatic shift: the very remedies – such as beetle pessaries – that were once evidence of the male medical fantasies by which women were tortured must now be seen as women's own chosen therapies, later appropriated and given a new theoretical overlay by male doctors. Ann Hanson has argued that men's theory is superimposed on women's remedies;[13] this recalls Aristotle's view that, in conception, woman provides the raw material and man the shaping force.[14] She has more recently shifted the emphasis by suggesting that Hippocratic doctors are the mediators 'between theory and the welter of data that came to them from cases of specific women'.[15]

One aspect of this shift in the questions being asked of Hippocratic medicine has been a renewed interest in the key issue of efficacy. In the 'weren't women treated abysmally' period, efficacy was of minor importance – if treatment and remedies were mainly an expression of male oppression of women, efficacy took a back seat. But if the remedies are to be seen as women's traditional knowledge, then either they work – in which case, women's traditional knowledge scores high marks and is to be admired – or they don't work, in which case these nameless women go back to being negatively valued as 'old wives'. Angus McLaren believes that the contraceptive recipes given in medical writers of the ancient world are 'clearly "female knowledge" of which male writers were simply the chroniclers', but he rates this knowledge as largely worthless, only 'working' in the sense that it gave women the illusion of some degree of control over their own bodies.[16] In contrast, John Riddle's book, *Contraception and Abortion from the Ancient World to the Renaissance*, gives an enthusiastically positive valuation of these recipes in arguing strongly that 'they' knew things which 'we' do not.[17] Riddle suggests that female networks transmitted knowledge of effective plant contraceptives, many of them pot herbs, for many hundreds of years; he ends by proposing that, for a woman, salad 'may have been her control over her own life and her family's life'.[18] He identifies so many plants as contraceptives and/or abortives that one ends up wondering, with him, 'why there is any population in the Mediterranean at all'.[19] This I would see as an example of going too far in the attempt to show how deeply knowledgeable our foremothers were. There are other problems with Riddle's approach to pharmacology; for example, in modern laboratory tests a plant may be shown to contain an active ingredient which inhibits fertility, but its precise mode of use in antiquity may have invalidated its efficacy.[20]

Are the recipes 'women's voices'? Nowhere in the Hippocratic texts is it said explicitly that the recipes given derive from women; they are called *gynaikeia*, 'women's things',[21] but so are women's diseases in general, female genitalia and menses. The modern idea that they do is largely based on the sheer number of such recipes in the gynaecological treatises, in comparison with other Hippocratic texts,[22] but also on similarities between ancient remedies and modern Greek folk medicine.[23] There are other hints, for example, Galen's reference to the midwife who uses 'the customary remedies' for a sick widow does at least suggest that some remedies were both 'customary' and known to women.[24]

I would suggest that part of the problem we need to face in assessing the recipes is our belief that this is the sort of thing mothers should pass to daughters, reflecting the nostalgia of women in today's world for a – real? imaginary? – time when such information was indeed handed down as women's knowledge. Even if they are 'women's voices', however, do they differ significantly from men's voices? One interesting aspect of this question concerns the ingredients. As von Staden has shown, a prominent feature of the gynaecological treatises is the use of 'dirt': bird droppings, mouse excrement inserted into the vagina, mule dung, goat dung and hawk droppings drunk in wine.[25] It is no good saying this is a simple 'if it is disgusting, it will cure an unpleasant condition' approach, since these substances are not used in the treatment of men. So, are the recipes in which they occur the expression by men of women's imagined impurity, or can they still come from a female tradition? In the latter case, should we see this as a tradition in which women have absorbed and accepted their 'dirty' natures, or should we try to find a more positive way in which the use of such substances could be interpreted?[26] The idea that the pharmacopoeia represents women's traditional remedies meets further problems in the use of dangerous substances which could cause birth defects[27] and in the rare, costly ingredients which are occasionally mentioned, such as Egyptian perfume, myrrh and narcissus oil. Are these likely to feature in women's home remedies or, as I have argued elsewhere,[28] do they owe more to Hippocratic men trying to outdo each other in thinking of ever more flamboyant recipes with which to impress their patients?[29]

I would further argue that the current focus on the recipes within the gynaecological texts, with the supplementary issue of their efficacy, may be damaging to our understanding of Hippocratic medicine. The substances used in the pharmacopaeia should not only be investigated in terms of their 'efficacy'; all natural matter carries rich cultural values, and these are not necessarily best determined by laboratory tests.[30] Furthermore, the recipes form only one aspect of the process of therapy; equally significant may be other facets of the medical encounter, from the doctor's presentation of self, his behaviour, confidence and startling skills in telling the past, the present and the future,[31] to his rhetorical powers which present his theories in such a way that he provides a convincing story embracing all the symptoms and other relevant facts, and ending with advice which will bring about a cure.[32]

One problem common to both the 'weren't women treated abysmally?' approach and the 'finding women's voices in otherwise unpromising materials' line is that they tend to assume the ancient texts are transparent. For example, Rousselle has written: 'The little we know from ancient doctors' writings about women's bodies is precious, particularly their reports of the questions women asked and their ideas about their own bodies.'[33] But how often are the medical writings of antiquity 'reports'? Are they not texts in which nothing should be taken at face value? Where women speak in these texts, they are as much the creation of male authors as is Clytemnestra, or Juvenal's Laronia.[34] But, as Jack Winkler reminded us, 'men's talk' is 'calculated bluff' and in reading we should always try to 'read against the grain'.[35] Just because the Hippocratic case histories contain named patients, and chart the progress of their disease by following the changes which occur day by day, this does not make them any less 'text' than a play, or a poem. This is not simply a point made by post-structuralist readers; Langholf, for example, has shown that the data of observation in the *Epidemics* is adjusted to fit the theory, so that when the crisis, or turning-point, in a condition fails to come on the day predicted by the theory of 'critical days', the writer simply states '*around* the twentieth day'.[36] These are not simple 'reports', but are always set in an enveloping context of culture and theory.

One of the central factors here is the medical writers' insistence that they are right, taken with the internal logical consistency of what they say. This is a seductive combination, one which has been significant in the historiography of ancient medicine, in which many of the historians themselves have been medical practitioners. In reading the texts, such writers recognise one of their own. Hippocratic medicine has the authority, the bedside manner and the internal consistency to make it sound convincing. Actually, of course, there are a number of different and even conflicting theories in the Hippocratic corpus, with disagreement on basic issues such as whether women's bodies are hotter or colder than those of men, and whether or not women contribute a 'seed' to the process of generation. But regardless of these differences the tendency has been, and still is, to look for one theory and to see one great man, Hippocrates himself, behind the corpus.

As I have noted elsewhere, this tendency seems to me to recall the trust an anthropologist may show towards his or her chief informant, the person who is chosen to act as the bridge between cultures.[37] Victor Turner wanted to trust his main Ndembu informant, Muchona the Hornet. Although Muchona was of marginal social status, Turner's fieldwork was swayed by the rounded, coherent and systematised world-view he offered; he found Muchona's explanations for aspects of ritual 'always fuller and internally more consistent', to be accepted even when they were directly at variance with what Turner reports as an eyewitness. Other Ndembu did not share this assessment of Muchona, saying 'He is just lying'.[38] It is possible that Muchona's testimony should be discredited as the work of an outsider desperately trying to be accepted by the anthropologist.

The trouble with the Hippocratic Corpus is that we do not know whether its writers were in a position analogous to that of Muchona. Were they central, or marginal? How intense was the competition between them and the other types of healer we glimpse through their writings – the root-cutters, prophets, cord-cutters and others? Were Hippocratic therapies used as first resort, or last resort – widely, rarely or even never? Would other members of their culture see them as 'just liars'? These are critical questions for our understanding of the relationship between Hippocratic medicine and any 'female tradition'; for example, Lesley Dean–Jones argues that the reason why there are twice as many male as female case histories in the *Epidemics* is that women tended to frequent traditional healers rather than Hippocratics,[39] but there is no evidence to support this view.

My third line of approach, 'strategies women used within the system,' sees Hippocratic medicine neither as a male system to oppress women, nor as a male take-over of women's traditional knowledge, but rather as a system within which men and women both had some power, and within which women as patients could become active agents in their own diagnosis and treatment.

Despite their desire to bolster their own authority, and their insistence on women's silence due to embarrassment, the medical writers of antiquity do not present women as being entirely without knowledge. Indeed, in certain cases the doctor is expected to defer to women's superior knowledge.

The main knowledge which women are accepted as having, or are imagined to have, concerns pregnancy. A woman 'knows' she has conceived by a sensation of closure in her womb or by observing that the seed does not leave her body. How do the Hippocratic writers 'know' what women 'know'? Their own answer to this critical question is that they know because women – or, at least, some women – tell them. In *Flesh* 19, the writer attributes his information to public *hetairai*. People will ask how he knows the amazing things he is telling, such as the 'fact' that all parts of the foetus are formed after seven days in the womb. The source is partly women – he says, 'and as for the rest, I know only what women have taught me' – and partly his own eyewitness evidence from the products of abortion.[40] The famous entertainer in *On Generation / Nature of the Child* 13 'had heard the sort of thing women say to each other, that when a woman is going to conceive, the seed remains inside her and does not fall out. She digested this information, and kept a watch'.[41]

Aristotle too gives information on women's 'feelings'. Many have 'choking feelings' and 'noises in the womb' before a period starts, and they have a distinctive sensation in the flanks and groin which tells them they have conceived.[42] The writer of the tenth book of *Historia animalium* notes several times that women emit what he calls 'seed' at the end of their erotic dreams.[43] Neither tells us how he knows what women dream or feel, although Rousselle states that the latter 'must have received his accounts of the sensations they experienced from women themselves'.[44] The possibility remains, however, that writers made up stories like this to impress their audiences; if you believe that the womb is a reversed jar with its own neck, mouth and lips, in sympathetic relationship with the corresponding parts of the upper female body,[45] then 'choking feelings' may be perfectly plausible as the womb prepares to open to bleed.

The highly positive evaluation of 'what women say to each other' by classical medical writers is noteworthy, since the few extant references to women's knowledge and its transmission among women in antiquity are otherwise far from flattering. Dean–Jones gives what she describes as two negative and two positive examples of ancient Greek assessments of women's transmission of knowledge.[46] The two 'negative' examples are not controversial; they are Semonides' description of the bee-woman, who does not enjoy sitting among women where they tell stories about love,[47] and the attack in Euripides' *Andromache* on women who lead each other on to wrongdoing, in which women are called 'teachers of evil'.[48] The supposedly 'positive' examples are however far from straightforward. In Aristophanes' *Ecclesiazusae*, Praxagora explains to her husband that her absence from home at night was due to going to help a friend in labour, not – as he suspects – a visit to a clandestine lover.[49] There is no specific reference here to the transmission of knowledge, only to practical support; far from giving a positive evaluation of women's knowledge, indeed, the passage serves to raise the fear that women's support networks may in fact be a cloak for adultery. It thus seems very close to the viewpoint of the Euripides passage. The second 'positive' example used by Dean–Jones is the passage from Chariton's *Chaereas and Callirrhoe* in which the steward's wife, Plangon, notices that Callirrhoe, having been sold into slavery, is two months pregnant by her absent husband Chaereas. Here Plangon is not, however, simply a confidante; she is acting for Callirrhoe's love-struck master, Dionysios, who is trying to use Plangon's knowledge of women to win Callirrhoe. When Plangon offers to help Callirrhoe to abort the child, this is really only pretence; she knows talk of abortion will instead serve to push Callirrhoe into wanting to keep the child and will thus further her own plans to help Dionysios.[50] Plangon's offer of knowledge to help Callirrhoe abort is only the prologue to the central part of the section, where Plangon suggests that, since Callirrhoe is a mere two months pregnant, her best option is to marry her master Dionysios and pass off the baby as his (premature) son.[51] Far from this being a positive evaluation of the sort of knowledge women pass on to each other, we could instead read this passage as a depiction of women's knowledge being used to deceive the male.

Callirrhoe's innocence and Plangon's knowledge also recall the distinction made between two types of woman, in terms of their reliability, in the Hippocratic Corpus. What Hanson has called 'the woman of experience'[52] is trusted, and cited as the doctor's source for women's oral tradition, while the woman who lacks 'experience' is doubted. Callirrhoe, being in Hippocratic terms an 'inexperienced' woman, does not even realise that she is pregnant: Plangon has the knowledge which enables her to detect and, if required, to end Callirrhoe's pregnancy. It is not only on the grounds of 'lack of experience' that Hippocratic writers are sometimes prepared to question women's knowledge; on a woman who claimed that she miscarried a male child at twenty days, a Hippocratic writer says, 'If this is true, I don't know.'[53] Fatty and bilious women, we are explicitly told, do not know whether they have conceived.[54]

Thus the ancient medical writers accept women's knowledge – with the important proviso that it may be a knowledge they have constructed for women – but they reserve to themselves the right to judge whose knowledge they will accept. This makes women as patients neither the 'passive victims of historical injustice' of the 'weren't women treated abysmally?' approach, nor the 'constant heroines struggling to change society' who are the goal of the 'finding women's voices' approach.[55] Within this finely balanced situation, women's knowledge must be constructed within the parameters of the male theory which states that the male is the appropriate provider of health care. Self-knowledge is permitted; self-help is not. Knowledge of the inside of one's body is encouraged, in order to report to the *iatros* the condition of the mouth of the womb as narrow, moist or closed,[56] and the model patient, Phrontis, reported the absence of her lochia to the doctor after feeling an obstruction in her vagina, and was subsequently cured.[57] Self-help, although rarely mentioned, is condemned in one passage which attributes ulceration of the womb to the harsh pessaries used by women to treat themselves and others.[58] Hanson has shown how a clyster to be used as a remedy for discomfort caused by strong pessaries is given twice in a chapter of *Diseases of Women*; in other sections of this text which appear to have been written later this same remedy comes to be applied more widely to cases of ulceration.[59] Here it appears that we have a negatively-valued piece of self-help – the pessaries – alongside a recipe for a clyster which may also derive from self-help but which enters the Hippocratic remedy-lists and is then extended to use in similar cases.

Even within the parameters of Hippocratic medicine, openings exist which may permit the woman patient to become an active agent during therapy. It is at least theoretically possible for the woman who believes herself to be pregnant, but does not want the child, to say to a doctor, 'I haven't had a period, I am worried that the blood is building up and causing these symptoms, and no, it certainly can't be pregnancy, because I saw the seed come out after intercourse and anyway I don't have any feeling of closure of my womb.' She could then be given an early abortion under the guise of 'bringing on the period'.[60]

There are also points at which a woman can stop a painful or otherwise unpleasant treatment by conforming to the male doctor's sometimes bizarre image of her body.[61] Denying that your womb has moved to your liver[62] gets you nowhere, but agreeing that it has moved, and adding that it is now safely back in place, stops the treatment. In fumigation, the patient is specifically asked 'if she can feel the mouth of the womb'; if she can (or at least says that she can) and it is correctly realigned so that menstrual blood can come out and male seed can enter, then the treatment can be ended.[63]

Women can also use to their own advantage the Hippocratic theory of critical days, by which the crisis point in a condition is expected to come on certain numbered days. *On the Seven Months' Child* says that the first and seventh days after conception are most likely for a miscarriage;[64] here, a woman who herself brings on an early abortion could avoid awkward questions afterwards by saying, 'Well, these things happen; after all, it is the seventh day since I felt myself conceive.'

The issue of timing can be critical to the interplay between female self-knowledge and male theory. Ann Hanson has drawn attention to the significance of defining a child as seven or eight months. She has convincingly demonstrated that both women and men could use the system for their own benefit, rather than it being a male system imposed on women.[65] It was believed that the child born in the eighth month – that is, after the completion of seven full months in the womb – never survived, while the child born in the seventh month may or may not survive. This may seem odd to us; surely the longer a child spends in the womb, the greater its chances of survival? It also seemed odd to Aristotle, who contrasted it with Egypt, where no such belief existed. In Greece, he says, most eighth month babies die for the simple reason that any eight month baby who lives is promptly redefined as a seventh or ninth month baby; once it lives, the women assume they must have miscalculated.[66] Hanson has further argued that, by calling a child born dead 'an eighth month child', mother, family, birth attendants and doctor are all freed from any blame for what has happened. However, logically, the problem here is the Hippocratic belief that women 'know' when they have conceived; yet the treatise *On the Seven Months' Child* says that it is precisely *women* who insist that the eight months' child never survives.[67] So it looks as if women are prepared to revise their 'knowledge', their estimate of the time the child spent in the womb, if that child is born dead or damaged, while a child born alive but sickly can be labelled 'a seven months' child' to prepare all concerned for the possibility of his or her death.

Thus women can be presented as conveniently silent, passive patients, but are also believed to have their own 'knowledge'. It may even be in their own interest to go back on it – to deny that they ever said this was a ninth month child – or to suppress it. Hippocratic doctors claim to be appropriating women's knowledge – 'You may wonder how I know this; well, women told me' – while also choosing when to discount what women say. The system allows women patients opportunities to negotiate, as an agent, within defined limits. This suggests that the interplay between women and men is rather more subtle than either the 'weren't women treated abysmally?' approach or the 'finding women's voices' approach would allow.

## NOTES

1  See for example Crawford 1978 and 1981: 49 n. 9 and 67, on the diary of Lady Frances Catchmay (*c.* 1625) and the spiritual diary of Sarah Savage (1687–8) as sources for women's menstrual experience and pregnancy; and Porter (ed.) 1985. Green 1989: 436 tries to look beyond

'the history of women practitioners' to 'the history of women patients', in the sense of the care received by women.

2  For example, the diary of Mary Poor, used by Brodie 1994 to provide an insight into a Victorian couple's attempts at family planning. The memoirs of Lady Ann Fanshawe (1625–80) record eighteen pregnancies; see Marshall 1905.

3  Manuli 1980.

4  *Diseases of Women* (henceforth *DW*), 1.62 (Littré (henceforth L) 8.126)

5  *On Prognosis*, 6. 2–110 (ed. Nutton 1979: 100–3).

6  On which see von Staden 1992.

7  For example, Lewis 1981 regards the attempt to restore the missing women to history as characteristic of the 1970s. Davis 1976 traces back the history of lists of 'women worthies' and biographies of individual notable women.

8  Cord-cutter, *DW* 1.46 (L 8.106); *iatreousa*, *DW* 1.68 (L 8.144).

9  For example, Phanostrate, *IG* II/III 3.2 6873 is *maia kai iatros* in a late fourth-century BC inscription; see Nickel 1979. On the dangers of distortion consequent upon studying 'a few exceptional women' see, for nursing history, Davies 1980: 11.

10  L 8.154–232; for Littré's assessment, see 8.155.

11  Rousselle 1980, 1988.

12  Some recipes, once written down, proved to be very long-lived, continuing to be repeated even when new medical theories should have made them redundant. An example is the use of sweet- and foul-smelling substances for 'uterine suffocation'; aromatics are rubbed on the groin and inner thighs in the Hippocratic *DW* 2.201 (L 8.384), and are probably the 'customary remedies' to which Galen, despite his rejection of the idea that the womb moves, alludes in his *On the Affected Parts* 6.5 (Kühn (henceforth K) 8.420). See King 1993. Despite its stability, the recipe tradition also shows flexibility, most notably in the recipes preserved on papyrus, which show changes to quantities and offer alternative ingredients (Ann Hanson: personal communication).

13  Hanson 1990: 309–110.

14  For example, Aristotle *GA* 729a 25–35; 729b 12–21; Horowitz 1976: 195–16.

15  Hanson 1992: 236.

16  McLaren 1990: 28. As Patricia Crawford (1994: 99) has pointed out for the early modern period in England, 'In practice, women's knowledge must have been less effective than people believed, otherwise there would not have been so many unwanted pregnancies outside marriage.'

17  Riddle 1992.

18  Riddle 1992: 155.

19  Riddle 1992: 38.

20  Nutton 1985; Lloyd 1979: 46–7.

21  Hanson 1990: 310: 'Elements of the oral tradition among women are *no doubt* preserved in the recipes of the gynecologies, for the medical writers refer to therapies for the care of women as *gynaikeia*' (my italics).

22  For example, Hanson 1992: 235: 'In no other segment of the early Greek medical writings are the medicaments that cure, or at least alleviate,

awarded such prominence'; Dean-Jones 1994: 30: 'The gynaecology incorporates more elements of folk practice, such as a wider *materia medica* . . . than other sections of the corpus.'

23  Hanson 1991b: 78 and n. 32.
24  *On the Affected Parts* 6.5 (K 8.420).
25  Von Staden 1992c.
26  Ann Hanson (pers. comm.) has recently pointed out to me that the use of dung could be interpreted in a more positive way, as 'fertiliser' for the field which is the womb. On the imagery of woman as earth, see duBois 1988.
27  Zivanovic 1982: 88 and 247: 'many elements used as remedies may lead to poisoning'.
28  King 1995.
29  Green 1989: 458, writing on early modern medicine, points out that male and female healers were sometimes using very similar remedies but, whereas women used everyday ingredients, men deliberately chose costly alternatives in order to distance their remedies from those of women.
30  Von Staden 1992c: 23–56.
31  *On Prognosis*; see also King 1991.
32  Jouanna 1984; King 1989a.
33  Rousselle 1988: 2.
34  See Chapter 14, this volume.
35  Winkler 1990b: 4 and 126.
36  Langholf 1990: 186–90 and 209.
37  King 1995.
38  Turner 1960 and 1969: 69.
39  Dean-Jones 1994: 136.
40  L 8.610 with *Flesh 1* (L 8.584).
41  *On the Nature of the Child* 13 (L 7.488–90); transl. Lonie 1981: 7 and see 160–2.
42  *Historiaanimalium* 582b10–12 and 583a35–b3; cf. 584a2–12.
43  *Historiaanimalium* 634b29–31; 635a34–36.
44  Rousselle 1988: 28.
45  Hanson and Armstrong 1986; sympathy between the upper and lower parts of the body means that loss of virginity changes the quality of a girl's voice.
46  Dean-Jones 1994: 28 and n. 85.
47  *Aphrodisioi logoi*, Semonides II. 90–1(Lloyd-Jones 1975: 59); it is of interest that Theodorus Prisicianus 2.11 (p. 133 Rose) advises men suffering from impotence to read 'tales of love' as a cure.
48  Eur. *Andromache* 943–6.
49  *Eccl.* 526–50.
50  Chariton *Chaereas and Callirrhoe* 2.8.4–11.6.
51  ibid. 2.10.5.
52  Hanson 1990: 309–10.
53  *Epidemics* 4.6 (L 5.146).
54  *Flesh* 19 (L 8.610).
55  The formulations are those of Davis 1976: 86.

56 *DW* 1.59 (L 8.118), cf. 2.155 (L 8.330); 3.213 (L 8.410); Rousselle 1980: 1095–6.
57 *DW* 1.40 (L 8.96–8).
58 *DW* 1.67 (L 8.140).
59 *DW* 2.209 (L 8.404); Hanson 1991b: 79–81.
60 *DW* 1.25 (L 8.66) lists, as something to be avoided, the activities which could cause miscarriage. Such knowledge is, of course, always available to those who in fact wish to induce a miscarriage. Furth 1986: 64–5 argues along similar lines for the period 1600–1850 in China, where lists of drugs to be avoided during pregnancy could be turned around and used as abortives, while Crawford 1981: 69 documents for seventeenth-century England the practice of seeking an abortion by asking to have a supposedly suppressed menstrual period induced. See also McLaren 1994: 267 on late nineteenth-century pills to remove 'obstructions', a code word for unwanted foetuses; and McLaren 1984: 102 on drugs euphemistically described as being intended 'to restore the menses'.
61 On a similar question, in relation to Aristotle, Dean-Jones 1994: 38 agrees that 'women must have acquiesced in the model to the extent of providing data to support it and acceding to therapy based on it' but she prefers to believe that women interpreted the model in a more positive way. I would instead see the advantage of these models to women as lying in the loopholes they provide to the patient.
62 Movement of the womb to the liver, in search of moisture: *DW* 1.7 (L 8.32–4); 2.127 (L 8.272–4).
63 *DW* 2.133 (L 8.286).
64 *Seven Months' Child* 9 (L 7.449).
65 Hanson 1987.
66 Aristotle *Historia animalium* 584b7–14.
67 *Seven Months' Child* 4 (L 7.442).

# Chapter 10

# Women who suffer from a man's disease

## The example of satyriasis and the debate on affections specific to the sexes

*Danielle Gourevitch\**

Antiquity asked the question whether there existed states peculiar to each sex and to women in particular, and which might concern medical science. Moreover, the ancients called several diseases *satyriasis* or *satyriasmos* because of certain natural peculiarities, physical and existential, which legend, sculpture and painting attributed to satyrs. The appearance of their skin had caused this name to be given to the first stage of leprosy,[1] and, because of their little horns, also to frontal exostoses. The existence of 'glands' beneath their ears lent the name to mumps, and certain warts also have this name.[2] Similarly, the appearance of their genitals gave the name both to a persistent erection of the penis (also called 'priapism'), and to a potentially fatal state of acute and painful erection.

This last, however paradoxical it might initially seem, could also afflict women.

## DO AFFECTIONS (πάθος,[3] *passio*) EXIST WHICH ARE PECULIAR TO WOMEN AND WHICH CONCERN MEDICAL SCIENCE?

This question is formally asked by Soranus of Ephesus in Book 3 of his gynaecological treatise;[4] he proceeds, according to his usual method, by a definition of the concept, an historico-critical overview and his own reflections within the frame of methodological doctrine.

> 'Do there exist affections peculiar to women?' The question may also be put thus: 'are there affections peculiar to the female sex, in the sense in which woman constitutes a species, the female a gender'. As for the expression 'peculiar to', ... it designates first that which does not belong to another. ... It is in this sense in

which the present question is posed. Elsewhere, 'affection' means at once that which is according to nature (for example, conception, giving birth, lactation), and that which is contrary to nature (for example, fever). Among those affections which are contrary to nature, some are considered to be general, i.e., applying to a whole genus (of pathology), like contractions, while others are considered partial and of limited duration, like frenzy or lethargy. This book concerns especially that which is contrary to nature, both in the particular and in the general senses.

Inquiry is very useful here for the sake of learning whether women also need treatment which is peculiar to them. But a disagreement has arisen, for some assume that affections arise which are peculiar to women, as do the Empiricists, Diocles in Book 1 of his *Gynaecology*, and, among the Erasitrateans,[5] Athenion and Miltiades, among the Asclepiadeans, Lucius, in Book 3 of his *Chronic Diseases*, and Demetrius of Apamea. Others, however, assume that no affections unique to women arise: for example, in the opinion of most people, Erasistratus, and, as has been implied, Herophilus[6]; also Apollonius Mys in the first and third books of his work, *On the Sect*, as well as Asclepiades (according to the general consensus), Alexander Philalethus, Themison, Thessalos and their disciples.

To support the opinion that there are specifically feminine affections, these are the arguments generally advanced: we call certain physicians 'women's doctors' because they treat women's diseases; when women suffer from affections which are peculiar to their sex and which they do not share with men, people generally rely upon midwives; moreover, the feminine differs naturally from the masculine, so much so that Aristotle and Zeno the Epicurean claim that the female is imperfect while the male is perfect: now, that which differs by the whole of its nature is also susceptible to particular affections. Also: the uterus is an organ peculiar to women and its functions — menstruation, conception, parturition — are manifest only among them. . . . In his *Midwifery*, Herophilus says that the uterus is woven from the same things as the other parts, is regulated by the same faculties, has the same material substances at hand, and is caused to be diseased by the same things, such as excessive quantity, thickness and disharmony in similars. Accordingly, says Herophilus, there is no affection peculiar to women except conceiving, giving birth, 'ripening' the milk and the opposite of these.[7] The disciples of Asclepiades, in an attempt to establish that there is no specifically feminine affection, affirm that the female is formed from the same types of elementary materials as the male, and falls ill under the effect of the same cause, obstruction, which is, according to these authors, directly responsible for most affections; finally, they add that the same procedures and prescriptions serve for her cure. Therefore there exists no affection peculiar to woman, since physiology, aetiology and treatment are the same for women as for men. Themison and Thessalos . . . say, consequently, that there is no affection unique to women.

We agree with the opinion of the authors just quoted and affirm that the others have resorted to erroneous demonstrations. . . . Next, owing to whatever combination of primary elements, it is possible that an original part of the whole was developed in women (in fact, Erasistratus asserts that the other parts became so different as a result of a particular assemblage of vessels). Even if this part does not differ from what it is in the other sex, it is possible for woman to be affected in a manner unique to her, since the same place also suffers now from contraction, now from laxation. It is necessary to use similar arguments against Herophilus and Asclepiades,[8] who are wrong as far as elementary particles are concerned, and, furthermore, over the causation of illness. . . .

Therefore, putting their thesis simply, all these authors conducted themselves correctly, but they were mistaken in their demonstrations. As for us, we assert that, among the affections in accordance with nature, there are those which are characteristic of women, like conception, parturition, lactation, if indeed one agrees to term these functions 'affections', but that, in the field of those affections contrary to nature, there is no generic affection which is feminine; there exist only specific or individual affections. In fact, regarding general affections, women and men alike suffer from contraction or laxation, acute or chronic; woman is subject to the same seasonal differences, to the same attacks of illness, to the same weakening, she has the same reactions to foreign bodies, ulcerations and injuries. It is only in those cases involving individual variations in detail that woman has affections which are peculiar to her, that is to say, symptoms of an original character: therefore demanding the same general treatment, as will be understood more easily upon reading that which follows.

It is apparent that this was a hotly debated topic, an argument to rage through the centuries. But in fact the problem is two-sided: a problem of the history of medical ideas, since the different Alexandrian and post-Alexandrian schools are taken into consideration by our author; and a problem of vocabulary: the meaning of the words πάθος and *passio*, which leads to a problem of practical medicine.

The quarrel between the schools is a complicated one, since, on this point as on so many others, the different schools not only disagreed among themselves, but also revealed internal discord.[9] We shall not enter into doctrinal detail here.

The Greek word πάθος denotes an experience which everyone can know and feel, as much psychically as physically; in this context we translate it by the word 'affection' (von Staden in his *Herophilus* translates it sometimes as 'affection', sometimes as 'disease'). In accordance with its etymology and in this context, it means 'that by which the subject is affected', something 'undergone', not necessarily a disease, but rather a somewhat disagreeable state, a discomfiture, an unavoidable physiological ('in accordance with nature') or pathological ('contrary to nature') condition which occurs to man, animals, plants leaving them unable to do anything about it.[10] But when the affection is not in accordance with nature, πάθος, just like the Latin *passio*, can take on the meaning of unwholesome process or, further, of a properly pathological state. And it is clear that the masters and the students of the schools, never famous for their good faith, enjoyed playing on these words.

It is important to distinguish clearly between the problem of specifically feminine (or masculine) states, and that of differential morbidity according to sex,[11] recognized at least since Hippocratic times,[12] and attributed as much to the partially different nature of men and women (biological factors), as to their different lifestyles: more active and oriented towards the outside world for men, more domestic and quieter for women (social factors). This sex-linked morbidity is connected with far more than the genital region.

For the disease which concerns us presently, the problem is one of practical medicine: no one, certainly, would bring the specificity of the female organs into question, nor, therefore, the special quality of the symptoms experienced. The therapeutic principles have nothing particular about them, but local treatments must be adapted. The surprising problem of female genital satyriasis is one of an apparent contradiction between the symptoms and the affected part.

## SATYRIASIS, ACUTE AND PAINFUL ERECTION OF THE PENIS

This disease of the male sexual organ seems to have found its way into medical literature in the first century BC, in the works of one of the founding fathers of the methodist school, as Caelius Aurelianus on Themison[13] reminds us. Actually, the first text to be preserved dates from the first century AD, and is part of the book of Aretaeus of Cappadocia.[14] The bizarre and disquieting nature of the disease is marked from the start by a mythological reference, and the chapter ends with the words: 'It is wholly an acute disorder, distressing and indecent. In fact, in the majority of cases, the patient dies within eight days.'

What follows is an inventory in chronological order, which I believe to be exhaustive, of other ancient texts, Greek and Latin, in which this meaning of satyriasis appears. These are often difficult texts, not translated into any modern language, and far from being comprehensively covered in dictionaries.

Rufus of Ephesus[15] describes a patient he had known, whose penis was seized by a continual and violent pulsing, accompanied by stiffening:

> When the affection spread, it took hold of the penis, as though this organ were inflating; thus the pain was diffused to the root of the penis and to the perinaeum. It was equally distressing to this individual to engage in coitus as it was for him to abstain from it: coitus rendered him extremely licentious, whereas abstinence aroused dishonourable passions in him.

Soranus of Ephesus' treatise on general medicine is lost, but we do possess an adaptation by Caelius Aurelianus who, in his *Acute Diseases*,[16] writes:

> Satyriasis is a violent desire for coitus, accompanied by stiffening, attributable to a diseased state. It derives its name, according to some, from the resemblance that sufferers bear to satyrs, which, as people say and as legend tells, are understood to be drawn to wine and prone to sexual intercourse; others, however, maintain that this name comes from the properties of a plant which is called *satyrion* by the Greeks, since those who consume it are driven to coitus and experience a sort of severe tension in the genital organs.
>
> The antecedent causes of this affection are: the taking of drugs

intended to arouse sexual desire, plants which the Greeks call *satyrica* or *entatica* [= tension producing], and which are bitter, stimulating and therefore bad for the sinews and tendons; also immoderate and ill-regulated sexual habits. It is an affection common to men and women, and which occurs mainly in middle age and youth. For the vigour of these ages tends towards the practice of coitus.

In the patients, the symptoms are the following: violent tension and rigidity of the genital organs, accompanied by pain and a burning sensation; also, an unbearable itching, which ardently incites sexual desire, bringing on derangement, rapid pulse, laboured breathing, which is shallow and rapid; a feeling of despair; insomnia; hallucinations, thirst; loss of appetite; difficulty in urination so pronounced that retention of the faeces is generally brought on; some patients may also experience fever. However, in all sufferers it results in a convulsion of the nerves which the Greeks call *spasmos*, and an involuntary ejaculation . . . Therefore, one must distinguish priapism from satyriasis to the extent to which satyriasis is an acute disease which is never of long duration, and which is accompanied by the contraction of the sinews and tendons, and by a frenzied desire for sexual pleasure.

Satyriasis is an affection of contraction, an acute and violent affection. In fact, all the nerves and sinews are affected, a fact which may be inferred from the accompanying mental derangement and the contraction of the limbs. . . .

In the Galenic tradition, one also encounters allusions to this disease. The Pseudo-Galen wrote (without doubt before Galen himself):[17]

Satyriasis is an affection which consists in the stiffening of the sexual organs, at the same time as their different parts become stretched. There are patients in whom ejaculation occurs, accompanied by sexual pleasure; the mind of these patients is touched, and there is a contraction of the nerves and of the spermatic ducts.

Galen himself returns to the subject in a number of passages. On the one hand, his concern is a problem of vocabulary and of nomenclature. In his *Dictionary*,[18] he explains the complex term 'satyrism', writing notably: 'some have meant by this tension in the sexual organs'. Elsewhere,[19] he alludes to 'elephantiasis', an affection which, in its initial stages carries the name *satyriasmos*, because the faces of its sufferers resemble those of satyrs ... just as some call the prolonged stiffening of the sexual organs which does not cease in accordance with nature *satyriasmos* or *priapismos*.

Oribasius[20] sets forth the opinion of Rufus according to which

the ancients have taught us nothing about elephantiasis. . . . The physicians who lived but a short time before us established in the following way the different forms which this affection could take: at its inception they called it *leontiasis* . . .; but, when the eyebrows swell, when the cheeks redden, and the patients are seized by a kind of ardour for coitus, the physicians give the name of *satyriasis* to this state which is not merely an affection of the genital parts, since the latter has derived its name from the chronic stiffening of these parts, whereas the former also takes its name from the general appearance of the affection.

Aetius,[21] who clumsily confounds satyriasis and priapism, further writes:

Priapism is a stiffening of the penis, and an increase in its length and thickness, without venerean desire, brought on by a kind of irritation, which arises along with a kind of inflammation and pain in the genitals. The name priapism comes from Priapus and Satyr, who are represented in painting and in sculpture as naturally having such a penis. . . . The sufferers feel a pain similar to that caused by tetanus. The penis, stretched and swollen with *pneuma*, suffers something resembling a spasm. These patients die rapidly if they are not given prompt attention. . . .

Among the Latin authors who are not Soranus' followers, the confusion is at its worst: Theodorus Priscianus[22] believes that satyriasis 'originates from a certain state of physical discomfiture which sometimes occurs even in women and which some have termed *metromania*; it produces an insatiable desire and a stiffening of the genital region, with frequent necessity of coitus'.

Isidore of Seville[23] writes that 'satyriasis is a chronic desire for sexual gratification, with stiffening and an increase in the volume of the genital organs; the affection takes its name from that of the satyrs'.

Finally, in the *Glossae medicinales*, collected in the seventh century AD and edited by Heiberg, there is the following definition:

Satyriasis, that is to say, the desire to fulfil the lover's obligation, is recognized by an exaggerated stiffening of the organs, accompanied by pain and a burning, itching sensation, or by an excessive search for the pleasures of the flesh, also rapid heartbeat, gasping and rapid breathing. It is a shameful and dangerous affection. Satyriasis therefore is an enflamed passion for the venerean pleasures accompanied by a strong and shameful erection of the genital organs; occasionally also with ejaculation of sperm and tension of the sinews and tendons or tremours; and, when the disease persists, the patients can do no more than ejaculate before fainting and their life is at grave risk. Satyriasis derives its name from its resemblance to the satyrs, whose reputation it is to be too much inclined to the pleasures of Venus.

## NEVERTHELESS, THIS LOCALIZED DISEASE, ATTACHED TO THE QUINTESSENTIALLY MASCULINE ORGAN, ALSO EXISTS AMONG WOMEN, ACCORDING TO CERTAIN AUTHORS

Starting from the most ancient descriptions of the masculine form of the disease, authors either confirm or bear witness to the testimony of others that the disease could take a feminine form.

Aretaeus[24] adds to his description: 'It is said that women may also suffer from this affection, and that they too experience an analogous impulse towards the pleasures of love, along with the rest.' Soranus of Ephesus[25] judges that

> satyriasis appears most often among men, and that is the reason we have dealt with it in our *Acute Diseases*, but it also exists among women. They succumb to an intense and painful itching of the sexual parts which makes them constantly touch this place with their hands. This gives rise to an irresistable desire for sexual relations, and, at the same time, to a certain mental derangement which, because of the sympathetic link between the meninges and the uterus, overrides all sense of modesty.
>
> It is a question of inflammation of the uterine regions. Now, the sexual impulse which occurs in the patients only serves to aggravate their condition. In fact, the afflicted parts of the body are stretched in the extreme, and the semen is not expelled because of the occlusion of the passages. . . . Therefore, one must take care first to bleed them, to restrict their diet, to place upon the pubic

region and the hips poultices capable of refreshing and gently compressing, and to rub the head with vinegar mixed with rose oil; to drink warm water; the diet should be liquid, and everything which causes flatulence or which may excite sexual desire must be eliminated from it. On the third day after the blood-letting, place upon the affected parts cupping-vessels without scarification. The rest of the treatment will be the same as that which will be described for inflammation.

Aretaeus' translator, Caelius Aurelianus, agrees in this respect and himself continues:[26]

All of these symptoms also occur in women afflicted with this affection, but in them the itching is particularly severe because of their nature. And, in fact, they place their hands upon their genitals in a shameful manner, since these shameful parts itch, and, if a man happens upon them, they accost him and, falling to their knees, beg him to give himself over to their desire. . . . Spermatorrhea, which is what we term discharge of semen, differs from satyriasis in that spermatorrhea is a chronic involuntary discharge of semen, without stiffening of the sexual organs; further-more, satyriasis is not an affection of protracted duration, such as the Greeks term chronic, but rather like the affection which the Greeks call priapism. . . .

Mustio is also in agreement with Soranus, in both of the manu-script forms in which we know his text; the version edited by Drabkin[27] (with the *Gynecology* of Caelius Aurelianus) summarizes:

Satyriasis is a disease shared by men and women. In women, satyr-iasis is an itching in the genital organs accompanied by pain so severe that they must bring their hands to the genitals, and an insatiable desire for the male, the women having lost all modesty with respect to their organs; but, if the meninges, which have a sympathetic link to the uterus, rob them of all modesty without enabling them to abandon themselves to coitus, they may also cause them to become somewhat delirious. As for the treatment, we apply the same as that which we have prescribed for contrac-tion and inflammation of the uterus.

And, in the version edited by Rose:[28]

Satyriasis is a disease common to men and women. This disease is found more often among men, which is why it receives the name of satyriasis from that of the satyrs: antiquity, which loved to tell fables, describes these creatures as inclined towards the pleasures of love. Among women, satyriasis is an itching of the genital organs. . . .

Theodorus Priscianus, who attributes the disease to 'a certain pathological condition of the body', believes that it 'sometimes occurs even among women, and that some have called it *metromania*'.[29]

## IF THE AUTHORS THROW DOUBT UPON THIS FEMININE FORM, WHY DO THEY DO SO?

In fact, only one author, Aretaeus, denies the existence of this disease in women, again in the chapter cited in note 15, which is adamant:

> For my part, I am convinced that there may occur a certain lubricity among women of a moist constitution, which may lead to the pouring out of the excess (of moisture), but it is not at all true satyriasis. In fact, the nature of women does not incline them to it, because their constitution is cold. And woman does not have erectile parts, as does the satyr, according to the name given to the disease. And, in fact, men do not suffer from suffocation, which originates in the uterus, for the good reason that the male does not have a uterus.

The problem thus would appear to be brutally solved by a writer who is archaizing and conservative as much in his style as in his concepts or morals, despite a clinical sense which is inspired and innovative. No penis, therefore no satyriasis. But can one generalize and establish the rule 'No organ, therefore no disease'? Aretaeus is tempted to go that far, and in this chapter also says, 'No uterus, therefore no hysteria.' In this passage, the affection in fact triumphs, since, precisely in the chapter devoted to hysterical suffocation,[30] he evokes another affection which greatly resembles this one, with two pathognomonic signs, namely suffocation and aphonia. This affection, however, could not originate in the uterus, since it also occurs in men. Has Aretaeus not come within a hair's breadth of understanding that there is a masculine form of hysteria?

As for feminine satyriasis, a position as extreme as that of Aretaeus is exceptional. Other authors who do not believe in the existence of the disease in women simply do not discuss it. Most frequently, the paradoxical character of this disease when it occurs in women is more subtly indicated.

## CERTAIN PROCEDURES FOR TREATMENT AND CERTAIN REMARKS ON THE CIRCUMSTANCES IN WHICH THE DISEASE OCCURS ARE NOT WITHOUT INTEREST FOR THE PRESENT PROBLEM

Rufus of Ephesus, after giving his description of the pathology, comes to treatment:[31]

> I shall set forth first the therapeutics of this palpitation, then that of the diseases ... into which it may tranform itself.... With regard to the position to adopt in the sickbed, it is better to lie on the side than on the back; since it is not appropriate to lie on the back: this position produces erotic dreams by the irritation of the genital organs. One must avoid conversations about sex, and lustful thoughts, and, above all, one must arm oneself against that which the eyes see, knowing that all of these things, even in fantasy, provoke a desire for copulation. ... As internal medicines, one should take the seed of the honeysuckle plant, and the root of the water-lily; this cures erotic dreams.... If the disease turns into spermatorrhea, one must make haste to drink infusions of honeysuckle and water-lily.... It is necessary to treat satyriasis by blood-letting, by a strict diet, with water to drink, by cooling medicines.... One may also prepare lotions; ... one pours the concoction into a tub and bathes the patient up to the lower abdomen, since this often relieves tensions.... Rue may be suitable for the treatment of individuals afflicted with spermatorrhea or satyriasis; mint is extremely harmful in cases of spermatorrhea; ... it may be helpful in satyriasis. One must avoid allowing satyriasis to turn into spermatorrhea; ... it is when the disease has just become fully blown that hot baths are necessary to assuage the affection; ... one must not allow coitus too soon; on the contrary, one must distance the patient from all licentious looks and allusions, all thoughts of love, all profligacy....

Caelius observes in his turn:[32]

One must prohibit male patients from receiving visitors, particularly young women and men. Because the beauty of the visitors stimulates the patients by a sort of reminiscence inasmuch as it is true that even men who are not ill, seeing such things, often arrive immediately at gratification, brought to it by the titilation of their organs. . . .

And, further on:[33]

Among the physicians, no one other than Themison wrote about this disease, although it seems not to have been rare, but rather often to have attacked in an epidemic manner. Themison thus recalls that often in Crete many men die of satyriasis, and it is believed that this occurs because of poor nutrition, and because a plant called satyrion is often consumed in great quantities.[34] In addition, Themison says that he himself has seen a young woman, otherwise very suitably married to a man of good family, die of satyriasis in the region of Milan. . . .

We note a certain parallelism in Aetius' treatment of spermatorrhea,[35] 'a discharge of sperm which occurs involuntarily and without stiffening. . . . This happens not only to men but to women, and in women, the affection is difficult to get rid of'. In the treatment of men, the patient must take care not to allow himself the slightest thought of the pleasures of physical love.

## CONCLUSION

In these texts relating to genital satyriasis, both masculine and feminine, three conceptions of the disease are superimposed.

1   Disease as a morbific process in general, in the texts that are conserved, is the same in all humans: doctrine of pores and particles in Asclepiades; doctrine of the communities in the methodists, etc. In this sense, there is neither peculiarly feminine disease nor masculine disease.

2   Disease as an attack on a specific part of the body, either exclusively or preferentially. Thus epilepsy is a disease of the brain, and hysteria a disease of the uterus. It is as impossible to imagine a man afflicted with a bout of hysteria as it is to imagine a woman afflicted with a disease of the penis. Hence the indignation of Aretaeus, who dilates upon this object of scandal and stamps it out with two witty stylistic touches.

3   Disease as the aggregate of symptoms which may make itself felt
    beyond the organ itself: in Soranus' time, it had been known for
    some time that hysterical sufferings were not limited to the uterus
    and lower abdomen, but might affect the whole of the person,
    including the psychological personality. It had also long since been
    established that there were very particular links between epilepsy
    and hysteria: if a man appeared to suffer from a hysteroid crisis,
    the physician was at a loss; he did not dare say that the crisis was
    hysterical, since his patient did not have a uterus; therefore he
    spoke of epilepsy, but often manifestly without conviction, and he
    hinted that the conditions for correct differential diagnosis were
    not there.

4   Moreover, Alexandrian anatomical medicine had more or less
    established that the organs of the male were repeated in the
    female, that is to say that there were equivalent organs in male
    and female. In addition, the common character of the symp-
    toms might allow one to ignore the fact that the organs were
    not exactly the same. Finally, as far as female satyriasis was
    concerned, only in name did it remain paradoxical, just as
    masculine hysteria was still long to appear as a contradiction in
    terms, hysteria being specific to women, since only women have
    a uterus.

Nevertheless, the treatment has some surprising aspects. First,
because the care given to men afflicted with satyriasis resembles in
some of its details the typical care given to women with genital problems. Next, because in the treatment of afflicted women there are
certain elements missing.

1   The sick man is plied with water: infusions are to be prepared
    for him, lotions to be applied; he is to be given baths, especially
    hot baths. All this 'cooking' is characteristic of therapies given to
    women. Afflicted in his most precious part, the man is emascu-
    lated by his disease which he considers as shameful, by its
    treatment as well — which is feminine and effeminating.

2   Great care shall be taken to avoid any opportunity for sexual
    arousal of the patient. However, one cannot help but remark that
    the poor male patient appears very weak, and that it takes but
    little to stir him. Therefore he should not be allowed the company
    of men, young men, honest women and prostitutes; one should
    not have any frivolous conversation with him, one should not even
    allow him the chance to fantasize in a cosy bed.

3   As for the woman, such precautions are not taken. Why? Virtue
    and self-control have no role to play here: recall the case of the
    young woman from Milan, very proper, married to a man equally
    proper, who nonetheless died of satyriasis.

This is because the sexual needs of women are different from those
of the man, an old notion that dates back at least to the Hippocratic
Corpus, and of which Soranus himself had not yet divested himself:
sexual desire in women does not need a particular object. Woman
desires sexual relations, and not this or that man whom she likes.
Just as her attitude towards sexual pleasure is not the same as that
of the man, so it is not to be judged by the same measure. Woman
is more bound by sexuality to the extent to which it is sex itself
that attracts her, not a particular object of desire. It is therefore useless to take precautions relevant to her psychic state: normally,
her need for the sexual act is purely physiological, and has nothing
emotional about it. In the case of satyriasis, it is this same need that
has become pathological. Thus the woman afflicted with the disease
makes a nuisance of herself, throwing herself at man in general rather
than at this or that particular man, and without being emotionally
touched by any. Even in the text of Soranus, who is disturbed to see
his poor female patients fall into such a degrading state, the negative
effects of this disease on men and women are not perceived alike:
the hideous and degrading character of the disease appears worse in
woman.

This is because socio-cultural elements cloud the issue. Obviously,
any patient suffering from satyriasis (and from several other diseases
with which it might be confused) causes some embarrassment to
whomever sees him or her; this condition has something dirty and
shameful about it. But the embarrassment is particularly felt in the
presence of the female patient, since, among the main virtues which
are expected of them, women must have domestic discretion; having
become a pitiful sub-human, highly difficult to treat, the woman with
satyriasis is intolerable and scandalous.[36]

Satyriasis is one of the 'shameful' diseases, the ensemble of which
we propose to study. Not only does its glaring ugliness shock everyone,
but it also excites curiosity; a curiosity which, although possibly
genuine in the physician, is nonetheless troubling if one considers
what Plutarch has to say about some other slightly indelicate situa-
tions:

Imagine Herophilus or Erasistratus or Asclepius himself, when he was a man, coming into a house with his drugs and instruments, and asking whether anyone had a fistula in the anus or any woman a cancer of the womb! Yet in medicine, curiosity spells salvation.[37]

Certainly, outside the field of medicine, such curiosity may be considered only malicious.

In the final analysis, what is all this really about? Certainly not the disease in men which the psychiatrist of the nineteenth century termed 'satyriasis': a 'disturbance of the libido in the male, which forces him to commit offences against public morality'; nor the nymphomania described for women: a 'pathological exaggeration of sexual desire in woman',[38] that is to say a sort of hunt after men, whimsical and unstable, which is destined never to succeed. It is perhaps a form of intoxication, which could be of alimentary origin, as Caelius effectively suggests when citing Themison. It was certainly not, in any case, a scourge, but more probably an extremely rare disease, even if it did occasionally touch groups of people. Its importance lies less in the details than in the discussions of the very notion of sexual disease to which it either gave rise or helped to sustain; less in the facts than in the imaginings which it fuelled in the past, and which it certainly remains capable of fuelling today.

## NOTES

\* The author and editors are grateful to Catherine McDonald for her help with the translation from the French.

1 I am presently preparing a medical, literary and iconographical study of this disease, to be published in *Medicina dei Secoli*.

2 Cf. my article to appear in *Traditio* (autumn 1994) in reply to W.D. Sharpe, 'A suggested emendation of Isodore of Sevilla, *Etymologiae* IV, 8, 9', in *Traditio* 14, 1958: 377–378.

3 Cf. E.P. Hamp, πάθος, *Glotta* 59, 1981: 157–159. This word is defined within a series: διάθεσις, νόσος, νόσημα, ἀρρώστημα, ἀρρωστία. See Aristotle, *Metaphysics* IV; the first part of *Anonymus Londoniensis*, ed. W.H.S. Jones, Cambridge 1947; and the Pseudo-Galenic *Definitiones medicae* in vol. XIX of Kühn's edition.

4 Soranus, *Diseases of Women* book III, vol. III, text established, translated and commented by Paul Burguière, Danielle Gourevitch and Yves Malinas, revised by Simon Byl and Mirko Grmek, Paris 1994.

5 Cf. I. Garofalo, *Erasistrati fragmenta*, Pisa 1988.

6 The Herophilean definition of πάθος is conserved in no. 134 of the *Definitiones medicae* (Kühn, XIX, 386–387), transl. after von Staden, *Herophilus*, 1989: 375, T 206:

An affection is an unwholesome impending of the natural activity, either of a certain, or of some, or of a single, or of all the operations of nature. Some people define it this way, as do the Herophileans: an affection is that which is not throughout resolved in the same time, but sometimes in less, sometimes in more.

For his part, the pseudo-Soranus writes: *quid est pathos? Herophilus dixit esse passionem quae non (bene) solvitur et bene mollitur, huius enim dixit esse causam in humoribus constitutam* (*Quaestiones medicinales* 103, von Staden, T 205b). Translated after von Staden, 1989: 365, T 194.

7    Translated after von Staden, 1989: 365, T 193.
8    Cf. D. Gourevitch, 'Asclépiade et Bithynie chez Pline. Problèmes de chronologie', in J. Pigeaud and J. Oroz (eds), *Pline l'ancien, témoin de son temps*, Salamanca and Nantes 1987: 647–681. And J.T. Vallance, *The Lost Theory of Asclepiades of Bithynia*, Oxford 1990.
9    Cf. D. Gourevitch, 'Le vie della conoscenza', in *Storia del pensiens medico occidentale*, ed. M.D. Grmek, Bari 1993: 120–165; and D. Gourevitch, 'Ce que disaient d'elles-memes les sectes médicales', *Revue de philologie* 66, 1992: 29–35.
10   Theophrastus *Historia plantarum* I.3.
11   Cf. D. Gourevitch, *Le mal d'être femme. La femme et la médecine à Rome*, Paris 1981: especially 56–59.
12   See in particular the famous descriptions in the Epidemics.
13   *Acute Diseases* III, XVII, 185.
14   *Symptoms of Acute Diseases* II, 13
15   *On satyriasis and gonnorrhea* = Daremberg, pp. 66ff.
16   III, XVIII, 175ff.
17   *Definitiones medicae* 279 = Kühn, XIX, 426.
18   ibid.
19   *De contra naturam . . .* , 14 = Kühn, VII, 728.
20   *Coll. med.* XLV 28 = Daremberg, V, 63–64.
21   *On satyriasis, or, if one prefers, on priapism. After Galen.* In *Rufus*, ed. Daremberg, pp. 119ff.
22   2, XI, 32.
23   *Etymologiae* IV, 7.
24   *Symptoms of Acute Diseases* II, 13.
25   *On Women's Diseases* (CUF) III, 3.
26   *Acute Diseases* III, XVIII, 178.
27   23, p. 75.
28   Page 57.
29   2, XI, 32. *Metromania* is a very rare word: besides this occurence, it is used in Cassius Felix (79, p. 191, 7) to refer to uterine disease: *metromaniam latino sermone matricis furores sive insaniam dicimus*; and in the Latin Oribasius, *Syn.* 9, 45 add. Aa, p. 136 extr. = Daremberg, VI, 361: *Item ex alio autore de suffone qui accidit ex umoribus aut de matrici causa, quae vocatur metromania (metromannia), vel ad eas qui suffocantur.*
30   *Symptoms of Acute Diseases* II, 11.
31   Daremberg, pp. 66ff.
32   *Acute Diseases* III, xvii, para 180.

33  ibid., para. 185.
34  A whole series of plants linked to the satyrs, sexual arousal, genital and procreative activity would need study.
35  *Rufus*, ed. Daremberg, pp. 121ff.: *On Spermatorrhea, after Galen.*
36  For other views of the female patient of satyriasis, cf. D. Gourevitch, 'Psychanalyse et vases grecs', *Mélanges d'archéologie et d'histoire de l'Ecole française de Rome* 90, 1978: 153–160.
37  *On Curiosity* = *Moralia* 518d, transl. D.A. Russell, 1993: 198.
38  *Dictionnaire de médecine Flammarion*, preface by Jean Hamburger, transl. K. MacDonald, 4th edn, Paris 1991.

# Chapter 11

# Re-reading (Vestal) virginity*

## Mary Beard

(one of) 16 Vestal Virgins, who were
   leaving for the coast,
– And although my eyes were open they might
   just as well have been closed. . . .
                    (Procul Harum, *A Whiter Shade of Pale*, 1967)

there was something queer about the Virgines Vestales. . . .
                    (Versnel 1993: 269)

The mythology of the Vestal Virgins is on the move. *Our* mythology. The spinster dons of ancient Rome (Balsdon's vision of a Julio-Claudian Oxbridge[1]) have had their day. So too have the pagan nuns of the Roman forum – Christian holiness and self-denial *avant la lettre*.[2] *Our* Vestals are much stranger than that: they are touched with a primitive, anthropological 'weirdness'; key players in a game of sexual ambiguity (interstitiality, marginality, anomaly, paradox and mediation) that in Balsdon's time would have seemed – if anything – the concern of ethnography rather than Classics. But not now. *We* have decided to take the Vestals seriously – at the cost of turning them into a model of primitive strangeness, forever lodged at the heart of sophisticated Rome.

   This paper is a critique of the new myth of the Vestals – and particularly of my own contribution to the formation of that myth.[3] It aims to expose the limitations and misdirections of the 'ambiguity model' for these priestesses; to suggest not so much that that model is incorrect (which it may or may not be), but that at a more fundamental level it 'misses the point' of Roman culture, and misdirects our attempts to reconstruct and analyse it. Also at stake in this argument, however, are issues much more specifically concerned with women's studies within ancient history: the limitations of our new myth of Vestal ambiguity are partly the limitations of a history of 'women' conceived without reference to a history of 'gender'; or rather the limitations of a history of 'gender' conceived as an objective category, without reference to its debated and contested *construction* within the wider cultural matrix.

## THE SEXUAL STATUS OF VESTAL VIRGINS: BEARD 1980

Beard 1980 made an engagingly simple point. It started from the well-worn debate on the origins of the Vestal priesthood at Rome. Were the very first Vestal Virgins the daughters of the early kings of Rome? Or were they the wives of those kings?[4] 'Daughters' might seem the obvious answer: Vestals were, after all, always (officially) virgins and always plural. Surely only an argument for early Roman polygamy (and a very strange version of polygamy at that) could see their origin in the *wives* of the early kings. But, at the same time, these priestesses always seemed to resist simple classification as daughters: their priestly dress was the *stola*, the traditional costume of the Roman married woman; they arranged their hair in the style of the Roman bride on the day of her wedding; and their legal relationship with the Pontifex Maximus seems, in some respects, to have mirrored the relationship of wives to their husbands. Maybe then their virginity was to be interpreted not so much as literal virginity, but as the more general, moral, *pudicitia* of the Roman matron. The Vestals, in other words, could originally have been wives.

My argument amounted to a refusal to choose between those two alternatives. Leaving aside any speculation about regal family life in earliest Rome, neither the (literally) virginal aspects, nor the matronal aspects of the Vestals could be ignored; any interpretation of the character of the priestesses (and of what I then called their 'sexual status' – probably meaning 'gender') had to allow them *both* aspects. And that, indeed, was precisely the point. Anthropology led the way. What Mary Douglas had done for the pangolin and for the prohibitions of Leviticus,[5] I could do for the Roman Vestals. So, the argument went, their ambiguity was not just 'odd', something to be explained away; it was an almost predictable marker of their sacred status. Their funny mix of categories, both/neither virgins and/nor matrons, was what showed them to be 'sacral'. Here was the *Purity and Danger* of the classical world.

Ambiguities multiply. The final flourish to *my* ambiguous Vestals turned out to be a tentative claim for a *male* dimension too. It was not just a matter of mixing virgins and matrons; some of the rights and privileges of these priestesses seem to have belonged character- istically to *men* – a lictor to attend them, seats at the games with the senators, testamentary powers equivalent to those of men. *Perhaps*, I argued, *perhaps*,[6] the sacrality of the Vestals was marked also by an ambiguity between the categories of male and female. Where would the confusion of gender categories end . . . ?

## REACTIONS AND RESPONSE

These arguments hit a chord. They had found their moment: 1980 something – historians of Roman culture were looking for 'theory', looking to legitimate the status of Roman culture as *culture* . . . and here was (anthropological) THEORY, on a plate, and at the same time deliciously neat and simple, solving a problem, confirming the serious import of at least one part of Roman religious custom. Pure magic. It was hard not to fall for it; and most of us did. Vestals now became uncontrovertibly 'ambiguous, in-between' (Scheid);[7] 'honorary men' (Hopkins);[8] '(extra)-sexuelle' (de Cazanove).[9] There was nothing hypothetical about it, no 'perhaps' or 'maybe'. It was a 'fact' (Hallett);[10] the ambiguity was 'notorious . . . manifest . . . convincingly elucidated' (Versnel);[11] Beard had 'shown' that the Vestals 'were' both daughters and wives (Scheid).[12]

Not everyone agreed wholeheartedly, of course. Jane Gardner deployed her legal expertise (and a lot more of it than was necessary in the circumstances) to show that the legal privileges of the Vestals did not strictly add up to *male* privileges.[13] And Ariadne Staples minutely re-examined, yet again, all the recorded attributes of the Vestals – arguing that these did not so much indicate 'ambiguity', as a status outside all known categories of gender: a perfect symbolic representation of the undivided collectivity of Rome.[14] But in all this learned enquiry, no-one seems to have stopped very long to question the overall approach, or the theoretical models employed. Nor have they stopped to ask what might follow from that approach, or where it might take us next. The fact is that Beard 1980 has so far led almost nowhere in the wider study of Roman religion and culture; that, for all its great revolutionary claims, it seems to have been a more or less dazzling dead end.[15] Why might that be? What went wrong?

This paper is an affectionate critique of Beard 1980. It is not concerned with 'how the facts fit'. (For what it is worth, I am still broadly convinced that they fit well enough; but, no doubt, I am not the best person to judge.[16]) I want instead to think about the method and approach; to try to explain why it has been a dead end; to reformulate some of the questions in the light of more recent studies of the construction of gender and its transgressions; to suggest some new directions to follow. This is an attempt to do 'better' second time around.

## RELIGION AND THE CONSTRUCTION OF GENDER

Gender categories are not objective, cultural 'givens'. The major error of Beard 1980 is to treat them as if they were. The structure of its argument assumes the existence of the 'male', the 'virginal' and the 'matronal', as categories whose definition we can take for granted – different from our own maybe, but pre-existing, unproblematic. The Vestals are then artfully placed in the middle, as a strange mixture of all three – and hence 'sacral'. True, there is an occasional glimmer of concern in the text and (especially) notes about the *pre-existence* of taxonomic categories. Which came first, as Mary Douglas eventually wondered, the ambiguity or the sacrality? And who created the normative categories in the first place?[17] But this concern stops short; it never dares to follow its own logic – to turn the whole argument on its head.

The inverted argument would run something like this. Yes, it is obviously the case that religion may *reflect* the gender differences and categories operating within society more generally; it is obviously the case, too, that any system of religious symbolism may in part *be constructed out of* (or parasitic on) gender categories defined in the wider cultural world. Yet at the same time, religion itself plays a major part in actively *constructing*, *defining* and *negotiating* those categories – in defining what it is to be female, what constitutes virginity or marriage and so on. In fact, to put it more strongly, religion regularly acts as a privileged space, a key place within any particular culture for the definition of gender roles, for debate on gender norms and trans-gressions. Beard 1980 fails to recognise this function; and so, it concentrates narrowly on the strange amalgam of genders that consti-tuted the Vestals – without exploring the implications of that amalgam in the wider social construction of gender at Rome.

Put simply, the Vestals constructed Roman gender, as much as gender (and its ambiguities) constructed the Vestals. What should lie at the heart of the 'problem' is not (as I chose to stress) the 'sexual status of Vestal Virgins', but the very terms out of which that 'sexual status' was defined: man, woman, virgin and matron.[18]

## POLYTHEISM, SYSTEM AND MEANING

Roman polytheism is a complex *system*. Its claims to 'meaning', its hermeneutic functions, depend on that *system(at)ic* quality. 'Meaning' resides not in any individual element of the polytheism (whether god, festival, priest, ritual . . .), but is constructed in the connections, oppositions and tensions within the system, between its different elements.[19]

That is, no doubt, to state the obvious. But if Beard 1980 fails to engage with the Vestals' role in the construction (rather than just the confusion) of normative gender categories at Rome, that is partly because it fails to see the Vestal priesthood as one element within a *system*. Sure enough, it offers plenty of comparisons between Vestals and pangolins (the scaly ant-eaters discussed at length by Mary Douglas, part fish/part tree-climbers[20]), but almost no comparison or connection with any other element of Roman religion or culture. The Vestals are treated as if they were a strange and isolated anomaly – weird and interesting maybe, but natives of some abstract world of cross-cultural ambiguity, not of Rome.[21]

In fact, you do not have to look very hard among the priestly groups of Rome to find a systematic concern with gender, its norms and transgressions; a series of debates on and around the definition of Roman sexual categories – of which the Vestal ambiguities are just one part. Let me give one example of how that system might be perceived.

The priests of Magna Mater (the *galli*) are almost as well known as the Vestals for breaking the gender rules: self-castrated eunuchs (it is said), flamboyantly female in appearance, loud cross-dressers; 'not-men' at loose in the city of Rome, discomfiting hangers-on of an eastern cult.[22] The normative categories of *our* scholarship, of course, keep these priests well away from the Vestal Virgins: 'oriental' cults inhabit different books from the 'native' religion of Rome; eastern excess doesn't belong with the ancient heart of the city. Romans too had an interest in policing those same boundaries: the *galli* were as 'not-Roman' as the Vestals were 'Roman'; the *galli* as 'other' as the Vestals were 'native'.[23] Yet, at the same time, that opposition was also a *connection*, made to be displayed in contiguity; Roman literature and culture put the Vestals and the *galli together* in order to parade their difference. Like all differences, it could only be perceived by comparison; difference inevitably entails system.

Consider, for example, the famous story of the introduction of the cult of Magna Mater with her priests. The ship bringing the cult image and its servants from the east gets stuck on a sandbank just outside Ostia – and it is only dislodged by the intervention of a woman, Claudia Quinta, who miraculously pulls the boat in. There are many versions of the story. In some, Claudia Quinta is a Roman matron suspected of unchastity, who proves her innocence by the performance of the miracle. For Herodian, she is a Vestal under suspicion of *incestum*. The logic of this account is clear: the Vestals and the *galli* are conjoined at the very moment of Magna Mater's entry into the city; the *galli* are brought to Rome through the intervention of a Vestal.[24] This conjunction also operates in the visual topography of the city of Rome. Close to the temple of Vesta on the Sacred Way, going into the Forum, was a shrine of Magna Mater; from the reign of Augustus, adjacent to the temple of Magna Mater on the Palatine, in the emperor's house itself, was a shrine of Vesta. Vestals and *galli* shared a field of vision – to see one was to see both.[25]

We do not know in detail how these proximities were perceived; or by what process (if it is a chronological development) the story of Claudia Quinta the matron 'became' the story of Claudia Quinta the Vestal. But at the very least the conflations and proximities are enough to suggest a different agenda in 'reading' the Vestals' virginity; to suggest that – never mind the far-flung pangolin – the anomalies of the Vestals are part of a gender story told, retold and re-debated *within* Roman religion itself; that the priestly officials at Rome (whether of 'native' or 'foreign' cults) *together* offer ways of imaging gender; and that the norms and transgression are to be identified and paraded at the intersections of those images, not only in the single frame. Beard 1980 fails precisely because it chooses to tell an ethnographic story *at the expense of* a Roman one; and it looks for ambiguity in isolation, not in system.[26]

## VIRGINITY AT THE CENTRE OF THE TEXT

Underlying Beard 1980 there is what can only be called a denial of reading. The ancient texts it considers are *excavated*, not *read*. The method is a familiar one: the Roman antiquarian literature is combed – a bit of Labeo (quoted by Aulus Gellius) is dug out here, some convenient lines of Festus on the Vestal hairdo deployed there, with plenty of snippets from Pliny the Elder and Valerius Maximus sprinkled on for good measure. The byways of Latin literature ransacked and minutely dismembered, all (as intended) making a very learned impression. But what is left out of the picture (what Ancient History, as a discipline, has consistently ignored) is the character, point and focus of the texts so expertly dissected: what were these writers writing *about* when they wrote about the Vestals? Who wrote about Vestals, to whom, and why?

If I had asked those questions, I would quickly have seen that the overwhelming preoccupation of ancient writers is the punishment of the Vestals, the Vestals who broke their oath of chastity, or those suspected of having done so. Perhaps it was the lurid bits that made the best read. But even so, the effect of this concentration is to turn the discourse of and around the priesthood into a discourse of virginity lost, as much as of virginity maintained; a discourse of transgression, of rules broken, rather than rules kept. The Vestals, in other words, can be seen not merely as a parade of anomaly, but a focus of negotiation around the category of virginity, a negotiation of the boundary between virginity and non-virginity.

The clearest examples of this negotiation (and some of the lengthiest surviving discussions of Vestals – which, significantly, did not find their way into Beard 1980) are found in the *Controversiae* of the Elder Seneca; written versions of some of the declamatory exercises, part rhetorical training, part after-dinner entertainment, for the Roman imperial elite; arguments offered on either side of fictional law-cases – cases based partly on Roman law, partly on a fantasy construction of a never-never land legal system.[27] Several of these cases are concerned, either explicitly or by implication, with the Vestals – and with the alleged breaking of their vow of chastity. 'A Vestal Virgin wrote the following verse: "How happy married women are! O may I die if marriage is not sweet." She is accused of unchastity' . . . and the pleasure of the text that follows lies in the arguments that are rehearsed for and against the accused priestess. For the virgin: poetry is not necessarily the mirror of life. Against her: 'A woman is unchaste if she wants sex, even if she has not had it'; any Vestal who had written in those terms had by definition broken her vows.[28] At much greater length, another case takes up the problem of the virginal status of the priestess at entry to the priesthood:[29]

A virgin was captured by pirates and sold; she was bought by a pimp and made a prostitute. When men came to her, she asked for alms [*stips*]. When she failed to get alms from a soldier who came to her, he struggled with her and tried to use force; she killed him. She was accused, acquitted and sent back to her family. She seeks a priesthood!

Let us suppose the preamble says that the law is 'A priestess must be chaste and of chaste parents, pure and of pure parents' – does she qualify for the priesthood? Again a series of arguments follow – for and (mostly) against her chastity. Could she count as chaste if she had been *kissed*? Who, anyway, could countenance a priestess who had lived in the company of whores? If she had been so virtuous, why had she not been ransomed? Had she not, on the other hand, defended her chastity with *greater* commitment than women usually displayed? She had literally fought for her virginity. But then again she was now a murderer, and yet judged innocent of the crime.

These arguments are extended over pages and pages of the text of Seneca, and of other declaimers. Within this elite male institution, at the centre of Roman declamatory culture, not only was female virginity (and its definitions) a major theme, but that theme was played out in the context of *Vestal* virginity. Re-reading the Vestals would necessarily involve a reinstatement of this kind of text at the centre of the argument; a reinstatement of virginity and its transgressions above the neat schematics of ambiguity.

## VESTALS AND THE PUZZLE OF 'BEING ROMAN'

All sorts of things about the Vestals were a puzzle to the Romans – a puzzle that Beard 1980 thinks it appropriate to try and solve. Romans confused; scholar knows best. But the process of reading the Roman discussion of the Vestals should have entailed taking those puzzles seriously – *as* puzzles. Maybe the puzzles were not always meant to be solved, but, as puzzles, they could have constituted a provocation and a proposition; the puzzle was the answer.

Let's take one. What (apart from the fire) was inside the temple of Vesta? Beard 1980 knows the important answer here – and can't resist falling for the wee passage of Pliny[30] that tells us about the . . . phallos. It is too good to be true: male sexuality lurking in the virgins' temple, a physical presence. Ambiguity again is writ large at the very centre of the cult. But in the excitement of that one apparent 'fit', the over-whelming bafflement of most ancient writers is overlooked. For the truth is, of course, that *everybody* knew that *nobody* (except the Vestals, who weren't telling) knew what was inside the temple. Not for sure, anyway. There were lots of guesses, lots of 'it is said', lots of candidates for inclusion – the Palladium rescued from Troy by Aeneas, the Samothracian images that Dardanus took *to* Troy when he founded the city, maybe *nothing* but the fire – but no one really *knew*.[31]

What kind of point could this very pointed bafflement have? At the centre of Rome, on the very hearth that ensured Rome's continuance and safety, its essence, there lay a puzzle, and a series of conjectures, of wonderings. This is no accident, no failure on the Romans' part to know their own culture properly. It is a strategic deferral – deferral of certainty on what the centre of Rome, real Romanness, could or should be. As often with Roman culture, we are brought back here at its very heart(h) to a sacralised parade of the question of what Rome was, where it came from, how Romanness was to be defined as Roman. Rome as foreign – Trojan, Samothracian even? Rome as male – phallic power? Rome as the representation of nothing other than itself – the hearth is the hearth is the hearth, and nothing more (or less)? 'Answers' are not at stake here, but 'questions'. Roman identity is shown to be debated, debatable, negotiated, negotiatable. This is a story not just about gender and its ambiguities (though it is no doubt partly that); it is a story about gender (and its uncertainties) mapped on to other cultural categories (and their uncertainties) – civic identity, nationhood and imperialism. The Vestals ask us to ask what it is to be Roman, what Rome is.[32]

## OUR STORY

Fifteen years ago it was very hard to rethink the Vestals: hard to identify the problem, hard to find the analogies, hard to deploy the anthropology of ambiguity. Yet at the same time, it was so easy to convince: so easy to feel that the effort had worked; so easy to show that the problem had been cracked; so easy to back a new orthodoxy. Yes, 'there *was* something queer about the Virgines Vestales'. The 'queerness' was the answer. If that is now changing, if what was easy now seems too easy, then it is, of course, because *our story* of Rome, and of gender within Roman culture, has moved on. Beard 1980 (and the work that followed from it) is in a sense a final flourish of a dead subject: 'the history of women'. Rewritten as 'the history

of gender' the simplicities and certainties of ambiguity ('the Vestals
were not *either* virgins *or* matrons; they were both, and . . . they were
also men'[33]) could not and should not convince. Not, then, 'women
in Roman history', but 'Roman history writes "woman"'; reading is
always preliminary, before you . . .[34]

## NOTES

\* This re-reading comes with thanks to John Henderson (for help with
the jokes); and with best wishes to Henk Versnel (who will enjoy them).

1 'Just as the halls of women's colleges in Oxford and in Cambridge have,
hanging on their walls, the portraits of former Principals, so round the
Atrium Vestae stood portrait statues of Senior Vestal Virgins' (Balsdon
1962: 242).

2 T. Cato Worsfold, *The History of the Vestal Virgins of Rome*, London 1932:
11 ('In modern days the sisterhoods of the nuns of the Church of Rome,
themselves of great antiquity, offer the closest resemblance'); Balsdon,
too, flirts with the image of the nun: 'To invent a parallel, you would
have to imagine that in the whole of modern Italy there was only one
body of Nuns, and that there were a mere six members of that body'
(Balsdon 1962: 235).

3 Beard 1980. This paper started life as a seminar presentation, in a series
organised by Keith Hopkins and Fergus Millar at the Institute of Classical
Studies in London in 1979; and it was changed and expanded for publication, partly at the insistence of the Editorial Committee of the *Journal
of Roman Studies*. In general, those changes did little to help the argument. I now have no interest whatsoever in the second part of the
published paper (with its silly comparisons between the Vestals and
various heroines of Greek tragedy); neither does anyone else – to judge,
at least, from the thumbed or unthumbed state of the pages in any library
copy I have checked. Consider them deleted.

4 Vestals as daughters: T. Mommsen, *Römische Strafrecht*, Leipzig 1899:
18; H.J. Rose, 'De Virginibus Vestalibus', *Mnemosyne* n.s. 54, 1926:
440–448. Vestals as wives: G. Wissowa, in Roscher, *Myth. Lex.* VI: 260;
F. Guizzi, *Aspetti giuridici del sacerdozio Romano: il sacerdozio di Vesta*, Naples
1968: 102.

5 Douglas 1966: 41–57; Douglas 1975: 27–46.

6 The '*perhaps*' has a nasty tendency to get left out in transmission. See,
for example, K. Mustakallio, 'The "crimen incesti" of the Vestal Virgins
and the Prodigious Pestilence', in T. Viljamaa, A. Timonen and C. Kritzel
(eds) *Crudelitas: The Politics of Cruelty in the Ancient and Medieval World*, Krems
1992: 'As Mary Beard stresses, the unfemale parts of their sacred role
were quite obvious.' Hopkins 1983 (see note 8) is another victim of this
overcertainty.

7 'In other words, the sexual status of the Vestal was ambiguous, in-
between' (Scheid 1992: 384).

8 'Vestal virgins, honorary men' (Hopkins 1983: index).

9  'Mais justement, les Vestales ne sont pas des matrones, mais leur exact contraire. Non seulement par leur condition (extra)-sexuelle' (de Cazanove 1987: 169).

10  'Additionally the fact that the Vestals were defined symbolically as *both* unmarried daughters and more mature wives helps to clarify why their membership in the order benefited their blood families in the way that it seems to have done' (Hallett 1984: 85).

11  'The notorious ambiguity manifest in their two co-existent and apparently contradictory roles, that of virgins *and* that of matrons, has been convincingly elucidated by Mary Beard' (Versnel 1992: 48); see also Versnel 1993: 270: 'Beard vindicates the ambiguity as an essential and structural feature of the Virgines Vestales.'

12  'On the other hand, Vestals were neither matrons nor maidens as Beard (1980) has shown' (Scheid 1992: 383).

13  'Beard's suggestion that the Vestals' sexual status was ambivalent, that they were in part, classified as male and that this is shown by their being given certain privileges almost exclusively associated with men, does not really fit the facts' (Gardner 1986: 24). Gardner recognises, at least, that my 'suggestion' was just a suggestion, but she makes the predictable lawyer's mistake – treating law only as a system of 'fact', rather than (also) a system of shifting cultural symbols. In other words, law can provide the Vestals with a penumbra of maleness, even if it does not technically invest them with exactly the same privileges as men.

14  A. Staples, 'The Uses of Virginity: the Vestals and Rome' (forthcoming) – a chapter of her Ph.D. thesis, 'Gender and Boundary in Roman Religion', Cambridge University, 1993. For other critiques, see H. Cancik–Lindemaier, 'Kultische Privilegierung und gesellschaftliche Realität: ein Beitrag zur Sozialgeschichte der virgines Vestae', *Saeculum* 41, 1990: 1–16 (esp. 14–15); Versnel 1993 (esp. 271–272 – a cogent attack on the idea of the Vestal fire as a sacred mirror of the ambiguity of the priestesses).

15  The most sustained attempt to develop the argument is Versnel 1992 and 1993: 228–288. There are also a few circulating samizdat copies, fading xeroxes, of Helen King's (*c.* 1981) thoughts on a similar theme.

16  It is, of course, a question of the basis of the argument, and of what counts as proof. It may well be that there are numerous individual errors, misinterpretations, misplaced emphases in Beard 1980; it may well be that there are other ways to write the Vestals into Roman socio-religious history (see Cancik and Staples, note 14). But I have seen nothing to convince me that the ambiguity I identified was merely *my* mirage. See also note 13.

17  Douglas 1975: 276–318; Beard 1980: 20–21.

18  Not that we should reify these terms either. For general discussion of these issues, see P. Caplan (ed.), *The Cultural Construction of Sexuality*, London 1987.

19  I suppose that one could – equally well? – argue that the point of Roman polytheism was that it was *no system at all*. If so, the arguments that follow apply even more forcefully.

20  Douglas 1975: 27–46. Dr Henderson points out to me that Mary Douglas
    appears to have missed an even more striking example of the pangolins'
    interstitiality: namely that they can walk on their hind legs – so confusing
    the categories of human and animal.
21  A consequence, maybe, of the undiluted structuralism at the heart of the
    paper. As the structuralist moment passes into the *post*-structuralist,
    cultural density and (at the same time) cultural specificity find their place
    again.
22  For a quick dissection Beard 1994; for loving detail, Sanders 1972.
23  The classic statement of policing the difference is Dion. Hal., *Ant. Rom.*
    2, 19. See also *Dig.* 48, 8, 4–6; Val. Max. 7, 6 – all discussed in Beard
    1994: 174–177.
24  Claudia Quinta as a matron suspected of unchastity: Livy *History* 29, 14,
    5–14; Ovid *Fasti* 4, 291–348. As a Vestal: Herodian *History* 1, 11, 4–5.
25  For Magna Mater on the Sacred Way: E. Nash, *Pictorial Dictionary of
    Ancient Rome*, vol. 2, London 1968: 34–35, read with L. Richardson, *A
    New Topographical Dictionary of Ancient Rome*, Baltimore, Md. and London
    1992: 243; the precise location adjacent to the temple of Vesta is discussed
    by F. Coarelli, 'I monumenti dei culti orientali in Roma', in U. Bianchi
    and M. J. Vermaseren (eds), *La soterologia dei culti orientali nell'impero Romano*,
    Leiden 1982: 33–67 (esp. 34–39). For Vesta and the Vestals on the
    Palatine: Nash, *Pictorial Dictionary*, vol. 2: 511–513; and (more judiciously)
    Richardson, *Topographical Dictionary* 413.
26  In other words, Beard 1980 fails because it 'primitivises' Rome; any
    cultural model that fails to take account of Rome's seething sophistica-
    tion, its multi-ethnic, multi-cultural cosmopolitan self-reflexivity, *must* be
    wrong.
27  For a general account of Senecan *Controversiae*, see H. Bornecque, *Les
    déclamations et les déclamateurs d'après Sénèque le père*, Lille 1902; J. Fairweather,
    *Seneca the Elder*, Cambridge 1981. Briefly, M. Beard, 'Looking (harder) for
    Roman myth: Dumézil, declamation and the problems of definition', in
    *Colloquium Rauricum* 3, Stuttgart and Leipzig 1993: 51–56.
28  Seneca *Cont.* 6, 8.
29  *Cont.* 1, 2.
30  Pliny *NH* 28, 39.
31  See, for example, Dion. Hal. *Rom. Ant.* 2, 66; Ovid *Fasti* 6, 295–298;
    Plutarch *Life of Camillus* 20.
32  Discuss.
33  Beard 1980: 18.
34  This is a (self-)parody. Cf. J. Henderson, 'Not "Women in Roman Satire"
    but "When Satire writes 'woman'" ', in Braund 1989.

# Chapter 12

# Male power and legitimacy through women:
the *domus Augusta* under the Julio-Claudians

*Mireille Corbier*

## THE HISTORIOGRAPHICAL IMAGE OF AUGUSTUS' FAMILY

### A *paterfamilias* and a *princeps* in search of an heir and successor

Augustus' family endured for six generations – that is, well over a century counting from the murder of Caesar in 44 BC to the suicide of Nero in AD 68. I do not pretend to compete with the author of the famous novel *I Claudius*. My intention is to analyse how a new family unit, different in many respects from the traditional patrilinear group – the *gens* – that was the traditional structure of the Roman family, was constructed, reproduced and continued, and particularly to examine why and how women were involved in the transmission of legitimacy.

From *c.* AD 15–20, there is evidence[1] that the princely status of this new unit was officially recognised in the phrase *domus Augusta* ('Augustan House'), while Tacitean usage invites us to call it the *domus Caesarum* ('The House of the Caesars'). The House of the Caesars was an original and intentional construction (Corbier 1994a).

The legacy Augustus had to leave was enormous – not just a name and a patrimony, clients and ties of *fides*, but power as well. This was new. Augustus had no sons, and so he was forced to provide legitimate male descendants with the help of his female relatives. His sister Octavia provided him with a nephew and his wife Livia with two stepsons, and he exploited the abundant females of his family (a daughter and four nieces) and ran the whole range of possibilities that marriage, divorce, remarriage after divorce or widowhood and adoption offered (Figures 12.1 and 12.2).

## Marriages within the family

The strategy of building alliances among kin, which was begun by Augustus in 25 BC, when he married his daughter (Iulia) to his nephew (Marcellus), and continued with the marriage of his younger stepson (Drusus) with his younger niece (Antonia Minor), led to the formation of a multi-branched imperial family over three to four generations, and it was possible consequently to keep renewing connections in a systematic way with the resulting personnel.

But we have to keep in mind that, after the death of Augustus, there were two competing sources of legitimacy: legitimacy through blood relationship with the founder, Augustus, and legitimacy through blood relationship with the actual ruler, for example, Tiberius or Claudius.

## A 'FAMILY' WHICH LACKED MEN AND HAD AN EXCESS OF WOMEN

From the beginning, the family lacked men, specially adult men, and always had an excess of women, particularly surviving women, even in periods when it was provided with male heirs.

Let us choose two characteristic dates: the year 13 BC, corresponding to the supposed date of the ceremonies represented on the *Ara Pacis*, and the year AD 23.

The familial procession depicted on the *AraPacis* gives an image of the imperial family at a stage where it was clearly perceived as a *domus* – a house – even if it was not yet named *domus Augusta* (which we do not know). If you consider the individuals and the couples represented there, one observation is apparent, given the fact that Augustus had no brothers and no sons: the priests apart, there is not a single man whose presence is justified otherwise than by his link to Augustus – as a cognate (*cognatus*) or an affine (*adfinis*) – through a woman who is herself a relation of Augustus – a daughter, a sister, a wife, a niece. The female group represented on the *Ara Pacis* is Augustus' family *stricto sensu*. The case of year AD 23 is different, as at that time Tiberius had a number of male relatives, nephews and grandsons, through two males related to him: his brother Drusus the Elder (Drusus I on the figures) and his son, Drusus the Younger (Drusus II on the Figures). In AD 23 when Tiberius' son, Drusus the Younger, died and after him when one of his twins, young Germanicus Gemellus, died too, the *domus Augusta* (as the imperial family was now

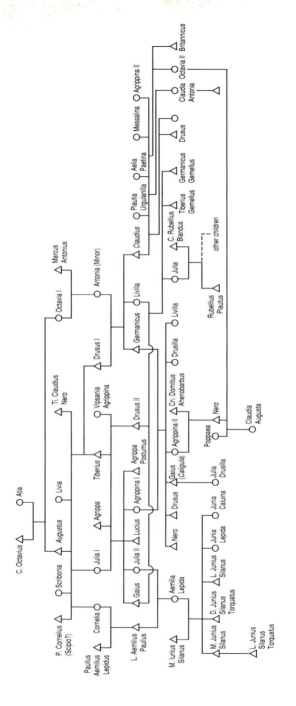

*Figure 12.1* The respective descendants of Augustus and Livia

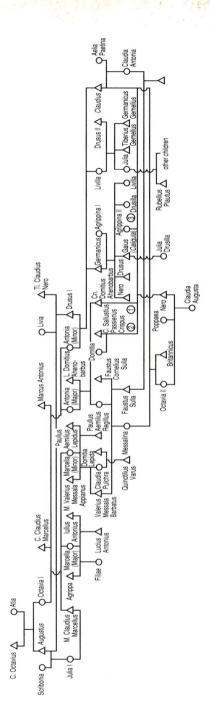

*Figure 12.2* Descendants of Octavia I, sister of Augustus

named) comprised not only a 65-year-old emperor and four 'Caesares' in the age-span 17 – 3 (Nero Caesar, Drusus Caesar, Gaius Caesar, Tiberius Gemellus), but also four widows (Livia, now named Julia Augusta, Antonia Minor, Agrippina the Elder – Agrippina I on the figures –, Livilla) and four 'Julian' princesses (three by Germanicus and one by Drusus), not forgetting Claudius. Young boys grew up with their sisters and female cousins in houses full of mature and older women, for women had greater prospects of survival than men.

## LEGITIMACY THROUGH WOMEN: MARRIAGES AND ADOPTIONS

Let us consider the role of women in transmitting legitimacy – for women were very much utilised as 'vehicles of power' in the phrase of Claude Lévi–Strauss (1983). Girls were, for example, betrothed while still infants; they were married soon after reaching puberty, between the ages of 13 and 15; those who married later had been kept in reserve for a precise relative, thus the elder Agrippina who married Germanicus. And they were remarried at once when divorced or widowed.

Using the prerogatives of a *paterfamilias* and the authority of a *princeps*, Augustus made several attempts to provide himself with a male heir when his marriage to Livia failed to produce a natural child. He had to perform the operation three times, since death kept depriving him of the chosen heirs.

The first two solutions centred on Augustus' daughter, Julia. In the absence of a brother, it was the responsibility of a daughter to produce a successor (in the anthropological meaning of the word). Augustus might adopt Julia's husband or Julia's son as well. Thus, in 25 BC, Julia was married to Marcellus, the son of Augustus' sister Octavia. But this classic combination – the marriage of first cousins – produced no descendants. And young Marcellus died prematurely.

Augustus had to wait for Julia's second marriage (after widowhood) to his friend Agrippa (who was obliged to divorce Augustus' niece, Marcella, to marry Augustus' daughter), a union which in 20 BC produced a son, Gaius, and in 17 BC another, Lucius, and between them a daughter. Augustus adopted his two grandsons as *his* sons and he himself taught them to read, and to write like himself, imitating his way of writing. However, by AD 4, Gaius and Lucius, the adoptive sons, were both dead – at about the age of 20 – and Augustus

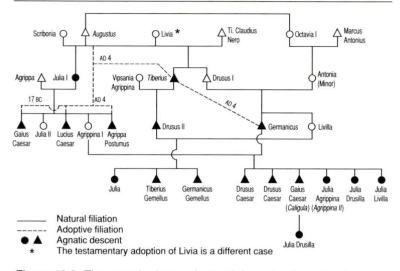

*Figure 12.3* The agnatic descendants of Augustus by natural or adoptive filiation

had to rebuild. By adoption, he gave himself two new sons, his stepson, Tiberius, and his last natural grandson, Agrippa Postumus. But Augustus also gave himself two grandsons, who biologically, were Livia's grandsons. He achieved this by constraining Tiberius to adopt his nephew Germanicus (son of his brother, Drusus the Elder) who automatically thereby took age precedence over Tiberius' natural son, Drusus the Younger (Figure 12.3).

After the adoptions, let us consider the marriages. To Gaius, his first adoptive son, Augustus married the sole granddaughter of his wife Livia – here we shall call her, as Suetonius does, Livilla. But the marriage produced no descendant.

After the adoptions of AD 4, Augustus had Germanicus, his adoptive grandson, marry his own granddaughter by blood, Agrippina the Elder, and he married Gaius' widow, Livilla (Livia's granddaughter), to Drusus the Younger, his second adoptive grandson. Thus, in the imperial family, he created two 'Julian' branches destined to produce his great-grandchildren – boys named Caesares and girls named Juliae. Although the two fathers concerned, Germanicus and Drusus the Younger, had been born Claudians, now, after the adoptions, they were members of the Julian family. The children born to the two couples, it turned out, were doubly cousins. Importantly, the marriage of Germanicus and Agrippina the Elder produced descendants common to Augustus and Livia, as Tacitus (*Ann.* 5, 1) notes.

The study of marriages allows the underlying strategies of alliance to be analysed. The choice lay between a 'closed' or 'open' matrimonial policy. The 'closed' policy – that is marriage between close kin – was usually followed for the older princes who were the potential successors. The 'open' policy – namely marriage not between close kin – was followed for the younger princes and the princesses, at least in the first generations. We shall note the change under Tiberius.

As shown above, direct exchanges were made between the respective grandchildren of Augustus and Livia, whose mothers, Julia (Augustus' daughter married Augustus' friend Agrippa) and Antonia Minor (Augustus' niece, married Livia's younger son), were first cousins: in 1 BC, Livilla was given to Gaius Caesar the heir apparent, and *c.* AD 4–5 Agrippina the Elder was given to Germanicus, who by this date had himself become the heir apparent. At about the same time, the widowed Livilla was remarried to Drusus the Younger.

In the two couples united in AD 4–5 in order to reign or to transmit power, the wife's birth was superior to that of her husband, as each were a closer blood relative to Augustus (a granddaughter and a grandniece) than her husband (a grandnephew and the son of a stepson). Germanicus spent years away from Rome and had his wife accompany him to increase his prestige and to spread the image of a princely couple destined one day to achieve the succession. At her husband's funeral, as the people of Rome shouted, Agrippina was recognised as *solum Augusti sanguinem* (Tac. *Ann.* 3, 4). The noble arrogance of the princess is confirmed by anecdotal evidence. Thus Agrippina, now Germanicus' widow, presented herself to Tiberius, the ruling Emperor, as the 'living image' of Augustus, 'born from his divine blood' (Tac. *Ann.* 4, 52).

In the generation of Augustus and Livia's great-grandchildren, couples were bound by multiple family ties (Figure 12.4). In AD 20, Tiberius arranged the marriage of Julia, his granddaughter by Drusus the Younger, and Nero Caesar, Germanicus and Agrippina's elder son. The young spouses were cross-cousins through Livilla and Germanicus, parallel cousins on their father' side, and cousins again through their common ancestor Agrippa. The two branches of the House were becoming one.

So the purpose of the ruling family was to have sufficient potential heirs, but not too many. Furthermore, for princes who were well placed

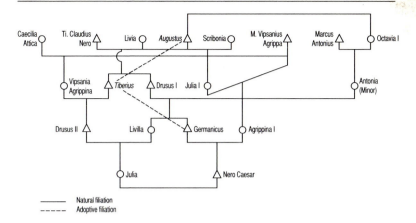

*Figure 12.4* Kinship between Nero Caesar and his wife Julia

to succeed to the principate, close-kin marriages served to make the kin closer still and increase the legitimacy of the chosen heir.

The wish to retain a link with Augustus, however, could be very strong: according to Suetonius (*Life of Gaius*, 23), Caligula (Agrippina's son) was prepared to deny that Agrippa was his maternal grandfather so that he could claim descent from an incestuous union between Augustus and his daughter Julia.

One final example will make the point clear. After Claudius was chosen by the praetorians in AD 41, as Germanicus' brother, to succeed his assassinated nephew, Caligula, he never failed to recall his kin-ties to preceding emperors (Caligula apart) as the sole legitimising basis of his power. In the absence of any adoption, he had simply to assume for himself the name Caesar. After his accession he had his grandmother Livia deified – Julia Augusta became Diva Julia – since it was she who connected him the more directly with Augustus. And he confirmed for his mother, Antonia Minor, the name Augusta (given by Caligula in 37): since, through her, he could refer to the deified Augustus as his *avunculus* – in fact *avunculus magnus* (but the link with a maternal uncle is stronger than with a great-uncle). So Claudius' legitimacy was due to these two women, Livia and Antonia (Octavia's daughter), and also, as said above, to his elder brother Germanicus.

Women had no official political roles to play, and so invested in their sons. Augustus' sister, Octavia, although a mother of four daughters, spent the rest of her life mourning her son Marcellus after his premature death at the age of 20; he had been meant to succeed Augustus, and Octavia was left to resent the interest Augustus subsequently took in Livia's sons.

But two emperors – Tiberius and Nero – were precisely their mother's sons: Tacitus (*Ann.* 1, 5, 4; 12, 68, 3) allows us to see how first Livia, in AD 14, then the second Agrippina, in AD 54, manoeuvered to guarantee the succession for their sons, Tiberius and Nero, when Augustus and Claudius died. Tiberius' accession was due as much to the machinations of his mother Livia as to the premature deaths of Gaius and Lucius, Augustus' adoptive sons. Augustus could then have chosen Germanicus his grandnephew as his successor, and adopted him; the sources say he considered the possibility, but was turned from it by his wife Livia. But he had another reason to prefer an older to a younger man: the principate was still judged a supreme magistracy. As for Nero: his accession was the result of Britannicus' eviction, contrived by his mother, Agrippina the Younger.

If one remembers that, in Rome, legitimate filiation derived from the father, and from the father only, we understand Tiberius' disappointment when, at the death of Augustus, the senate suggested to add to his name 'Julia's son' (Julia being now Livia's name). He was perfectly right in considering himself as Augustus' son, as Augustus had adopted him ten years before, and he did not want to be reminded that this adoption – and subsequently his accession – was the consequence of his mother's remarriage with the *princeps*. But Livia's testamentary adoption and change of name to Julia Augusta might have the precise purpose, in Augustus' intention, of enhancing Tiberius' legitimacy.

However the honour which was denied by Tiberius to his mother, Livia, was in one sense accorded to Agrippina the Younger, Nero's mother. In the *Acts of the Arval Brethren*, dating to between AD 50 and 54, Nero is twice described as 'the progeny (*suboles*) of Agrippina Augusta and the son (*filius*) of Claudius'. The Latin vocabulary respects here a distinction between a biological relation – the maternal filiation – and a social one – the paternal filiation.

## DANGER PRESENTED BY WOMEN

The Julio-Claudians did not hesitate to eliminate those who could, potentially, produce rival legitimate heirs. Augustus had set the precedent as early as 29 BC when, after the defeat of Antony and Cleopatra, he executed Cleopatra's presumed son by Julius Caesar and Mark Antony's elder son by his wife Fulvia. And his example was not forgotten. When Tiberius came to power, the order was given for the killing of Augustus' grandson, Agrippa Postumus (even though he was no longer an adoptive son after being 'abdicated' from the family in AD 6). And, less than a year after Caligula acceded, his cousin Tiberius Gemellus was driven to suicide. Claudius' son Britannicus did not live beyond the first six months of his adoptive brother's reign.

But what about the women?

The women of the imperial family were much less affected at first. The two Julias were only exiled by Augustus, not killed, for instance. But the two daughters of Claudius were both victimised by Nero, their adoptive brother, one (Octavia) for having married him, the other (Antonia) for refusing to do so. The two Claudian princesses had received names which referred to Claudius' mother and grandmother, the two women who linked Claudius by blood to the founder, Augustus. Claudia Antonia and Claudia Octavia wore as surnames (*cognomina*) the *gentilicia* of these ladies. So the prestige of names extended to the princesses and was transmitted by them. And it explains their popularity: at the news that Nero was going to divorce Octavia (Claudius' younger daughter), the populace at Rome demonstrated in her favour and Nero had to abandon his design. He could break the people's loyalty to Claudius' family only by levelling a charge of adultery and abortion against Octavia.

After the death of his second wife Poppaea, Nero wanted to repair the damage caused to his popularity by his divorce with Octavia, the Emperor Claudius' younger daughter. By marrying Claudius' elder daughter, Claudia Antonia, now a widow, he hoped to reinforce his legitimacy. Thus Antonia was offered an unexpected role: that of legitimising the ruler, her adoptive brother. Her refusal was the cause of her death.

The potential danger represented by the widows who had children and who might remarry was well understood. Augustus and Tiberius adopted opposite policies.

Agrippa was scarcely dead when his widow Julia (mother of the two adopted sons of Augustus) was remarried by her father, Augustus, to his stepson Tiberius – the latter being compelled to divorce a wife he loved, Vipsania Agrippina, who had given him a son and who was again pregnant.

But Agrippina the Elder and Livilla, the two daughters-in-law of Tiberius, were not allowed to remarry when, in AD 19 and AD 23 their husbands, Germanicus and Drusus the Younger, died. In AD 25, Tiberius specifically refused Livilla permission to marry Sejanus, the ambitious praetorian prefect. In his dilatory reply to Sejanus's request, Tiberius, according to Tacitus (*Ann.*, 4, 39–41) would have echoed Augustus's hesitation over the choice of a husband for his daughter Julia: foreseeing[6] 'to what height the product of such a union would be raised above all others'. In AD 26, Agrippina I in her turn was refused permission to remarry. But not all women were used in the construction of legitimacy, as illustrated by the marriages of the year AD 33. In the absence of sons, daughters were useful until they produced successors. But if an emperor had sons or grandsons in the agnatic line, sisters were no longer needed. After the first generation, the imperial family had no need of new matrimonial alliances with senatorial families. However, celibacy was not the norm at Rome. It was a duty for a *paterfamilias* to marry all his daughters and grand-daughters: Tiberius had four of them, three by Germanicus and one by Drusus the Younger. So in the year AD 33, Tiberius adopted the course of 'eliminating' the excess women by marrying them outside the imperial family. He married off his two younger granddaughters by Germanicus – Drusilla and Livilla – and the one by Drusus – Julia, first married to the presumptive heir Nero Caesar, Germanicus' son, now a widow – and to senators who although of consular rank did not bear very prestigious names. This meant that, in AD 33, the prospective heirs, at that time, Caligula and Tiberius Gemellus (as all the other males were dead) could be presented in isolation.

Five years before, in AD 28, Agrippina the Younger (Agrippina II, Nero's mother), Germanicus and Agrippina's elder daughter, had each been married to a close relative, as was previously the custom for princesses.

Agrippina's matrimonial history is in fact a textbook case. She was married at the age of thirteen by her grandfather Tiberius to her cousin Domitius Ahenobarbus, and then, being twice widowed, chose her future husbands herself, one for his wealth, the other for his power. Her first husband was chosen by Tiberius within the *domus Augusta*. As Tacitus says (*Ann.* 4, 75), 'in selecting Domitius, [Tiberius] looked not only to his ancient lineage, but also to his alliance with the blood of the Caesars [*propinquum Caesaris sanguinem*], for he could point to Octavia as his grandmother and *through her* to Augustus as his great-uncle'. At the time of their marriage in AD 28 (young

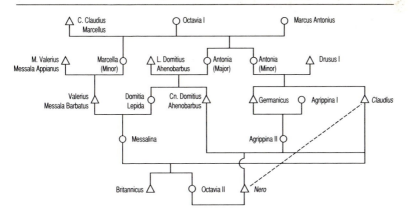

*Figure 12.5* Kinship between Nero and his wife Octavia II

Domitius and Agrippina probably had been betrothed from infancy), there was no prospect of succession: since Agrippina had three living brothers (the elder one being married to Tiberius' granddaughter Julia) and a young cousin, Tiberius Gemellus. Provided with four Caesares, Tiberius could marry his granddaughter inside the imperial *domus* without any danger.

Her second husband, C. Sallustius Passienus Crispus, a man much older than she, took away from her cousin and sister-in-law, Domitia, and secured his fortune for her son Nero who inherited from his father-in-law.

The third husband, the Emperor Claudius, her paternal uncle, she captivated in 49, after Messalina's death, and so placed Nero in line to succeed his new stepfather. According to Tacitus (*Ann.* 12, 2, 3), the argument developed by Pallas, Augustus' freedman, in favour of Agrippina was this: 'She would bring with her Germanicus' grandson, who was thoroughly worthy of imperial rank, the scion of a noble race and a link to unite the descendants of the Claudian family.' 'He hoped that a woman who had proved her fertility and was still in the freshness of youth, would not carry off the grandeur of the Caesars to some other house.'

However, even though he shared Augustus' blood through his mother Agrippina, Nero would not have become an emperor if the Emperor Claudius, his great-uncle, had not adopted him as a Claudius. But Claudius had a son, Britannicus. Agrippina had to prepare his removal. By marrying Claudius, she made Nero the

Emperor's stepson. With the betrothals of Nero and Claudius' daughter, Octavia, she made Nero the Emperor's son-in-law. Then she had to persuade Claudius that he should imitate Tiberius, who having himself a son, Drusus, had adopted another, Germanicus (Figure 12.5). But (she probably did not remind him of this point) Tiberius had been compelled by Augustus to do so.

## DOMUS AUGUSTA

Augustus laid the foundations of a *domus* – a 'house' in the sense that Claude Lévi–Strauss (1990) from an anthropological point of view has suggested giving to the familial structure of this kind. A *domus* that fused together two principal lines – Julian and Claudian – and the social and symbolic capital of each, but which also drew in other lines such as those of the *Antonii* and the *Domitii*.

Deprived of sons, Augustus lived surrounded by women and it was their marriages that provided members for the *domus*. Not all members of the *domus Augusta* were members of the *gens Iulia*; but in case of need, new men from the *domus* could be incorporated into the *gens* as Augustus' sons or grandsons. The *domus* functioned as a source, a reservoir (Corbier 1994a).

Because power and legitimacy were at stake, Augustus and his successors had to draw the boundaries of the *domus* so as to exclude unworthy members and create by adoption internal hierarchies to define an order of succession within the *domus*. It was the responsibility of the *princeps*, and of him alone, to delineate this internal hierarchy. As the succession remained bound up with filiation, members of the gens *Iulia* – males in the first rank – constituted the backbone of the *domus Augusta*. The tactics followed in building the *domus* had the effect of placing on an agnatic line men who were still Augustus' relatives with the status of cognate or affine. Thus Germanicus, who was at the same time Octavia's grandson and Livia's grandson, became in AD 4 Augustus' grandson (in agnatic line) after his adoption by Tiberius, himself adopted by Augustus. His marriage with Agrippina the Elder provided Augustus with children who legally were his great-grandsons in agnatic line and biologically his great-grandsons by blood.

Conversely, men and women who were members of the *domus*, and even of the *gens*, like Julia, Augustus' daughter, and Agrippa Postumus, Augustus' last adoptive son, could be discarded from the circle of the family. Others like Claudius, even though he was a member of the *domus* (like his brother Germanicus, he was Octavia's grandson and Livia's grandson), never entered the *gens*. He remained within the circle, but close to the boundaries, so that contemporaries themselves sometimes doubted if he was a member of the *domus* or not (Tac. *Ann.*, 3, 18).

The *domus Augusta* was a closed circle. How could one get in, if not by marriage? Sejanus, the praetorian prefect of Tiberius, tried twice to force the doors: in AD 25, when he asked for the hand of Livilla, widow of Drusus the Younger, and found himself turned down by Tiberius. But in AD 31, apparently, at the time of his downfall, he had obtained the longed-for *adfinitas* with a promise of marriage which made him a *gener* of the Emperor and a member of the *domus*, even if the identity of his fiancée – Livilla herself, or her daughter Julia, widow of Nero Caesar – is not certain.

In AD 41, after Caligula's murder, according to the Jewish historian Josephus (*Jewish Antiquities* 19, 251),

> there were some who aspired to the throne by reason both of their distinguished birth and of their marriage connections. For instance, Marcus Vinicius had a good claim both because of his noble birth and by his marriage to Gaius' sister Julia [Livilla].

From this passage, we can conclude that, in the absence of a male successor, marriage with a princess could give some hope of the succession.

## CONCLUSION

It is worth comparing the complex network of marriage alliances and adoptions formed by the respective descendants of Augustus and Livia, or by the descendants of Octavia, Augustus' sister, with the Flavian family.

The Flavians had so many males that they could invest in their *gens* and were not encouraged to construct a large *domus*. Vespasian had two sons (and a daughter) and at the very beginning of his reign he announced in the Senate that no one other than his sons would be his successor. He also had a brother who himself had two grandsons by his son.[2] There was no need to incorporate new young men into the *gens*.

But Augustus' lesson was not forgotten: the Flavians married the women of their blood (the grand-nephews of Vespasian, Sabinus and Clemens, married his granddaughters Julia and Domitilla); they did not give them to outsiders. So, even if Domitian adopted two grand-nephews by his sister, Flavia Domitilla, and his niece, his relationship with the two boys was not only an avuncular one: the boys, born from his patrilateral cousin, T. Flavius Clemens, still were Flavii; they only moved from one branch of the *gens* to another. The Flavian dynasty had a short life – but as a familial structure it was a *gens Flavia*.

It remains to say only that the construction of the *domus Augusta* by Augustus was purely casual. Augustus had no choice. If he had had sons, there would probably have been no scope for prominent women like his granddaughter and his great-granddaughter – the two Agrippinas.

A new reality, which would come to acquire the lasting name of *domus*, and specifically, in the first decades following the death of Augustus, officially bore the name *domus Augusta*, was long years in the process of definition. The varying nature of its composition posed a more general question: that of the construction of a kinship group sufficiently large to ensure its reproduction and survival by internal alliances, and sufficiently exclusive to avoid the distribution of rights of succession among too many rival candidates. Such a construction was made possible within Roman traditions by divorce, remarriage and adoption (Corbier 1987, 1990, 1991), rights which offered possibilities for adaptation to circumstances, but which would in due course be denied to the dynasts of Christian Europe. For a new problem, solutions were borrowed from the classic armoury of Roman law: if the *domus* was constructed initially with the family relationships of the founder, its composition and internal hierarchy were subsequently modified on several occasions by the decisions of the 'patriarch'. It was he who decided remarriages, divorces or adoptions, but he had to take account of premature deaths, psychological incapacities and the misbehaviour of individual members of the *domus*.

Augustus was constrained to operate within a context that was both general – the tradition of alliances between the great families of the Roman aristocracy – and particular – the relative lack in his family of males, and especially males who survived long enough to become heirs, and the corresponding superabundance of females who thus found themselves entrusted with a responsibility never before theirs in Rome: that of the transmission of legitimacy.

## NOTES

1 From the *Senatus Consultum* of December AD 19 on the funerary honours accorded to Germanicus, recorded on the *Tabula Siarensis* (*L'Année Épigraphique* 1984: 508) and from the *SC de Cn. Pisone patre* soon to be published by W. Eck (for a preliminary commentary, see Eck 1993).

2 According to the genealogy currently accepted: see Raepsaet-Charlier 1987: table 12.

# Chapter 13

# Women and elections in Pompeii

## Liisa Savunen

*L(ucium) P(opidium) S(ecundum) Aed(ilem) O(ro) V(os) F(aciatis) D(ignum) R(ei) P(ublicae) Successa Rog(at)*

(*CIL* IV, 1062)

A number of electoral inscriptions from electoral campaign posters are still visible in the main streets of Pompeii. These posters, *pro-grammata*, are a unique source for scholars of municipal elections in the ancient world.[1] The elective *comitia* in which upper magistrates, aediles and *duoviri*, were elected for a year, was held every year in March.

Women also participated in canvassing. Although many scholars have considered their role important, it has never been systematically studied.[2] My aim in this paper is to analyse in detail the electoral posters made by Pompeian women and to discuss the role of women in Pompeian municipal politics. Why did women endorse candidates publicly? What were the relationships between candidates and supporters? I work on the assumption that the women were not a homogeneous group, but differed in terms of, for example, social status. I also assume that the *programmata* made by women did not differ from those made by men or groups in terms of either format or motives. In this way analysis of *programmata* made by women can also shed light on the background and underlying motives of *program-mata* in general.

*Programmata* fall into two categories: *programmata antiquissima*, dating back to the period immediately following the establishment of the Roman colony in 80 BC, and *programmata recentiora*, originating in the last 17 years of Pompeii.[3] The two types differ in a number of ways, the most obvious of which is that in *programmata antiquissima* the supporter (= *rogator*) is seldom mentioned and is never a woman.

The simplest of the *programmata recentiora* consisted of the candidate's name – or merely his initials – and the office, both in the accusative case. The name was usually followed by standard phrases and abbreviations such as *OVF* = *oro vos faciatis*, *VB* = *virum bonum*, *DRP* = *dignum reipublicae*. The name of the supporter was not required. Of the more than 2,500 *programmata* discovered only about 30 per cent include the supporter's name.

Fifty-two posters were made by women, and in all we have 54 women supporting 28 different candidates.[4] Fifty-two of these women used their own name, either *cognomen* or *nomen gentilicium*. Most women (33) had a poster of their own, but some featured alongside a man (13) or another woman (four). Behind two women there seems to have been a larger group called *suis*. Two inscriptions have preserved an attribute which probably refers to a woman: *CIL* IV, 913, *Hilario cum sua*, and *CIL* IV, 7213, *Amandio cum sua*. However, *sua* can also refer to *familia* or *domus*.[5] Scholars have found it difficult to assign Pompeian women and the electoral notices they produced to a specific place within the more general framework. Bernstein and Mouritsen have both tried to clarify the role of kinship in the *programmata*. According to Mouritsen, the direct involvement of women in an election campaign would have cast a doubtful light on the candidate, unless the women featured in the capacity of members of the candidate's *clientela*.[6] Mouritsen's general idea concerning personal connections is interesting, but his theories on women's involvement are far from convincing.

## FEMINA POLITICA

A great deal of satisfactory work has been written on the role of women in politics and public life. The most substantial work has been done in the field of Roman law by studying the duties and status of women.[7]

According to the well-known Ulpian passage, women were excluded from all duties whether civil or public, and were thus unable to become judges or magistrates.[8] Only free-born and emancipated male citizens had the right of access to the magistracy and to vote in *comitia*. Women, slaves, condemned persons and foreigners who did not have permanent residence in the city were not allowed to vote.[9] Women could take part in *contiones*, preliminary public meetings, in which citizens appeared unsorted.[10] It is very likely – although we have no evidence – that women also participated in *contiones* in Pompeii.

The analysis of powerful women known from literary sources has also been valuable. During the Republic upper-class women took part in political affairs, and in the principate the women of the imperial family in particular were able to influence Rome's destiny. The lack of franchise was not the crucial point, as women could exercise political power through *amicitia* and *clientela*.[11]

Bauman has recently argued that the entire basis of male politics changed under one-man rule and the system became more advantageous to women. In Rome elections and voting for proposals in *comitia* were in decline: the decreased importance of the popular assembly made the denial of the franchise to women less relevant.[12] However, as electoral notices show, in small municipal towns like Pompeii political life was on the increase.[13] The participation of women in elections in Pompeii seems to call into question the significance of the franchise and the idea of citizenship.

## WOMEN IN POMPEIAN POLITICS

In order to be able to study *programmata* made by women, one first has to collect, count and classify all posters of all candidates.[14] This is no easy task, as the names of both the candidates and supporters are fragmented and therefore open to various interpretations. There are many candidates with the same *nomen*, and it is difficult to decide which candidate is concerned in any given case. For example, Franklin and Mouritsen have arrived at different results, and the numbers in this paper differ from theirs.[15]

The next step after collecting the posters is to divide candidates into two categories, those with women supporters and those without. The *programmata* of each candidate can also be divided into those with *rogator* support and those with non-*rogator* support. The latter means posters with no mention of a supporter. The *rogator* support category can in turn be divided into individual and collective support. Individual support means that the names of individual men or women were given. Collective support refers to posters made by specific groups, such as *fullones universi, dormientes, furunculi*, etc., some of which may even seem ridiculous. There are thus four distinct categories of support: women, men, groups and non-*rogator* support.

One poster can include more than one supporter and also more than one candidate. In this paper I use the concept of support expression, which includes all supporters and non-*rogator* support of one candidate. It has to be emphasised that poster and support expression are two totally different concepts. One poster can contain more than one support expression (e.g. in *CIL* IV, 171, *Caprasia cum Nymphio* there are two).

Comparison of different groups highlights some very interesting details. First, no candidate had only women supporters. Second, only 28 candidates had women supporters, but they got 1,286 posters and 1,356 expressions of support. In the group without women supporters there were 110 candidates with a total of just 1,253 posters and 1,298 expressions of support. Third, in a survey of all posters and expressions of support the percentual distribution between non-*rogator* support and *rogator* support is relatively similar regardless of whether or not there were women among the supporters (69 per cent if there were women, 75 per cent if not). Fourth, the distribution of collective support is also the same in both groups (5 per cent). Fifth, in the relative division of support the share of women is 2 per cent (men 21 per cent, collective 5 per cent, non-*rogator* support 72 per cent).

The similar distributions show that we are dealing with a random sample and in fact the groups are similar. The greatest difference between the groups lies not in the support of women but in the number of posters and thus in the number of support expressions. The division between women supporters and others is artificial. It was very likely that a candidate would have women among his supporters, the more so if he had at least 50 support expressions. If he did not have women among his supporters, this was more a result of having fewer posters and thus fewer support expressions.

There are, however, exceptions to this rule. Aedile candidate C. Cuspius Pansa had so many posters (ninety-six) and support expressions (twenty-eight men plus seven collective) that he could have been expected to have had women among his supporters – but he did not. On the other hand, the *duovir* candidate C. Iulius Polybius had just eighteen support expressions, of which seven were from women. Aedile candidate Cn. Helvius Sabinus and *duovir* candidate L. Ceius Secundus likewise had more women supporters than their total level of support would lead one to presume. However, as the sample is not statistically very representative, one has to be cautious about drawing far-reaching conclusions.

It has already been mentioned that electoral posters were rather uniform in character. The supporter's being a man or a woman had no impact on the text of the poster. The same abbreviations, verbs and phrases were used in either case. The laudatory formulae used were also, with few exceptions, very similar. The only exceptional formula to be found among women's *programmata* is *CIL* IV, 3678, *M(arcum) Casellium et L(ucium) Albucium aed(iles) O(ro) V(os) F(aciatis) Statia et Petronia rog(ant) tales cives in colonia in perpetuo.*[16]

The choice of verbs (*facere, rogare, cupere, volere*) has presented several problems.[17] Of all the theories put forward on this question, that of Gründel is the most interesting. He argues that the perfect tense *fecit* refers to supporters who wished to convey to the candidate after the election that they had voted for him.[18] *Facere* was used six times by women, but only once in the perfect tense.[19] In men's *programmata* this tense was also very rare.[20] This leaves Gründel's theory based on very poor evidence and unfortunately we have no other proof that Taedia Secunda or any other woman would ever have voted in the elective *comitia* of Pompeii. It does seem to me, however, that *facere* could imply a close relationship between supporter and candidate.

Women supported the same candidates as men and their posters were similar – there was no feminine way of producing posters. The candidates supported by women were also those with the most posters and support expressions. Women supporters cannot be distinguished from any others. On the contrary, it would seem that female support constituted part of a candidate's campaign and as such was as acceptable and as legitimate as posters produced by men and groups. There is nothing that would indicate clearly that candidates supported by women needed more posters than others on account of their being less well-known or of less distinguished descent.[21]

## SOCIAL STANDING AND POLITICAL POWER

There can be four derogative motives underlying *programmata*: gender, social status, disrepute or shameful profession. It has been argued above that there appears to have been no difference between women supporters and others. It is therefore likely that gender itself was not considered suspicious by Pompeians. The fact that women often produced *programmata* together with men reinforces this hypothesis.[22]

Assessing the social standing of supporters is a difficult enough task, but research into profession and possible disrepute presents even greater problems. In most cases a name is preserved in only one inscription. Indications of status are very rare in electoral inscriptions. The identification of supporters as slaves or freedwomen is of course a feasible proposition but accuracy cannot be guaranteed. The site of the inscription can also provide clues as to identity but is highly problematic. Most inscriptions cannot be dated exactly, and the function of the building may have changed in the course of time.

Della Corte[23] identified persons who featured as supporters in an electoral notice on the exterior of a house as occupants of that very building. However, this is mere conjecture, as it is unclear whether Pompeians actually wrote electoral *programmata* on the walls of their own houses or on those of others.[24] There are indications that walls were regarded as parts of public streets and would thus have been at the disposal of scribes.[25]

The only indicator of a supporter's social status is his or her name. However, even though onomastic analysis allows us to determine a supporter's social status, there remains the task of demonstrating the extent of the supporter's personal prestige and/or influence over the election process. This is greatly complicated by the fact that we do not know which candidates were elected.

In our sample of women we have twenty-four different *nomina gentilicia*. Two women had both *gentilicium* and *cognomen* (Sutoria Primigenia, Taedia Secunda); all the others used either *gentilicium* or *cognomen*. It may be that the others had only a *gentilicium* or that they had a *cognomen* but they did not use it. Posters had to be short, and the use of the whole name formula would have taken up too much wall space. Forty-three per cent of these *gentilicia* belonged to politically active families.[26]

Twenty-three women featured only by *cognomina*. Helpis Afra had a double *cognomen*, one Latin and the other Greek. The proportion of Latin and non-Latin *cognomina* is otherwise equal. The question of Greek *cognomina* and the social status they implied is a widely disputed one. According to Solin,[27] Greek names in Rome were a sign of servile origin in the first or second generation. This also seems to have been valid in Pompeii.

A *nomen gentilicium* indicates at least the status of a freedwoman. On the other hand, a *cognomen* implies a slave. However, the distinction is not quite so clear-cut. In a number of posters written by men only a *cognomen* was used, and in some cases that same *cognomen* is known to have belonged to a person who was undoubtedly free-born.[28] This could suggest that certain supporters were so well-known that the use of *cognomen* alone was sufficient to convey the person's identity. It could also suggest that the *cognomen* was the name normally used by Pompeians. A candidate's support also seems to have been published only in certain districts of the city, and as supporters were well-known among their immediate neighbours the use of the whole name formula was unnecessary. The number of *gentilicia* is noteworthy and shows that the low status of women cannot be taken for granted. This is confirmed by the number of non-Latin *cognomina*. Only 25 per cent of the total names were Greek *cognomina* and hence belonged to lower-class women.

In certain cases the archaeological evidence, in other words the original physical context of the inscription, can play a part in the identification. However, as the problems occurring in the following example illustrate, one has to be very cautious.

The electoral posters of four women – Asellina, Maria, Zmyrina and Aegle – may be seen to this day in the Via dell'Abbondanza on the wall of a house identified as a *thermopolium*. On the basis of this location della Corte identified Asellina as the owner (the place is commonly called Caupona di Asellina) and the others as her barmaids.[29] In fact, there is no other evidence to identify them and even onomastic analysis is of little help.[30] The evidence of the location is also disputable because bars in main streets were ideal sites for electoral posters as there they could be seen by as many people as possible. The disreputable character and suspicious profession of these women is a very feasible proposition but not certain.

It is important to note that the social structure of Pompeii changed in the last period of the city. The clearest evidence for this is in the construction boom following the earthquake in AD 62. Reconstruction took time because the Pompeians were impoverished. Aristocratic families moved to their country estates, abandoning town life and political activity. Their houses were turned into workshops. In contrast to the earlier period, builders were now freedmen or freedwomen. According to Castrén, many completely new families as well as sons of freedmen gained access to the Pompeian *ordo* in this period.[31] *Lex Malacitana* from about the year AD 84 also suggests that already in the first century there was a shortage of people voluntarily applying for office. If this were the case, it would be no wonder that the majority of supporters were freedmen or freedwomen.

## CLIENTELA OR INDIVIDUAL MANIFESTATION?

The most interesting point regarding *programmata* is the relationship between candidates and supporters. Was there a personal connection underlying *programmata* or did supporters have more general motives when choosing whom to endorse?

Unfortunately very little is known about electoral procedure or the official organisation of elections. Who was responsible for posters? Was it the candidate himself or persons connected with him who selected the supporters?[32] Or did people go to the organisers and grant them licence to use their names in electoral posters? Or was there any organisation at all?

The significance of electoral districts is another problem that remains unsolved. It seems that the town area of Pompeii was divided into four districts probably known as *vici*. The fifth district lay outside the town walls. However, it is not known whether these administrative districts also formed the basis of the voting districts. It appears that the electoral procedure required a candidate to secure a majority of the districts in order to be elected. Thus each candidate had to ensure that he won in at least his own electoral district.[33] This in turn would suggest that the inhabitants of a district supported the candidates chosen by that district.

Among women's *programmata*, the posters of candidates such as L. Albucius Celsus, M. Cerrinius Vatia, C. Iulius Polybius and M. Licinius Faustinus seem to have been concentrated in certain areas. In some cases, the candidate's own house can also be traced back to that same area. The support of Minia, Pollia, Caprasia, Miscenia, Specla, Zmyrina, Cuculla and Euhodia follows this pattern.[34]

However, the concentration of posters is not a full explanation of the *programmata*. Political merit also appears to have played a role. The praise of Statia and Petronia for L. Albucius Celsus and M. Casellius Marcellus, *tales cives in colonia in perpetuo*, probably refers to the aediles' responsibility for organising games. This was probably also Olympionica's motive for supporting M. Casellius Marcellus. Primigenia is likely to have referred to the *duovir*'s role as custodian of the public funds.[35]

Personal relationships between supporters and candidates, such as kinship (Taedia Secunda was grandmother of her candidate), vicinity (Appuleia), religion (Biria?), *clientela* or *amicitia* (Caprasia, Primilla),[36] were undoubtedly important, but as we do not know the *nomen gentilicium* of all the women it is difficult to determine the extent of the significance of patronage or *clientela*.

## CONCLUSIONS

Although personal connection between supporters and candidates seems to have played an important part in elections, it was not the sole motive for producing posters. It seems only natural that people who endorsed candidates were in some way closely connected with them. If different districts had their own candidates, it is also natural that candidates received support from their local constituents. The latter also had a chance to participate in preliminary assemblies where the candidates were nominated. In this way they were informed about the elections and candidates.

The problems of electoral organisation may seem crucial, but from the point of view of women supporters they are, in fact, of lesser importance. If women produced posters by themselves it was because they knew how to make them. If, and this is more likely, professional *scriptores* painted posters on their behalf, they must have been allowed to do so.[37] Had it been illegal or otherwise undesirable the *scriptores* would either not have painted the posters at all or if they had the candidates would have defaced them. Even if the campaigns were controlled by the candidates themselves and supporters selected beforehand, this would have no effect on the role of women, who would also have been selected beforehand along with the male supporters. As supporters women and men were equal. Posters produced by women had the same basis as those of men and as such they can be considered to have been as independent as the *programmata* of men and groups. No magisterial lists have been preserved and therefore we are not even able to assess the influence of men's *programmata*. It seems that *programmata* made by women constituted a part of a candidate's campaign. However, there is no evidence to suggest that women ever voted in Pompeii.

Other researchers have already observed that gender was not the sole determinant of public capacity.[38] In Roman society citizens were not equal and therefore all citizens did not have identical rights and duties. The same holds true in the question of Pompeian *programmata*. Among male supporters there were some excluded from the franchise who nevertheless took part in the *programmata*. There is thus no reason to overstate the denial of franchise to women. The crucial issue beyond women's *programmata* is the whole question of the significance of elections and of electoral *programmata* in Pompeii.

Elections were part of Pompeian public life. Posters did remain *in situ* after elections and revealed to newly elected magistrates who had supported them. The *programmata* may be regarded as a collective activity in which women took part not only as members or clients of the family but also as members of the community and the electoral district. Participation in the *programmata* could have been more important than the elections themselves.

## NOTES

* I would like to thank Professor Päivi Setälä, Professor Paavo Castrén and Dr Katariina Mustakallio for their valuable comments and suggestions. All errors remain mine.

1 There is no reason to assume that they were typical only of Pompeii, however. Literary and epigraphical sources show that they existed elsewhere as well. *CIL* V, 1490, 1641; *CIL* VI, 14313, 29942; *CIL* IX, 4126. See Zangemeister in *CIL* IV, p. 10. For the magistrates and election in Pompeii see Castrén 1983; Franklin 1980; Jongman 1988; and Mouritsen 1988.

2 For example, Castrén 1983: 79; Mouritsen 1988: 60f. The only existing study on the role of Pompeian women is d'Avino 1967, which does not fulfil scientific requirements. The article of Will 1979 is only superficial. I shall pursue Pompeian women and also the subject of this article in more detail and with more extensive documentation in my forthcoming book, *Women and the Public Sphere in Pompeii*. For women and elections in Pompeii see Scalera 1919: 387–405; and more recently Bernstein 1988: 1–18.

3 For the survival of *programmata*, problems of dating the magistrates and reconstructing the Pompeian *fasti* see Franklin 1980: 33f.; Castrén 1983: 113–114; Mouritsen 1988: 37f.

4 It is not always easy to ascertain sex because there are some contentious names. The names Heracla, Ascla and Sucula have usually been interpreted as women's names but they are men's. Cf. Solin 1982: 355–356 and 482–483; and Kajanto 1965: 329. The sex of Cuculla and Animula is unknown but these names are more likely to have belonged to women, cf. Kajanto 1965: 345, 365. *CIL* IV, 99 has been preserved in a fragmentary state and there are three different ways of interpreting it. Della Corte 1965: 31 n. 2 reads *Cæpari*; Mouritsen 1988: 175 *cupari*; the amendment in *CIL* IV, p. 460 *Chypare*, which is preferred also in this paper.

5 *CIL* IV, 1053 *Lollia cum suis*; and *CIL* IV, 7464 *Sutoria Primigenia cum suis*. Cf. *cum suis* in the following posters *CIL* IV, 235, 707, 1053, 3482, 7191, 7464, 7708, 9919; and Giordano and Casale 1990: 278 no. 10. Scalera 1919: 391, 400 argues that in the case of Lollia *cum suis* is similar to *cum familia* while the expression *cum sua* refers to a woman whose participation remains almost concealed but shows more serious participation.

6 Bernstein 1988: 6f.; Mouritsen 1988: 62.

7 Gardner 1986; and especially Gardner 1993: 85–109.

8 Ulp. *D.* 50, 17, 2; Paul. *D.* 5, 1, 12, 2. See especially Gardner 1993: 87–89.

9    Scholars are unanimous that when *contio* changed into *comitia*, the non-voters were removed. For example, Ross Taylor 1966: 3. The formula giving dismissal is known from Festus (*Gloss. Lat.* 72): *Exesto, extra esto. Sic enim lictor in quibusdam sacris clamitabat: hostis, vinctus, mulier, virgo exesto; scilicet interesse prohibebatur.*

10   During the early Republic women were not allowed to participate even in *contiones*, but attitudes became more permissive later. It is not known when this change took place or what lay behind it. Val. Max. 3, 8, 6. states *Quid feminae cum contione? Si patrius mos servetur, nihil.* Gell. *NA* 5, 19, 10. See also Botsford 1909: 326 n. 1. Livy 34, 2, 11 puts into Cato the Elder's mouth (234–149 BC) that before his generation women were not allowed to take part in politics or to be present at meetings and assemblies (*comitiis contionibus immisceri*), which is, however, an exaggeration. After the time of Gracchi, women could also speak at *contiones*, as did Hortensia in 43 BC: see Dio Cass. 83, 8; Val. Max. 3, 8, 6 and 8, 3; App. *BCiv.* 4, 32–34.

11   Bauman 1992; Dixon 1983: 91–112; Saxonhouse 1985: 100, f.

12   Bauman 1992: 5.

13   Staveley 1972: 223f. However, the *Lex Malacitana* of about AD 84 points to the fact that this interest was of short duration. According to Franklin 1980: 120, in the last years of Pompeii there were never more than two *duoviral* candidates for the two places to be filled. Cf. also Macrob. *Sat.* 2.3.11–12 where Cicero says to his friend P. Mallius who asks his support to obtain a *decurionate* for his stepson in Pompeii: *Romae, si vis, habebit; Pompeis difficile est.*

14   There are, of course, posters in which the name is no longer legible. If the name seems to have been in the plural, it has been classified among groups, otherwise among the posters of men.

15   Mouritsen 1988: 125f. *Catalogue of programmata recentiora*; Franklin 1980: 96–97, tables 8, 9; and especially J. L. Franklin, 'The Chronology and Sequence of Candidates for the Municipal Magistracies Attested in the Pompeiian Parietal inscriptions AD 71–79', dissertation, Ann Arbor 1975: 162f. appendix B.

16   Other examples include *CIL* IV, 187, 429, 597, 720, 4999, 6626.

17   Castrén 1983: 79 suggested that this problem and the role played by women in the Pompeian elections may have a joint solution. It was suggested already by Willems 1887: 84f. that the verbs *facere* and *rogare* correspond to two different stages of the election procedure. See also Mau 1889: 298–305.

18   Gründel 1967.

19   *CIL* IV, 7469 *L(ucium) Popi(dium) S(ecun)d(u)m aed(ilem) O(ro) V(os) F(aciatis) / Taedia Secunda cupiens avia rog(at?) et fecit.* Other cases *CIL* IV, 425 (*Animula facit*), 7873 (*Appuleia f*), 923 (*Caprasia fac*), 457 (*Iphigenia facit*), 7347 (*Vatinia facit*).

20   In all *fecit* was used at least twelve times. In individual support *CIL* IV, 98 (p. 192), 221, 297, 935bd, 3582, 3583, 3760, 7618. 6667 is disputable. In collective support *CIL* IV, 1122. *CIL* IV, 7187 *multis fecit benigne* is more a laudatory formula.

21   In the year AD 79 there were six candidates. Aedile candidates gained

posters and support expressions as follows: C. Cuspius Pansa 96/101/no women; L. Popidius Secundus 71/73/3 women; M. Samellius Modestus 52/55/2 women; and Cn. Helvius Sabinus 140/153/10 women. *Duovir* candidates: C. Gavius Rufus 35/36/no women; and M. Holconius Priscus 38/51/no women. This could suggest that women especially supported aedile candidates who, applying for office for the first time, also needed more posters and more supporters than *duoviral* candidates (C. Cuspius Pansa is the only exception). However, C. Iulius Polybius gained a total of 21 (one woman) support expressions when applying for aedile office but 40 (seven women) as candidate for *duovir*. L. Ceius Secundus gained 23 (one woman) support expressions as an aedile candidate but 95 (six women) as *duovir* candidate. See also Franklin 1980: 98–100.

22  *CIL* IV, 3527 *Appuleia cum Mustio*; 207 *Nymph(odot)us cum Caprasia*; 171 *Caprasia cum Nymphio*; 7669 *Acratopinon cum Cassia*; 6610 *Epidia nec sine C[osm]o*; 3595 *Acceptus rog Euhodia rog*; 1171 *Min[ia?] Sprvois?*; 3674 *Pyramus Olympionica Calvos*; 3403 *Parthope cum Rufino*; 1083 *Recepta nec sine Thalamo*; 7658 *Scymnis nec sine Trebio*; 3746 *Ambriaeus cum Vibia*; 913 *Hilario cum sua*; 7213 *Amandio cum sua*. Some of these men were even magistrates, e.g. 7658 Trebius is very probably A. Trebius Valens who was an aedile candidate during the Flavian period.

23  Della Corte 1965: 20.

24  According to Mouritsen 1988: 18–19, the homes of only 21 *rogatores* can be located with reasonable certainty.

25  *CIL* IV, 7621 *Lanternari tene scalam* may show that posters were written at night.

26  *Gens* Vibia, Statia, Maria, Lollia, Iunia, Fabia, Epidia, Cornelia, Cassia and Appuleia.

27  H. Solin, *Beiträge zur Kenntnis der griechischen Personennamen in Rom*, Commentatiories Humanarum Litterarum 48, Helsinki 1971: 135f.

28  For example Balbus in *CIL* IV, 935bdh, 2958 might be *duovir* candidate Q. Bruttius Balbus and Vatia in *CIL* IV, 132 aedile candidate M. Cerrinius Vatia.

29  *CIL* IV, 7862, 7863, 7864, 7866, 7873. See della Corte 1965: 307–309. Bars often functioned as brothels and prostitution was considered as a shameful profession. See Gardner 1993: 135f.; Evans 1991: 133f.

30  In the case of Asellina and Maria the names could have been either *gentilicium* or *cognomen*. See Kajanto 1965: 326; and Castrén 1983: 139 no. 47, 189 no. 242. For the name Asellina see also Väänänen 1937: 197–199. If Maria is a *cognomen* it is not Jewish as argued by della Corte 1965: 308, but Syrian. Cf. Solin 1983: 725. Zmyrina and Aegle are names of foreign origin which very probably belonged to slave women: see Solin 1982: 526 and 612–613.

31  Richardson 1988: 21 and 261f. Cf. *CIL* X, 846 concerning N. Popidius Celsinus who was co-opted into the *ordo decurionum* at the age of 6 after having restored the Temple of Isis following the earthquake. The Temple of Venus was still under restoration. For the rise of new families see Castrén 1983: 118f.

32  This is the idea of Mouritsen 1988: 44f.

33  Castrén 1983: 78f.; Jongman 1988: 289f.
34  *CIL* IV, 1171, 368, 207, 239, 7167, 7864, 7841, 3595.
35  *CIL* IV, 3674, 3773.
36  *CIL* IV, 7469, 3527. For Biria, *CIL* IV, 9885 and Bernstein 1988: 14. Caprasia, *CIL* IV, 171 supported A. Vettius Firmus. The existence of such a person as A. Vettius Caprasius Felix suggests that the *gens Caprasia* and the *gens Vettia* were in alliance. Primilla supported in *CIL* IV, 7230, C. Calventius Sittius Magnus. From the funerary inscription (d'Ambrosio and de Caro 1987: 216, 218) we know Calventia Primilla who may be the same woman.
37  The literacy of women is a much disputed problem. According to Harris 1983: 108, less than 20 per cent of Pompeian women were literate. He admits, however, that it is possible that Pompeian literacy was above the Italian norm.
38  For example, Gardner 1993: 85f.

# Chapter 14

# A woman's voice? – Laronia's role in Juvenal *Satire* 2

## *S.H. Braund*

Rarely in Roman satire do we hear a woman's voice: the speaking role of Laronia in Juvenal's second *Satire* is an exception which this paper seeks to explore.[1] Laronia is brought on stage (so to speak) to participate in the condemnation of hypocritical homosexuals. She speaks for just twenty-five lines of a poem one hundred and seventy lines long. What is her role in *Satire* 2? To what extent is she an autonomous character and to what extent is hers an authentic female voice?[2]

*Satire* 2 opens with an attack by the speaker on hypocritical moralists who uphold strict ancient Roman morality and criticise effeminates and homosexuals while indulging in such practices themselves in secret (lines 1–35).[3] The opening theme is *frontis nulla fides* (8), in effect, 'you can't trust appearances'.[4] The speaker in this poem is immediately revealed as the same raging bigot of *Satire* 1, who pictures Rome as a city seething with corruption.[5] His loathing for these hypocritical moralists is conveyed by telling oxymora,[6] by a series of analogies of hypocrites drawn from Republican times (24–8) and the single developed example of Domitian's hypocrisy in sexual matters (29–33), by angry questions (8–10, 24–8, 34–5) and by vocabulary typical of anger (*quis tulerit . . .?* 'who could endure . . .?', 24).[7] The laughter of the doctor (*medico ridente*, 13) who, called in to lance piles, discovers the hypocrite's anus smoothed (*podice leui*, 12) by anal intercourse firmly establishes that in this poem the speaker's victims, or 'out-group', to use Richlin's term, are hypocritical pathics, men who take the passive role in same-sex intercourse.[8]

After this indignant condemnation of hypocrisy by the speaker, Laronia is introduced into the poem, as if she had been standing in the wings, listening. She is provoked into speech by the continual criticisms of the immorality of *women* uttered by one of these hypocrites (36–7):

> non tulit ex illis toruum Laronia quendam
> clamantem totiens 'ubi nunc, lex Iulia, dormis?'

> 'Laronia could not stand one of those grim fellows so often shouting, 'Where are you now, Julian Law – asleep?'

Laronia is often assumed to be of low status, a prostitute, although there is no evidence for this.[9] This view may, I suggest, be an assumption by (male?) critics that a woman who dares to offer criticism of men must be of humble status and/or 'dubious' morality: the validity of her views is thus undermined.[10] However, all the evidence of the poem points to Laronia being of relatively high social status, albeit an adulteress. First, she is provoked into speech by the hypocrite's invocation of the *lex Iulia*, which made adultery by a married woman a criminal act (37).[11] This alone suggests that Laronia is a married woman who has infringed the *lex Iulia* by committing adultery. Second, the following section of the poem portrays adulteresses arraigned in court by a hypocritical moralist (65–70), not one of the covert moralists attacked in the opening section of the poem, but one whose hypocrisy is patent, thanks to his choice of a see-through toga to wear in court. This hypocrite, Creticus, is clearly prosecuting women for adultery: *est moecha Fabulla*, 'Fabulla is an adulteress' (68); this is the only charge mentioned. Moreover, we know that a Quintus Laronius was suffect consul in 33 BC: it is possible that Laronia is envisaged as this man's descendant,[12] perhaps also as Martial's (2.32.5–6),[13] a rich and influential widow (*orba est, diues, anus, uidua*). Therefore, Juvenal's Laronia may well be viewed as an elderly woman, so that the poem can be read as an inversion of Roman misogynistic literature attacking old women, e.g. Horace *Epodes* 8 and 12.[14]

I turn to Laronia's words. As she begins her speech, Laronia is introduced as smiling, *subridens* (38), a mark of irony.[15] Indeed, her first words are grimly ironic (38–40):

> felicia tempora, quae te
> moribus opponunt. habeat iam Roma pudorem:
> tertius e caelo cecidit Cato.

> What happy times, which set you up as the enemy of [corrupt] morality. Let Rome now acquire a sense of shame: a third Cato has fallen from heaven.

She proclaims the 'happy times' that have set up this pseudo-moralist as a censor of morals, as a third Cato,[16] to provide Rome's sense of shame. Her irony figures history thrown into reverse and the return of a Golden Age of blessed morality.[17] In lines 40–2 she adopts a more beguiling tone of voice:

> sed tamen unde
> haec emis, hirsuto spirant opobalsama collo
> quae tibi? ne pudeat dominum monstrare tabernae.

But, all the same, where did you buy this, the perfume which wafts from your shaggy neck? Don't be embarrassed to name the shop-owner.

She disingenuously feigns interest in the origin of the hypocritical moralist's perfume. This supposed community of interest is a disarming prelude to the point that follows, that if these 'moralists' are *really* interested in invoking the law in order to combat immorality, they will invoke not the *lex Iulia* but the *lex Scantinia*, the law outlawing sodomy which, she alleges, is widely practised among men (43–7):[18]

> quod si uexantur leges ac iura, citari
> ante omnis debet Scantinia. respice primum
> et scrutare uiros, faciunt peiora; sed illos
> defendit numerus iunctaeque umbone phalanges.
> magna inter molles concordia.

But if laws and statutes are to be disturbed [from their sleep], before all others should be summoned the Scantinian. Look at *men*, examine *them* first; their behaviour is worse, but they are protected by their number and their phalanxes joined by shield-boss. Great is the solidarity between effeminates.

Ironically, she borrows the term *concordia* from the discourse of marriage.[19] Laronia asserts that *women*'s conduct is irreproachable in comparison with *men*'s (47–8):

> non erit ullum
> exemplum in nostro tam detestabile sexu.

There will not be [found] any example so abominable in *our* sex,

and, as proof of this, proceeds to describe the behaviour of effeminate men.

* * *

Her proof of the need to invoke the *lex Scantinia* simultaneously initiates a series of allegations that (effeminate) men usurp female roles, in contrast with women who do not participate in male spheres of activity. The first of these concerns the active/passive and male/female sexual roles. Laronia alleges that women do not engage in practices of homosexuality or practices which deviate from the prescribed passive role (*Tedia non lambit Cluuiam nec Flora Catullam*, 'Tedia does not lick Cluvia nor Flora Catulla', 49) whereas men do, taking both the active and passive roles in intercourse (*Hispo subit iuuenes et morbo pallet utroque*, 'Hispo submits to young men and is pale from both diseases', 50):[20] hence the need for the *lex Scantinia*. Then, via the logical but unenunciated connection that the passive partner in male homosexual intercourse is considered to occupy the 'female' position,[21] Laronia asserts that, while *women* do not seek participation in such male spheres as litigation or athletics, *men*, by contrast, usurp female roles, such as spinning and weaving (51–7):

> numquid nos agimus causas, ciuilia iura
> nouimus aut ullo strepitu fora uestra mouemus?
> luctantur paucae, comedunt coloephia paucae.
> uos lanam trahitis calathisque peracta refertis
> uellera, uos tenui praegnantem stamine fusum
> Penelope melius, leuius torquetis Arachne,
> horrida quale facit residens in codice paelex.

> Do *we* ever conduct [legal] cases, are we familiar with the civil laws, do *we* disturb your court-rooms with any din? Few women wrestle, few women consume the meat-rich diet; *you* card the wool and carry back in baskets the prepared fleeces, *you* turn the spindle pregnant with slender thread better than Penelope, more delicately than Arachne, the sort of task the dishevelled concubine does as she sits on the [punishment] block.

Finally, in lines 58–61, she reverts to allegations of (male) homosexuality, but discreetly and indirectly, through understatement, and offers the young wife ironic advice of expediency, that she should acquiesce in her situation because her homosexual husband will pay her to keep quiet about his male lover:

> notum est cur solo tabulas inpleuerit Hister
> liberto, dederit uiuus cur multa puella.
> diues erit magno quae dormit tertia lecto.
> tu nube atque tace: donant arcana cylindros.

It is common knowledge why Hister filled up his will in favour of his freedman alone, why in his life-time he made many gifts to his young wife; she who sleeps third in a large bed will be rich. Marry and keep quiet [girl]: secrets bestow jewels.

Laronia rounds off her speech with a riposte to the hypocrite's invocation of the *lex Iulia* which compelled her to speak in the first place. She reiterates the point that men deserve criticism and prosecution before women do and condemns her male critics as corrupt (62–3):

de nobis post haec tristis sententia fertur?
dat ueniam coruis, uexat censura columbas.

After this, is a verdict of 'guilty' passed on *us*? [Your] moral judgement grants pardon to the ravens and attacks the doves.

\* \* \*

Evidently, there are two elements in Laronia's speech: an attack on male hypocrites and a defence of women. The primary function of the speech is to attack the hypocritical moralists. But we should also remember that Laronia is responding to an attack on women by a hypocrite: this accounts for the material in defence of women. It seems that what Juvenal has done here is not to present a fully-fledged invective against hypocritical moralists – which the speaker has already delivered in the opening 35 lines – but to incorporate a reply to some of the accusations typically made against women.

Hence there emerges a striking overlap of material between *Satire* 2 and *Satire* 6, Juvenal's massive misogynistic poem attacking Roman wives and above all their adultery.[22] Although Laronia does not respond to the accusation of adultery in *Satire* 2, she does rebut others that occur in *Satire* 6 (and in other misogynistic texts). What underlies Laronia's question to the effeminate about the shop where he bought his perfume (40–2) is the standard allegation that women's chief or sole interest in life is in cosmetics, clothes and fashion. This accusation occurs in Juvenal 6 in lines 457–73, where the wealthy woman is criticised for her extravagant jewellery and her use of face-packs and perfumes, and in lines 486–511, where the beautification of the woman, in particular by the creation of an elevated hairdo, is portrayed as a matter of the profoundest seriousness for both the woman and her household. (Earlier, for example, Ovid at *Remedia*

*Amoris* 343–56 criticises women's deceit of their lovers by their clothing and cosmetics).[23] Laronia does not deny this allegation, but her question suggests that this is not an exclusively female preserve and that effeminate men are (at least) equally interested in such matters.[24]

Next she denies that women engage in homosexuality or usurp the male role in intercourse (49). This reflects and responds to the allegation of lesbianism made against women, albeit infrequent.[25] Juvenal apparently devotes merely half a line out of his seven hundred in *Satire* 6 to a portrayal of lesbians: *in . . . uices equitant*, 'they take it in turns to ride' (6.311).[26] In other texts women breach the active/passive boundary to take a masculine role in sexual matters[27] and, ultimately, abandon the passive role in heterosexual intercourse.[28] Besides assimilation to the male physical role, this usurpation is manifested more frequently in the allegations of women taking the sexual *initiative* with men, ranging from the woman who uses lewd speech (Juv. 6.184–99) to the nymphomaniacs at the perversion of the Bona Dea rites (Juv. 6.314–45). However, Laronia redirects the allegation against men, claiming that men assume the passive (or 'female') role in homosexual intercourse (50). This allows her to move on smoothly to the assertion that whereas women generally keep out of male spheres of activity, effeminate men usurp female roles.

Her first case is litigation (51–2). The accusation that women invade this male sphere occurs in Juvenal *Satire* 6, where female lawyers feature in the catalogue of outrageous women (242–5):

> nulla fere causa est in qua non femina litem
> mouerit. accusat Manilia, si rea non est.
> componunt ipsae per se formantque libellos,
> principium atque locos Celso dictare paratae.

> There's hardly a case that comes to court that is not set moving by a woman. Manilia is the prosecutor, if she is not the defendant. They themselves compose and prepare the briefs on their own, prepared to dictate to Celsus how to open his speech and how to make his points.

Valerius Maximus exhibits a similar attitude of disapproval as he cites three examples of female lawyers, including a woman whose manly spirit caused her to be called Androgyne (8.3): evidently her transgression of the bounds of female behaviour involves a loss of sexual identity. Laronia, by contrast, asserts that women keep out of this area.

Laronia's second example of female avoidance of male spheres of activity is wrestling and athletics (53), and she claims that few women invade this apparently male preserve. Attacks on female athletes feature at Juvenal 6.246–67 and Seneca *Ep.* 95.21 and Martial 7.67, in which women are attacked for wrestling (among other male activities) as an indicative prelude to their assumption of the male role in intercourse, mentioned on p. 212.[29]

Having denied these standard accusations against women, Laronia sets up equivalent accusations against effeminate men. First, she alleges that they usurp the (for the ancients) quintessentially female job of spinning and weaving and, what is more, surpass even the most renowned female weavers of mythology, Penelope and Arachne (54–7).[30] Next, Laronia alleges that a man will leave his entire fortune to a freedman in return for (she implies) his sexual compliance (58–9), redirecting an allegation made against women in *Satire* 6, that a woman will insist that her lover or idol is included in her husband's will (218): *non unus tibi riualis dictabitur heres*, 'more than one of your rivals will have to be written down as your heir'. Given that the vast majority of women were not allowed by law to make wills,[31] this is the closest possible equivalent allegation in the male sphere.

Finally, she pictures the scene of three-in-a-bed: the woman with her husband and his (male) lover (60). There is no exact equivalent to this three-in-a-bed scene in misogynistic texts (which I suppose would require husband and wife and *her* lover in bed together), but a parallel is provided by the numerous accusations of adultery in *Satire* 6.[32]

* * *

It seems, then, that Laronia's speech is in part an inversion of standard themes of misogynistic invective: stereotypical accusations against women are refuted or denied or diminished in significance by Laronia's redirecting of those accusations against effeminate men.[33] So, we might ask, can Laronia on this account be described as a 'real' woman? Is she an autonomous woman given a free voice to defend womankind? At first sight, the answer might seem to be encouraging. A woman *is* permitted to speak in this poem, to speak without malice or a lust for vengeance, to speak justifiedly in response to the long-endured provocation of the hypocritical male attack on adulteresses. Her controlled, ironic and detached manner – so appealing and persuasive, because it seems so reasoned and reasonable – is a striking contrast with the *indignatio* of the speaker.[34] Her speech is not a 'harangue' or a 'tirade'.[35] Unlike the speaker, Laronia appears rational: she concedes points and qualifies statements. And, moreover, her participation in the poem is portrayed as highly effective: she simply tells the truth (64 and 65: *uera ac manifesta* and *quid enim falsi Laronia?*) and as a result the false moralists run away (64–5: *fugerunt trepidi . . . Stoicidae*). Or, perhaps, not so 'simply': the verb *canentem* seems to bestow a prophet-like status on Laronia;[36] moreover, the positioning of her name at the end of the sentence and the episode, with verbal ellipse, may lend her a superhuman status.

That is the most positive view which can be taken of Laronia. Whether this is 'realistically' what a woman in such circumstances might say, however, is another question. Laronia is, after all and inevitably, the construct of a male author. She is introduced here to expose the hypocrisy of the effeminates. But the effect of her words is to bolster a masculine view of the world, a view which condemns the assimilation of men to women. Laronia adapts the allegations made against women in misogynistic texts to attack the effeminates. Where *women* are generally portrayed by such stereotypical accusations as 'other',[37] that label of 'other' is here attached to the *effeminates* through Laronia's words. Both women and effeminates are portrayed as 'other', and the standard from which their deviation is charted is that of the manly male.[38] That is, effeminate/pathic men are assimilated to women or, rather, given the status of a third, intermediate, gender.[39] Laronia is no more autonomous than that of the anonymous interlocutor in Persius' first *Satire*, whom Persius makes clear is nothing more than a fiction convenient to his argument (*Sat.* 1.44): *quisquis es, o modo quem ex aduerso dicere feci*, 'You, whoever you are, my fictitious debating opponent'. Juvenal does not draw attention as blatantly as Persius does to the fiction, yet this does not diminish the fictive quality of Laronia's presence: her part in this little drama is secondary and subsidiary.

This is confirmed most significantly when the speaker inserts into her speech a male point of view for a moment, at line 52, where Laronia is made to 'defend' women's non-participation in litigation with the words *numquid nos . . . ullo strepitu fora uestra mouemus?* 'Do *we* ever . . . disturb your courtrooms with any din?' A woman defending women would not characterise female advocacy as 'din'. The loading of this word with invective against women confirms the secondary and subsidiary role played by Laronia in *Satire* 2.

Moreover, Laronia's appearance in the poem is brief, contained and controlled: she is used to achieve an effect, and once that effect has been achieved she is dispensed with. The next scene to be enacted on the stage now empty but for the speaker, who acts as a kind of ring-master or master of ceremonies, is a reconfiguration of the conflict between Laronia the adulteress and the hypocritical moralists, but with the initiative bestowed this time upon the moralists. Creticus, the overt hypocrite, is presented prosecuting adulterous women – and is duly exposed and pilloried by the speaker as the hypocrite he is. In effect, then, the Laronia episode is, simply, that: a fleeting dramatic episode in a many-pronged attack on effeminates and pathics. Laronia, then, is subordinate to and manipulated by a speaker who, as in the rest of the poems of Books I and II, victimises anyone and everyone that fails to conform to his narrow concept of acceptability in terms of gender, race, social status or sexual preference. Once she has fulfilled her role, she is marginalised, pushed off stage. Juvenal has created a master of ceremonies who hogs the limelight with his vitriolic attacks upon his victims. Among his victims is the woman who shares his outrage, whom he mobilises but then marginalises in his attack upon his *other* victims, the men who fail to be men.

In conclusion, the theme mentioned at the start of *Satire* 2 also seems to be valid at a metapoetic level: 'you can't trust appearances'. What sounded like a woman's voice turns out to be *écriture masculin*.[40] Satire, ancient and probably modern too, is a male, or rather a masculine, mode of discourse;[41] there is no woman in this text, only the construct of the speaker, himself a construct of the man-satirist.[42]

## NOTES

1 Discussions of *Satire* 2 devote little attention to Laronia: Anderson 1982: 209–19; Braund and Cloud 1981: 203–8; Courtney 1980: 32–3; Henderson, '. . . when Satire writes "Woman" ', in Braund 1989: 116–18; Henderson 1989: 66–7; Konstan 1993; Richlin 1983: esp. 201–2; Richlin 1993; A.C. Romano *Irony in Juvenal*, Hildesheim, 1979: 82–3; Winkler 1983: esp. 90–107.

2 Henderson (in Braund 1989: 116–18), his text bristling with question-marks, raises a number of possibilities (e.g. 'ventriloquising a "Woman"'; 'Does it take a woman to know a woman . . .? . . . Or is Laronia the Satirist-in-drag . . .?') but (as often) leaves the reader to decide.

3 The modern terms 'effeminate' and particularly 'homosexual' are at best misleading when applied to Roman antiquity. As Konstan 1993: 12 helpfully writes:

the relevant distinction is not between those who are attracted to people of the opposite sex and those who are attracted to their own, but between those who assume the dominant role in a sexual relationship and those who assume the submissive role

and 'dominance is associated with conventionally masculine characteristics, while submissiveness is associated with effeminacy', referring to Gleason 1990. For a full discussion see Richlin 1993: 523–73.

4   Cf. Martial 1.24 where a man's unkempt hair, gloomy scowl (*incomptis . . . capillis, triste supercilium*) and talk of Curii and Camilli belie his passive homosexuality: *nolito fronti credere: nupsit heri*, 'don't trust his appearance: yesterday he was a bride'.

5   I call the character whose voice we hear 'the speaker', to distinguish him from his creator, the poet Juvenal. On *persona* (or 'speaker') theory, see Anderson 1982: 3–10. The speaker of *Satire* 1 is a character at once repelled and fascinated by the lurid and seamy side of life. On the one-sidedness and exaggeration of the portrayal of life in Rome in Juvenal Book I see e.g. Braund, 'City and Country in Roman Satire', in Braund 1989: 23–47.

6   The speaker's oxymora: *qui Curios simulant et Bacchanalia uiuunt*, 'those who pretend to be Curii and live like Bacchanals', 3; *quis enim non uicus abundat / tristibus obscenis?*, 'for which street is not full of grim perverts?', 8–9; *Socraticos . . . cinaedos*, 'Socratic pathics', 10; *de uirtute locuti / clunem agitant*, 'while talking about virtue heave their buttocks', 20–1.

7   On the language characteristic of anger see Anderson 1982: 278–9: words of 'enduring' (*ferre; pati; tolerare*) are of prime importance.

8   On 'out-groups' see Richlin 1984: 67.

9   Laronia as prostitute: P. Green, *Juvenal: The Sixteen Satires*, Harmondsworth, 1967: 76: 'a courtesan'; G. Highet, *Juvenal the Satirist*, Oxford, 1954: 61: 'a hearty whore'; M. Coffey, *Roman Satire*, London, 1976: 125: 'representative of the class of prostitutes'; Winkler 1983: 96: 'the *meretrix* Laronia'.

10   R.A. LaFleur's ingenious but unnecessary suggestion ('Catullus and Catulla in Juvenal', *Rev. Phil.* 48, 1974: 73 n.4) that her name is *Latronia* may subscribe to the similar stereotype of woman as barking bitch (like Hecuba?); Laronia is notably *not* 'barking'.

11   Martial writing under Domitian speaks of the 'rebirth' of the law enacted by Augustus (6.7; cf. Stat. *Silv.* 5.2.101–2) and a letter of Pliny shows the law's strictest provisions in force under Trajan (*Ep.* 6.31.4–6, c. AD 107). For discussion of the legislation and attitudes to adultery see Gardner 1986: 127–31; Treggiari 1991b: 277–98; Edwards 1993: 34–62: and Fantham 1991.

12   Cf. J. Ferguson, *A Prosopography to the Poems of Juvenal*, Brussels, 1987; 133 who describes Laronia's family as 'respectable enough'.

13   R.E. Colton's many articles detail links between Martial and Juvenal, but in Colton 1965: 68–71 he omits any mention of their shared Laronia. Syme 1984: 1140 has wise words on some of the names shared by Juvenal and Martial.

14   On invective against old women see Richlin 1983: 109–16; J. Henderson,

'Suck It and See (Horace *Epode* 8)', in M. Whitby, P. Hardie, and M. Whitby (eds) *Homo Viator*, Bristol, 1987: 105–18; E. Oliensis, 'Canidia, Canicula, and the Decorum of Horace's *Epodes*', *Arethusa* 24, 1991: 107–38; W. Fitzgerald, 'Power and Impotence in Horace's *Epodes*', *Ramus* 17, 1988: 176–91.

15 Her smile is a mark of anger controlled, recalling the memorable moment in the *Aeneid* when Jupiter *olli subridens hominum rerumque repertor* (12.829) urges Juno to put an end to her anger (830–2, e.g. *inceptum frustra submitte furorem*); Jupiter's words disguise his own anger, rather like Mezentius at 10.742 *ad quae subridens mixta Mezentius ira*. On the manifestations of irony in Laronia's speech see Braund 1988: 10–11. I do not wish to assert that irony is characteristic of women and *indignatio* of men, not least because Juvenal will adopt irony as his predominant mode in his later Satires (see Braund 1988). However, in the context of his early Satires, which present male voice(s) attacking a variety of victims, the association of ironic attack with a female voice is an effective artistic strategy which serves to highlight the uncontrolled anger of the male voice(s).

16 A 'third Cato', after the two paragons of Republican morality, Marcus Porcius Cato (234–149 BC), censor in 184 BC, and his great-grandson of the same name (95–46 BC), a Stoic who committed suicide. For a similar phrase used similarly ironically cf. Hor. *Sat.* 2.3.296 *Stertinius, sapientum octauus*.

17 The motif of 'Cato . . . fallen from heaven' reverses the ancient story of the departure of the virgin goddess in horror at the wickedness of humankind, satirically presented by Juvenal at 6.1–20. This *tertius . . . Cato* is, of course, not a true moralist (unlike his namesakes: see note 16) and hence is ultimately compelled to flee (line 64 below).

18 The *lex Scantinia de Venere nefanda*, enforced by Domitian (Suet. *Dom.* 8.3), apparently outlawed sodomy: see Fantham 1991: 285–7. On the relation of the *lex Iulia* and the *lex Scantinia* and the nature of the debate see J.D. Cloud, 'Satirists and the Law', in Braund 1989: 55; Edwards 1993: 71; and Richlin 1993: 554–5.

19 See Bradley 1991a: 6–8; Treggiari 1991b: 251–3.

20 For imagery of disease applied to homosexuality cf. Juv. 2.17, 9.49; Hor. *Od.* 1.37.10 with Nisbet and Hubbard; Manil. 5.155; Sen. *Ep.* 83.20; and J.C. Bramble, *Persius and the Programmatic Satire*, Cambridge, 1974: 150 n.3.

21 On the female role of the pathic see Richlin 1993: 523–40.

22 See Braund 1992.

23 The inverse of such criticisms also occurs: prescriptions of ideal female behaviour in the matter of self-adornment are found in, e.g. Xen. *Oecon.* 10; Pythagorean treatise = Lefkowitz and Fant 1992: no. 107; for some comparative material see also Fidelis Morgan, *A Misogynist's Source Book*, London, 1989: section entitled 'Looks'.

24 Earlier, the Elder Seneca delivers a similar judgement of contemporary youth at *Contr.* 1 pref. 8, discussed by Edwards 1993: 81–2, a topic taken up by the Younger Seneca at *N.Q.* 7.31.2.

25 Evidence for lesbianism at Rome is minimal: Hallett 1989.

26 Cf. Elder Seneca *Contr.* 1.2.23: 'the *controversia* about the man who caught his wife and another woman in bed and killed them both'.

27  For example, Martial's attacks on Bassa (1.90) and Philaenis (7.67, 70) as women who assume the active male role in sexual relations with women (Bassa) and with both boys and girls (Philaenis).

28  Sen. *Ep.* 95.21: *adeo peruersum commentae genus inpudicitiae uiros ineunt*, 'They devise the most impossible varieties of unchastity, and in the company of men play the part of men.'

29  The close correspondence (missed by Colton 1965) of details between Martial 7.67 and Juvenal *Satires* 2 and 6 suggests that Martial provided the inspiration here. For possible inspiration of Martial by Seneca see Hallett 1989: 216.

30  For the allegation that men engage in spinning see Courtney 1980: *ad* 2.54; cf. Cic. *De orat.* 2.277 for a Roman example.

31  See Gardner 1986: 165–9.

32  See Braund 1992. The closest equivalent would seem to be the stories typical of 'Milesian tales' such as those in Apuleius' *Metamorphoses*.

33  Hence there is no difficulty in the apparent contradiction pointed out by commentators between 2.51–2, where Laronia suggests that no women engage in litigation, and 6.242–5, where female lawyers are added to the catalogue of outrageous women. Courtney 1980: 33 unnecessarily attempts to reconcile the two passages in his conclusion that women *could* plead in the courts, but did so rarely. The differing views in *Satires* 2 and 6 are offered by two very different speakers and in differing contexts for different purposes: it is Laronia's role to defend women; it is the role of the misogynist *persona*, created by Juvenal, to deliver the invective of *Satire* 6, to make every possible allegation against women (see Braund 1992). Neither passage can, or should, be treated as offering reliable evidence about Roman life; rather, these passages indicate the extremes of the ideological spectrum. Thus, the interpretation of *Satire* 2 offered here rebuts the reading of *Satire* 6 as the expression of Juvenal's own misogyny, as e.g. by G. Highet (*Juvenal the Satirist*, Oxford, 1954: 103).

34  On Laronia's reasonableness, see Winkler 1983: 99.

35  For example, Syme 1984: 1365: 'the harangue in which a woman called Laronia denounces hypocrisy and vice in Stoic philosophers'; Winkler 1983: 96: 'Laronia continues the satirist's tirade against the effeminates.'

36  *Cano* is an elevated word which likens Laronia to a prophetess, cf. Hor. *Carm. Saec.* 25; Virg. *Aen.* 6.98–100, 8.49.

37  On the 'otherness' of women: Simone de Beauvoir, *The Second Sex* (including the title); J.P. Hallett, 'Women as *Same* and *Other* in Classical Roman Elite', *Helios* 16, 1989: 59–78; A. Richlin, 'Zeus and Metis: Foucault, Feminism, Classics', *Helios* 18, 1991: 160–80.

38  Cf. Elder and Younger Senecas in note 24, where criticism of effeminates is couched in terms of their assimilation to women. On *mollitia* see Edwards 1993: 63–97.

39  See Edwards 1993: 78–81, e.g. n.68, on the assimilation of the non-man, the eunuch, to the female. Cf. Claudian's presentation of eunuchs as a kind of 'third sex', *alter ... sexus* (*In Eutr.* 2.223–4, also 1.467), a categorisation accommodated by the 'sliding scale' of gender proposed by Gleason 1990: 390–1; see also her discussion of the *androgynos/cinaedus*, 396–9. Juvenal's second *Satire* utilises many of the strategies of attack

upon effeminate/pathic males found in earlier classical literature, e.g. the condemnation through cross-dressing, found most memorably in Aristophanes' *Thesmophoriazusae*: in such texts accusations are turned back upon 'men' who are represented as a third sex (= inadequate males). For abuse of pathics in Aristophanes see J. Henderson, *The Maculate Muse*, 2nd edn, New York, 1991: 209–13; and for effeminacy manifested as transvestism ibid. 219–20.

40 By analogy with *Ecriture feminin*. On the value of this phrase for its neat elision of the nature/nurture distinction present in the two equivalent English terms 'female' and 'feminine': see Toril Moi, *Sexual/Textual Politics*, London, 1985: 97, also 108–26.

41 On the essentially (?) male nature of (Roman) satire, see Richlin 1983. On the transgressive paradox of the Roman *woman* satirist Sulpicia see H. Parker, 'Other Remarks on the Other Sulpicia', and A. Richlin, 'Sulpicia the Satirist', *CW* 86, 1992: 89–98 and 125–40 respectively.

42 My thanks are due to the responsive audience at the 'Women in Antiquity' conference held in Oxford in September 1993 for a number of astute observations and provoking questions and to David Braund for streamlining my thoughts and expressions.

# Chapter 14

# Aemilia Pudentilla: or the wealthy widow's choice

*Elaine Fantham*

I suspect that most modern readers at least begin with a false picture of society in Roman North Africa, one both less urban and less wealthy than the attested realities of Africa Proconsularis and Tripolitania from the first to the third centuries of our era.

In fact the fertile maritime regions had come early under Roman control, after the fall of Carthage in the mid-second century BC, and received many settlements of Roman veterans in the following centuries. If we consider the Roman families who descended from these veterans, the local magistrates and their citizen descendants, and the influential commercial residents who formed the *conventus* or core of the metropolitan Roman and Italian elite, the Africa of the early and middle empire was at least as Romanized as southern Gaul or Mediterranean Spain, its nearest neighbour.[1]

This high level of civilization and wealth is confirmed by the inscriptions of Proconsular Africa and Byzacena (northern and southern Tunisia) and of Tripolitania with its cities of Leptis, Oea (Tripoli) and Sabratha, communities that sprouted *fora*, public buildings and theatres even before the patronage of the African Emperor Severus and his dynasty. My concern is with the women of the most privileged families in these communities in the second century of our era: unfortunately outside the single literary text that is my primary source, the texts or inscriptions that mention such women do so chiefly in connection with male provincial or municipal leaders; even when named they are essentially identified through their kinsmen. Indeed the fullest recent prosopography of elite women in the imperial period can offer virtually no information beyond the offices held by their fathers, brothers, husbands and sons.[2] The record probably represents the reality of power: the wife or daughter of a senator, *vir clarissimus*, was by this period herself a *femina clarissima* but inevitably limited in what she could achieve outside the influence she wielded with and through her husband and family.

However the inscriptions of Africa do add some personal details: inscriptions can illustrate not only the virtues for which women were praised but the ways in which they enjoyed public status. These are essentially two – by priestly office or by benefaction – and occur in three types of inscription: sepulchral, dedicatory and honorific, on tomb, altar or statue-base. Funeral inscriptions attest women's tenure of priesthoods – either the priesthood of the woman's cult of the Ceres goddesses[3] (plural in post-Carthaginian Africa) or the Flaminicate of the imperial cult, which would usually be held by the wife or widow of the Flamen, a prominent man, often the head of the community's leading family.[4]

Thus in a typical elite family, the Flavii of the Vespasianic colony of Thelepte, the funeral monuments of their mausoleum (*CIL* VIII, 211–216[5]) show that the veteran soldier T. Flavius Secundus, one of the founding colonists, had a son of the same name, who became Flamen of the imperial cult for life, and erected the mausoleum for his parents and family. Two women of the family held the position of Flaminica: the son's first wife Aemilia Pacata, Flaminica for life, who died at sixty, and another family member, Flavia T. filia Pacata, who died at the age of fifteen. A later inscription on the right wall of this mausoleum shows that T. Flavius Receptus, perhaps the veteran's grandson, was Aedile or mayor of Thelepte before he died aged thirty-six.[6]

Family and well placed munificence earned women these priest-hoods. The base of a statue erected by the citizens of Thugga to Asicia Victoria records that she bought the office of Flaminica for her daughter Ulbia Asiciane with a gift of 100,000 sesterces, from which to finance stage games and hampers for the town councillors.[7] The principle of exchanging money for status is confirmed by another pair of inscriptions *CIL* VIII, 12317 shows that Modia Quinta of Turca, herself daughter of the Flamen Q. Modius Felix, paid an unre-coverable amount of sesterces in return for her flaminical office; other inscriptions from the same town (12353, 12354) show that her brother P. Modius Primus and his widow, Gallia Optata, received honorific statues for his benefaction in financing a new market building and her generosity in completing it after his death.

In rarer cases benefactors' wives and daughters were actually named by their communities as *patronae*.[8] More instances are known from Africa than from any other province, but all eleven African *patronae* are wives or daughters either of local men who had reached the Roman senate, or of proconsular governors of the province, from whatever origin. This paper now moves from epigraphic evidence for the lives and status of these elite women to a single woman, the earliest individual north African woman whose life we can recover in any detail.

About fifty years before Septimus Severus became emperor, before the Christian Tertullian wrote on the proper behaviour of women,[9] and the educated and well-born Christian wife Vibia Perpetua was imprisoned and martyred in the arena at Carthage in 202,[10] the wealthy widow Aemilia Pudentilla of Oea suffered a different kind of humiliation – from the scandal and accusations raised by her sons over her second marriage to Apuleius of Madaura, the future author of the *Golden Ass*. Her story would never have been known if Apuleius had not already been famous as an orator, philosopher and polymath, or if he had not been accused of practising magic, for our only source for Pudentilla's tale, Apuleius' *Apology*, is the *post eventum* version of his defence against the charge of using magical arts to seduce Pudentilla into marriage.

In a defence speech one naturally assumes manipulation of the facts, and we shall see that while Apuleius' defence depends on asserting Pudentilla's independence, he may falsify her situation in other respects. Just as it helped his case to maximize her autonomy and sound judgement, so it was crucial to minimize the socio-economic gap between their positions.[11]

We learn that Aemilia Pudentilla came from a wealthy family, whose property Apuleius gives as 4 million sesterces: when she married Sicinius Amicus, her dowry was commensurately large – 300,000 sesterces. Amicus died young, leaving her with two sons: at his death the elder, Pontianus, was about eight or nine, the younger, Pudens, three or four years old. No doubt Amicus' family was also fairly well off, but it is understandable that Pudentilla's father-in-law would want to keep the widow's wealth within his family, and to protect his grandsons' financial future. According to Apuleius, old Sicinius repeatedly urged her to marry another of his sons, Sicinius Clarus, but although she signed a betrothal contract she managed to prevaricate until the death of the old man. As head of his own descent family old Sicinius would have had no legal control over Pudentilla, since she would be married without *manus*. It would seem that widows at this period enjoyed considerable de facto independence, and could even function as guardians for their children, although they had no status in law.[12] Yet Roman families tended to keep male descendants under their control; though Pudentilla had the wealth to live independently, she may have stayed in the household of the Sicinii, at least while her sons were minors. This would certainly reinforce their pressure to prevent her remarriage outside the family or impose marriage within it; it is possible too that there was a local custom of widows marrying their husband's next of kin, like that which married Ruth to Boaz,[13] since we hear of the same pressures being applied to Pudentilla's younger son.[14] If Pudentilla did not feel free to marry whom she chose, custom or emotional blackmail could be a stronger factor than any legal issue.[15]

Fourteen years into her widowhood Pudentilla was freed by the old man's death, and indicated to her now adult son Pontianus, currently studying at Rome, that she would like to remarry, since he would soon be married and his brother would soon put on the toga of manhood. Again we see the sons' interests taking precedence. Pontianus, we are told, hurried back from Rome, afraid that some future husband might steal his inheritance (*Apol.* 69–71). It was at this time that the mature Apuleius visited his young student friend Pontianus on his way to Alexandria, fell ill and had to stay at Oea for some months. According to Apuleius, Pontianus himself urged him to move into his family home – where Apuleius lived for a year – and encouraged him to propose marriage to Pudentilla (*Apol.* 73). Since Pontianus was dead by the time of the trial we have only Apuleius' word for his attitude. It is somewhat difficult to reconcile with later events.

Within a year of introducing Apuleius into his home, Pontianus had married the daughter of Herennius Rufinus, had changed his mind about his mother marrying Apuleius, had quarrelled with and been reconciled to Apuleius (*Apol.* 94), had gone to Carthage to train as an orator, and died (96). With him perished not only a key witness, but the one man whose support of Apuleius could have forestalled the prosecution – and whose hostility would have damned him. After Pontianus' death his brother, Sicinius Pudens, now of age, was taken up by Herennius Rufinus, with whom he went to live, and looked likely to marry Pontianus' widow. Meanwhile Apuleius had married Pudentilla quietly at one of her country estates, ostensibly to avoid the expense of a more public occasion,[16] and became the subject, first of scandal, then of legal charges spread by Pontianus' father-in-law Herennius in association with young Sicinius Pudens and his uncle Sicinius Aemilianus.

Obviously the Sicinii would be alarmed at this marriage of the wealthy widow to a stranger, and it is hardly surprising that they used whatever means they could find to eliminate the interloper.

What I hope to do in the remaining pages is to enhance and correct Apuleius' picture of Pudentilla's rank and circumstances as a widow, to highlight prejudices about widows and other older women that emerge from Apuleius' self-justification, and to examine the situation from the widow Pudentilla's point of view.

First a word about Pudentilla's class and standing. We know that she was immensely wealthy and can surmise that her natal and marital families headed the local elite. Among the sparse epigraphical evidence from Oea in *Inscriptions of Roman Tripolitania*[17] three inscriptions honour Aemilii who may have come from her side. *IRT* 230, in particular, from the entablature of the temple of the *genius* of the colony of Oea, reports the benefaction of a younger kinsman, L. Aemilius Frontinus, consul and proconsul of Asia a generation later. Another inscription attests a senator from her husband's family, L. Sicinius Pontianus, perhaps the son of the young Sicinius Pudens. Pudentilla can be compared with the benefactresses discussed on p. 221 in the lavishness of her public gifts of 50,000 sesterces on the occasion of Pontianus' marriage and Pudens' coming of age (*Apol.* 88).

It is not in Apuleius' interest to overstress the importance of Pudentilla's own family, but her inheritance of 4 million sesterces in her own right (as well as the unspecified share of her husband's wealth that would go to her sons) would make her by far the most important woman of the community. Pudentilla's income is derived largely from her many estates, with revenues in corn, oil, wine and stockbreeding of horses and cattle, plus additional revenue from money placed at interest. In turn the size of her household and estates can be measured by the gift she was able to make to her sons of 400 slaves (*Apol.* 93). She can fairly be compared with the Domina seen in the luxurious fourth-century AD Dominus Julius mosaic from Carthage receiving homage and first fruits from loyal tenants, and in another vignette reclining at ease in her garden enclosure.[18]

Yet even Pontianus' supposedly disreputable father-in-law had inherited by Apuleius' admission 3 million sesterces (*Apol.* 75) – a fortune comparable with that of Pudentilla – and provided a dowry, as we later learn (92), of 400,000 sesterces. At over an eighth of his property this is indeed generous, and so Apuleius initially (76) suppresses the amount, alleging instead that it was money borrowed on the expectation of Pudentilla's death.

How does the outsider Apuleius compare? Apuleius first defends his financial standing by the claim that he and his brother were left 2 million sesterces by their father, but that he had reduced his share by studies, travel and acts of generosity (*Apol.* 23). Then his social standing: he is not some half-Numidian, half-Gaetulian native, but the son of a Duumvir or joint mayor of the colony of Madaura (*Apol.* 24), who has himself served as a member of the Curia. However the speed with which Apuleius returns to attack Pudentilla's brother-in-law, the landholding Aemilianus, strongly suggests that unlike these settled landowners Apuleius has reduced his million sesterces considerably and can point to no property held in his own name. He does not, and presumably cannot, cite the sources of his present income. However fluent his public lectures, he may well have looked like a fortune hunter once he addressed himself to Pudentilla.

Pudentilla deserves our sympathy on other counts. The prosecution had challenged Apuleius to explain (*Apol.* 67) why this free woman married him after fourteen years of widowhood and why, being a much older woman, she accepted a young man? We know his answer to the first question. Next he considers her age and widowhood. The accusers have said she was sixty – most unlikely, given the age of her children. Appealing to public and private records (*Apol.* 89) Apuleius argues that she is 'in *not much more* than her fortieth year of life' (emphasis added).[19] This seems to be confirmed by the clause in the marriage contract that allowed for redistribution of her dowry to any child she might have by him.[20] Up to what age would we accept that diagnosis or this expectation? Hardly more than forty-five, I suspect. In fact Apuleius has already suggested Pudentilla's relative youth by his tales of the physical illness induced by sexual abstinence (*Apol.* 69) that drove her to announce her intention of remarriage.

Whatever his original hopes, in court Apuleius is able to show documentation that he has accepted as dowry a mere 300,000 sesterces and ensured that this will pass on to Pudentilla's sons. At his urging she has also made them immediate gifts of substantial parts of her estate and 400 slaves from her slaveholdings (*Apol.* 93). But he precedes this financial accounting by a prejudicial account of his generosity in considering marriage to a widow with such a modest dowry.

Here we meet the standard negative arguments against marriage to older women, whether widowed or divorced. Such wives lack the chief dowry, that of virginity; they are difficult to control (*minime docilis*) and contemptuous of their new household. If they are widowed they should be suspect for not having kept their husband alive; if divorced they lose both ways: either the woman was so unbearable that she was divorced, or so arrogant that she initiated the divorce. That these prejudices were generally held has recently been argued by Peter Walcot.[21] To stress these notions rather than Pudentilla's many virtues of character (briefly mentioned along with her *mediocris facies* at *Apol.* 73) is certainly more in his interest than hers.

Pudentilla cannot, of course, be her own witness. For all her wealth and her capacity, as we hear it, to keep the accounts and run the affairs of her stock farms, she still has to have a tutor, Cassius Longinus, for legal purposes, and has used Apuleius himself as her advocate in a lawsuit against the Granii at Leptis.[22] Can we hope that at least she did not hear how she was treated in the case? According to Apuleius, one of his enemies' main charges was a letter written by Pudentilla *in Greek* to her son Pontianus begging him to come and save her while she was still in her senses because Apuleius was a magician and had bewitched her. Such claims if false could hardly have been made in her presence.

To us the correspondence cited in court carries additional interest for its evidence of levels of bilingualism and for the variety of languages in use in Roman North Africa.[23] Admittedly the Hellenism of Roman Africa may have been exaggerated in the past simply on the basis of Apuleius' extraordinary education, or Pontianus' library. But both Pudentilla's letter to her son and the letter she allegedly received from Apuleius are in Greek, whereas Aemilianus' letter to Pontianus (*Apol.* 70) is in Latin. Apuleius derides the Latin-speaking Aemilianus as a rustic, and insults the younger son, Sicinius Pudens, claiming he barely speaks even Latin, 'only Punic and whatever bits of Greek he can still remember from his mother's teaching'.[24] Pudentilla's literacy and bilingualism alike confirm her elite standing.

## THE WIDOW'S CHOICE

We return now to Pudentilla's letter, and her real attitude to the man we know her to have married. Was she infatuated or did she know what she was doing when she accepted the hand of Apuleius in marriage, and, if she freely chose him, why did she do so? By quoting at length from Pudentilla's letter Apuleius is able to show that the

very words cited to demonstrate her admission of folly and witchcraft
are in fact an allegation of her enemies that she is repudiating: this
is his supplemented if not emended text:

> Pontianus, when I wanted to marry for the reasons I mentioned,
> you yourself urged me to take this man before all others, out of
> your admiration for him and eagerness to bind him to you through
> the link with me. But now *as our illnatured accusers want to persuade
> you*, Apuleius has suddenly become a wizard and I am bewitched
> by him and in love. Come then to me while I am still sane. I tell
> you that I am neither bewitched nor in love. But fate . . . etc.
>
> (*Apol.* 82, 3–4; emphasis added)

Were these her own words? It is not beyond our very clever advocate to have concocted this version of Pudentilla's letter, with or
without her cooperation, to invalidate the document displayed by his
enemies.[25] The handwriting would not be questioned, since well-born
men and women like Pudentilla used slave secretaries to write letters
they dictated.[26] But this was hardly a letter to entrust to a scribe;
thus let us assume the letter, or the sentiments it attributes to
Pudentilla, are genuine.

What Apuleius has given us is a picture of a very self-possessed
and shrewd woman – as she must have been to protect herself from
all the men attracted by her fortune. Like other elite women of North
Africa, whether Vibia Perpetua or the Empress Julia Domna or
Monica the mother of Augustine, the Pudentilla we meet in the text
shows both strength of character and independence of judgement.[27]
She was certainly in her right mind. She may well have taken Apuleius
with her eyes fully open to his self-interest, but aware too of his attrac-
tions of youth, wit and person, and the fact that her outsider husband
would remain dependent upon her in ways that she could not have
expected from a local magnate. It is often wiser for a pre-eminent
woman to take an outsider as her consort, and social history from
comparable societies such as medieval England and Europe affords
parallels for this situation of 'the widow's choice'.[28]

Let me quote from a sample of treatments and circumstances. In
the chapter 'The Widow and Her Lands' of *The English Noblewoman*,
Ward describes the inconvenience to families when rich widows
continued to outlive their husbands in the enjoyment not only of their
own estate but of the lands and property in their dower and join-
ture: it was presumably in part for their protection that noble widows
had to have royal permission to remarry, but protection from whom?

Ward notes that they were put under pressure to remarry 'from families, friends, prospective husbands and the Crown'.[29] In fact their freedom of choice over a second husband was the subject of more than one clause of the Magna Carta.[30]

In most respects the position and estates of these ladies might be compared to Pudentilla's. Ward concludes that although many of these noble widows remarried, older ones might remain unmarried because they enjoyed the independence which widowhood gave to them: 'although they were not completely free of outside pressures . . . they had more say in making decisions affecting their own lives, households and estates than they had as wives' (Ward 1992: 48).

Archer, more concerned with the damage that widows could do by their extravagance to the rights of succession of their husband's families, opens her paper, 'Rich Old Ladies', with an excerpt from a satirical report by an Italian visitor to the court of Henry VII:

> no Englishman can. . .find fault with his mother for marrying again during his childhood, because from very ancient custom this license has become so sanctioned that *it is not considered any discredit to marry again every time that she is left a widow, however unsuitable the match may be as to age, rank and fortune.* (emphasis added.)[31]

Matters may have changed by the fifteenth century and morality would probably be freer in court circles, but what widow would not take the opportunity, if she might, of marrying for her own pleasure the sort of 'unsuitable' younger man of whom her in-laws would disapprove, if not a former household servant, at least a man whose lower social standing would make him subservient to her?[32] Since Apuleius clearly had a good opinion of himself, Pudentilla may have married him more for his youthful appeal than out of any expectation of controlling him; but he probably needed her financial support.

Let me bring in the last factor; the effect of a mother's remarriage on the interest of young children, especially sons. We have seen that the Italian diplomat thought in terms of a son's approval or disapproval of his mother's behaviour, and Ward (1992: 43) notes that the King of England might on occasions authorize a mother to serve as guardian of her sons. Hanawalt speaks in terms of 'children whose property a new husband might hope to manage until the child reached the age of twenty-one'.[33] A whole chapter of Humbert's *Le remarriage à Rome* deals with the separation of the wife's property from that of her next husband in the interest of her children by the first marriage.[34] Such fears explain both the interference of

Pudentilla's father-in-law with her free choice of a second marriage, and the age at which Pontianus began to encourage his mother to remarry.

A good parallel for Pudentilla from a more urban culture is the fifteenth-century Alessandra Macinghi Strozzi, the widow of a wealthy Florentine banker with three young sons.[35] The evidence of her letters suggests many ways in which she resembles our portrait of Pudentilla. These start when she is forty, and has been a widow some years. She is from a wealthy family, and has married into one, and she is a good businesswoman trained in reading, writing and accounting. Like Pudentilla, Strozzi had to manage her own lands and 'was involved in legal contracts for which she needed a male facilitator, but this could be a formality'.[36] Demographically the pattern of Florentine widowhood resembled the Roman one, in that women were on average married to men twelve years older than themselves, but differed in the likelihood of remarriage.[37] Strozzi lived at different times with many households of her husband's family, but she also lived some years as head of her own household and as she remained a widow, acted as guardian of her sons in their minority.

Later Alessandra Strozzi's sons went away on business, as Pontianus did to Rome and Carthage for his education. But whereas Alessandra's letters show that she looked forward to returning to live with her sons once they should marry, Pudentilla chose the other path, and now felt free to find herself a marriage. If Pontianus really did introduce his old friend Apuleius to his mother with this intention, he may have wished to keep her from joining his own new marital household, but he must also have felt no fear that he would lose financially from her remarriage. His new wife and father-in-law thought otherwise, and so, we are to believe, Pudentilla was once again subject to the interference of *adfines*, but now it was her son's *adfines* who saw her and her marriage as obstacles to their own enrichment.

Although Apuleius' portrait of Pudentilla's circumstances cannot be entirely trusted, it must have been plausible enough to convince the local community. Even as he emphasizes his own merits and generosity in settling to marry an older and relatively plain woman, we can see through his pleading why Pudentilla in turn may have seen through her fine young husband, and still expect a more free and pleasant life in his company. One is reminded of the young, dashing and ambitious Disraeli and his wealthy widow

Mary Ann.[38] And one can only hope Pudentilla lived as comfortably with her famous and self-confident Lucius as Mary Ann with her Disraeli.

## NOTES

1  On the civilization of Roman North Africa in the first two centuries of our era consult P. Garnsey 'Rome's African Empire under the Principate', in P. Garnsey and C.R. Whittaker (eds.) *Imperialism in the Ancient World*, Cambridge 1978: 223–254; Susan Raven, *Rome in Africa*, rev. edn, London 1993; and the introduction of A.R. Birley, *Septimius Severus: The African Emperor*, London 1975, which also has a chapter specifically on the trial of Apuleius.

2  See M.-T. Rapsaet–Charlier, *Prosopographie des femmes de l'ordre senatorial (I<sup>er</sup>–II<sup>e</sup> s.)*, Louvain 1987, reviewed by R.J.A. Talbert in *American Journal of Philology* 111, 1990: 123–127.

3  For example, *CIL* VIII, 579, the tomb of Fortunata, Priestess of the Cereres (Ceres Goddesses), 11306 Numisa, priestess of the Cereres, 1623 an altar dedicated by Valeria Saturnina, the senior priestess and lifetime priestess of the Cereres: or 591, a *cippus* from Hr Djenim with a relief of a woman sacrificing: the inscription shows that it was erected 'To Helvia Severa, most chaste priestess: she lived 85 years with wise judgement; she reached a deserved old age and an exemplary death. *Here is honour for piety; gratitude persists for the past service.*' The final phrases, both drawn from the African books of the *Aeneid* (1.253, 4.539) reflect local education.

4  Compare the funeral inscriptions of *CIL* VIII, 211–213 and two honorific inscriptions on bases of statues erected to benefactresses: VIII, 1495 and VIII, 12317 cited and discussed on p. 221.

5  All inscriptions cited are my own translation from *CIL* VIII, North Africa.

6  *CIL* VIII, 216 gives his career in the usual reverse order as 'T. Flavius Receptus of the tribe Papiria, ex-Aedile, secretary of the treasury and councillor of the colony of Thelepte.'

7  *CIL* VIII, 1495: *Asiciae Victoriae/C Thuggenses ob muni/ficentiam et singula/rem liberalitatem eius/in rem p. quae ob flamonium/ulbiae Asicianes fil. suae HS C/mil. N pollicita est quorum red/itu ludi scaenici et sportulae/decurionibus darentur d.d./utriusque ordinis posuerunt.*

8  See J. Nicols, '*Patrona Civitatis*: Gender and Civic Patronage', in *Studies in Latin Literature and History Presented to Charles Deroux*, vol. 5, Brussels 1983: 117–142.

9  Besides books advocating male chastity and commending monogamy, Tertullian wrote two books 'To His Wife', two on women's dress, one on the veiling of virgins, and an influential book on female chastity (*De Pudicitia*).

10  See now Brent Shaw, 'The Passion of Perpetua', *Past and Present* 139, 1993: 3–45.

11  A good, if brief, socio-economic assessment is offered by Pavis d'Escurac 1974.

12  On the position of propertied widows in general see Treggiari 1991b: 500–503. Clark 1993: 59 (following I. Thomas, 'La division des sexes en droit Romain', in C. Duby and M. Perrot (eds), *Histoire des femmes en Occident*, Paris 1990) points to widows (and divorcees) left in control of their children from the late Republic but dates their effective control of the property which their children would inherit 'from the late second century [AD]'. But if Pudentilla had effective control of her own dowry and estate, it is not so clear that she would have controlled that of her husband so long as his father lived.

13  In the book of Ruth, Ruth, the Moabite widow of Naomi's son insists on following her mother-in-law to Judah, although Naomi declares *she has no other sons to marry Ruth* and is too old to conceive new ones. Later Naomi's kinsman Boaz tells Ruth that if a nearer (and younger) kinsman of her late husband is not willing to take responsibility for her, he will do so. When the young kinsman declines on grounds of poverty, Boaz publicly declares that he has made Ruth his wife; Like *epikleros*-marriages in Greece, these marriages may have imposed a duty to protect poor single women but offered a privilege where there was wealth.

14  As alleged in *Apologia* 97: the dead Pontianus' father-in-law Rufinus pressured his younger brother to marry Pontianus' widow 'thrusting into the face and bed of the poor boy a woman quite a bit older and his brother's widow'.

15  On Pudentilla's delayed remarriage see Treggiari 1991b: 499 and n. 116; on the remarriage of widows/widowers at Rome in general, see Humbert 1972; and Treggiari 1991b: ch. 14, esp. 499–502.

16  *Apol.* 88, on which see Treggiari 1991a: 166, 169–170.

17  Cf. J. Guey 'L'apologie d'Apulée et les inscriptions romaines de Tripolitanie', *Revue des études Latines* 32, 1954: 115–120.

18  On the Dominus Julius mosaic see K. Dunbabin, *Roman Mosaics from Tunisia*, Oxford 1983: 119–120, pl. 109; A. Merlin, 'Le mosaique du Seigneur Julius', *Bulletin archéologique* 1921, 95–114; W. Raeck, '*Publica non despiciens*: Ergänzungen zur Interpretation des Dominus Julius Mosaik aus Karthago', *Römische Mitteilungen* 94, 1987: 295f.

19  The vague *haud multo amplius* is surely suspicious. How many years have been subtracted?

20  *Apol.* 91; cf. Treggiari 1991a: 393, citing parallel evidence from *Digest* 32, 37, 4 and 31, 67, 10.

21  Walcot 1991. Compare also Bremmer 1994.

22  *Apol.* 87 (accounts), 101 (Cassius Longinus), and 1 (suit against Granii).

23  See F. Millar, 'Local Cultures in the Roman Empire: Libyan, Punic and Latin in Roman Africa', *Journal of Roman Studies* 58, 1968: 126–134.

24  *Loquitur numquam nisi punice et si quid adhuc a matre graecissat: enim Latine neque vult neque potest* (*Apol.* 98, cited by Millar, 'Local Cultures': 130).

25  Can we really believe either that Rufinus carried round only a copy of these words, or showed only these few phrases of the letter on the writing tablets he was carrying round? This is the claim of *Apol.* 82.

26  Compare the surviving letter dictated by the Roman officer's wife Sulpicia Lepidina described in A. Bowman and J.D. Thomas, 'New Texts from Vindolanda', *Britannia* 18, 1987: 125–142.

27  Cf. Treggiari 1991b: 136.
28  Compare B. Hanawalt, 'The Window's Mite', and A. Moston Crabb, 'How Typical was Alessandro Macinghi Strozzi' in Mirrer 1992; Archer, 'Rich Old Ladies', in Pollard 1984; and Ward 1992.
29  Ward 1992: 42. Compare Hanawalt, 'The Widow's Mite': 35–36.
30  J. Loengard 'English Dower in the Year 1200', in Kirschner and Wemple 1985: 235–236 cites Magna Carta 7: 'a widow after the death of her husband shall at once and without difficulty have her marriage portion and inheritance, nor shall she give anything for her dower, nor for her marriage portion nor for her inheritance'. Chapter 8 provided that a widow should not be compelled to remarry so long as she preferred to remain without a husband, but give security not to marry without the consent of the king if she was a widow of a tenant-in-chief or of her immediate lord otherwise.
31  Archer, 'Rich Old Ladies', citing *A Relation or Rather a True Account of the Island of England*, ed. C.A. Sneyd, Camden Society XXVII, London, 1847: 26–27.
32  Cf. Archer, 'Rich Old Ladies': 27–28, citing Joan of Acre, Elizabeth Fitzalan and others.
33  In Mirrer 1992: 36.
34  Humbert 1972: 197f. Neglect of children in a mother's will is a standard ground for the *querela inofficiosi testamenti*.
35  See Crabb 'How typical': 47–68.
36  Crabb, 'How Typical': 51.
37  Crabb, 'How Typical': 49 notes that 'two thirds of women widowed in their twenties [like Pudentilla?] never remarried, and nine tenths of those widowed at thirty or older, ... good mothers were discouraged from remarrying for their children's sake'.
38  Our rosy picture of Disraeli's marriage (cf. A. Maurois, Disraeli, Paris 1927: 125–138; R. Blake, *Disraeli*, London and New York 1967: 150–161) stems from the words of Mary Ann Disraeli herself: although he had money troubles which he tried to conceal from her, Disraeli did not disappoint Mary Ann, and was essentially a kind and considerate husband.

# Chapter 16

# Female sanctity in the Greek calendar: the *Synaxarion* of Constantinople

*Anna Wilson*

Women saints, holy women – mystics and pious ascetics spring first to mind: in the West, St Frideswide, St Theresa or even Augustine's Monica; in the East the nun Macrina, the women pilgrims and settlers of the Holy Land, perhaps Chrysostom's friend the deaconess Olympias. All women of whose lives we know a good deal. Yet this approach is unsystematic. Vaguely at the back of our minds are all those martyrs, St Catherine and her wheel, St Ursula and the 11,000 virgins, as Carpaccio painted them.

In the twentieth-century western world few celebrate saints on a daily basis. How then to assess female sanctity in cultures foreign to our own? How to avoid generalizing from a small and misleadingly famous sample? To digest all sixty-eight volumes of the Bollandist *Acta Sanctorum* might deserve canonization in its own right, yet is not a practicable proposition. A comprehensive yet manageable dossier is required. Nor are female saints a special case; the same problems apply to the still more numerous male saints.

Church festal calendars may offer the best solution. Among the most helpful is the tenth-century Byzantine *Synaxarion* of the Church of Constantinople.[1] This compilation contains brief précis of the Lives or Passions of about three-quarters of its entries. Apart from the Bible and apocrypha, its main sources are saints' Lives or Passions of mixed literary and historical merit, most dating originally from the fourth to sixth centuries. They are supplemented with material from encomia, from the church historians and the chroniclers of monasticism. Frequently the source can be dated by content, literary style and vocabulary, even when no longer extant. A few post-Iconoclastic saints have been added to those of earlier date and are usually identifiable by their sobriquet 'the New'.[2]

The *Synaxarion* is a literary gathering of saints comparable with the visual one on the walls of most Byzantine churches. In their serried ranks they march through the days of the Church's year, the major biblical characters and scenes, the prophets, patriarchs and apostles, the martyrs, the ascetics, the bishops, even the odd Imperial saint – and quite a few are women. Here is a body of information running into thousands of main entries, needing only a key or two to open its doors. Little is strictly historical; much is close to pure fiction, strained through half a dozen retellings with embellishments, as well as through the compiler's sieve. Yet it is highly informative about audience expectation, perception and taste, and about their manipulation across half a millenium.

I have tabulated data from the first two months of the ecclesiastical year, September and October.[3] Table 16.1 shows the numbers of male and female saints of different types whose names, individually or in groups, head their entries. To avoid distortion, anonymous groups of martyrs, whether of five or forty, are treated as single entries. Saints who qualify under more than one heading, such as martyred monastics, appear in both of the relevant columns, and duplicates of the same saint are included on the grounds that their impact is greater. Thus at least four women saints are counted twice. The group entitled 'Other' covers saints of unknown type (three women here), references to events in Christ's life and major religious phenomena such as ecumenical councils and earthquakes.

Women make up 22 per cent of the total, 25 per cent compared with the men, and martyrdom is the best route to sanctity for either sex. The biblical figures for the Old and New Testaments are predictable. In column 2, excluding brief Marian references to the celebrations of the Theotokos or her icon in this or that Constantinopolitan church, there are only five female entries, all drawing heavily on apocryphal material. One of these, St Thecla, also appears in both martyr and monastic columns. Her standing as female protomartyr and apostle is higher than that of most New Testament bishop martyrs; indeed she receives a whole day of the calendar to herself.[4] The female monastic entry, a third of those for men, is distorted in that six, including Thecla, are really there as martyrs.[5] Only five are purely monastic. The low figure accurately reflects the histories of monasticism, which include few women, sometimes confining them to a separate subsection.[6] In the male entries, the number of bishops is similarly inflated by the entries for martyrs. Women do comparatively well in the tiny Imperial category and the

Table 16.1 Main entries by gender and type for September and October

| | OT | NT & Apocr. | Martyr (ma.) | Monastic (mon.) | Bishop (bp) | Imperial | Other | Total |
|---|---|---|---|---|---|---|---|---|
| Female | – | 11 (6 Marian, 1 ma.) | 78 (6 mon.) | 11 (6 ma. 1 NT) | – | 3 (1 mon.) | – | 103 |
| Male | 11 | 23 (8 ma., 6 bp) | 296 (25 bp) | 33 (1 ma.) | 56 (6 NT, 25 ma.) | 4 | – | 423 |
| Other | – | – | – | – | – | – | 30 (3 fem.) | 30 |
| Total | 11 | 34 | 374 | 44 | 56 | 7 | 30 (3 fem.) | 556 |

Note:   In this table double-counting is used for saints who occur under several types, but multiple anonymous martyrdoms have been treated as single entries. Four cases of duplicate female saints are included.

figure is roughly right for the year as a whole. From Constantine's Helena on, charitable and pious empresses who spent their money on almshouses and churches and discovered holy relics got a good hagiographical press, and the process was self-perpetuating.

Excluding Table 16.1's double-counting and including its three unidentified women saints, there are 102 women's names and anonymous groups of women for the two-month period, a substantial figure. The picture is sharpened by examining the distribution of women between all-female and mixed-sex entries as shown in Tables 16.2 and 16.3. Table 16.2 gives eighty-one women in independent female entries. Less the anonymous groups and Marian entries, that figure drops to sixty-one, of whom only thirty-eight rate an individual entry. Again, a group of thirty-two anonymous women in the massive Armenian martyrdom celebrated on 30 September distorts the number of women in the mixed entries in Table 16.3. Only thirty-five women are named, and only eleven of these as part of a male-female pair. In group entries women usually come last. For example, in family martyrdoms the usual order is father, mother, sons, daughters.[7]

Tables 16.2 and 16.3 produce ninety-six women's names, including duplicates. Yet it is instructive that the twenty-eight individual women martyrs in Table 16.2 are half the number of bishops (who themselves divide roughly in half as to martyrs and non-martyrs) in Table 16.1. Thus female sanctity should not be exaggerated between the fifth and tenth centuries in eastern Christendom. Yet there is sufficient evidence to merit consideration. In line with male saints the main emphasis is on martyrdom.

The picture can be filled out a little by looking at the women who play subordinate roles in these short narratives and provide a backdrop to the women saints. These are summarized in Table 16.4. Some are anonymous: 'a certain woman/mother/daughter'. Brief references to empresses as wife or mother are found, but more usually they have an active role as patron of a saint,[8] or in Helena's case playing second fiddle to Constantine over the discovery of the relics of the True Cross in a lengthy entry.[9] Normally martyrdom guarantees a position at the head of the *Synaxarion* entry, not a subordinate reference, so female martyrs are few in this category. There is one example from an atypical summary which introduces extra male and female martyrs within its narrative[10] and an anonymous mother and daughter pair from a horrifying massacre in sixth-century Ethiopia.[11] The monastic four cover the leader, Sophia, and three

Table 16.2 Number of women heading all-female main entries

| | Indivi-duals | Pairs | Larger groups | Anonymous groups | Total |
|---|---|---|---|---|---|
| Imperial | 3 | – | – | – | 3 |
| Martyrs | 28 | 6 | 11 | 10 (2 sets of 5) | 55 |
| Monastic | 5 | – | – | – | 5 |
| NT & Apocr. | 7 (6 Marian) | 4 | – | 4 (1 set of 4) | 15 (6 Mar.) |
| Other | 1 | 2 | – | – | 3 |
| Totals | 44 (6 Marian) | 12 | 11 | 14 | 81 |

Note: No double-counting, although two individual duplicate references are included, one pair recurs as part of a mixed grouping in Table 16.3. Monastic martyrs are listed as martyrs here, but they comprise three individuals, one pair and both anonymous groups of five.

Table 16.3 Number of women jointly heading mixed entries

| | Pairs | Trios | Quartets | Larger groups | Anony-mous groups | Totals |
|---|---|---|---|---|---|---|
| Imperial | – | – | – | – | – | – |
| Martyrs | 11 (11 pairs) | 6 (4 grps) | 7 (5 grps) | 10 (3 grps) | 32 | 66 |
| Monastic | – | – | – | – | – | – |
| NT & Apocr. | 1 | – | – | – | – | 1 |
| Other | – | – | – | – | – | – |
| Totals | 12 | 6 | 7 | 10 | 32 | 67 |

Note: No double-counting, but see Table 16.2 above for a duplicate pair. Here also a pair of monastic martyrs occurs within one particular trio, to which the group of 32 anonymous women is also linked.

*Table 16.4*  Categories of women mentioned in subordinate roles in the summaries

| Type | Number | Additional information |
|------|--------|------------------------|
| Imperial | 6 | Includes 1 parent |
| Martyr | 3 | Includes 2 anonymous Ethiopian women |
| Monastic | 4 | 3 anonymous |
| OT | 2 | 1 wife, 1 prophet |
| NT & Apocrypha | 11 | 2 Marian references; all the rest drawing on apocryphal: material, and including 4 converts and 4 prophets |
| Convert | 8 | Includes several wives |
| Wife | 2 | – |
| Parent | 8 | Includes 1 adoptive mother, and 1 mother as part of a cross-reference to a different date |
| Villain | 6 | Includes 1 mother, stepmother and 1 nurse, as well as a noble lady who torments her saintly slave-girl |
| Other | 1 | Accompanies a tortured martyr driven from town to town and collects his blood as a relic |
| Total | 51 | |

*Note:*    The table is based on hierarchy of types and there is no double counting. To arrive at the full number of wives, for example, it is necessary to add those included under 'NT' and 'Convert'.

anonymous nuns of a community from within which St Anastasia's outspoken insults to the Roman establishment are said to have earned her martyrdom.[12] Biblical and apocryphal references are relatively frequent and emphasize conversion. Yet the four prophets come from a single entry on the four daughters of St Philip.[13] The whole category witnesses to the emphasis on men that we know from its source material. Converts are a significant group but most who are not also martyrs belong to the apocryphal tradition.

It is rare to find a woman named purely as wife. Wives are normally involved in the main entries for group martyrdoms or in group conversions, yet in two cases we know only of their marital status. Reference to women as parents, if less common than in full-scale saints' lives, has survived the excerpting process quite well. Seven subordinate characters are supplemented by a considerable number among the main martyr lists.

The category that I have titled 'villain' is varied, and female examples are rather more individual than their numerous male equivalents. The major classes of male villain tend to be persecuting emperors and governors, occasionally jealous betrayers. The women come from exemplary tales with a certain zest to their brief treatments of evil women, stereotypical as in some sense they may be. An Isaurian stepmother betrays her five stepchildren's Christianity to get at their patrimony.[14] She receives a male counterpart in a pagan son's betrayal of his Christian mother who later adopts a new son in prison and is satisfactorily martyred with him.[15] In a highly romanticized tale, St Pelagia of Tarsus is let down badly by her mother and her former nurse. After sneaking out to receive baptism, Pelagia is turned from her nurse's door and rejected by her mother on account of her humble baptismal garb – she has deposited her costly veil at the bishop's feet.[16] One feels a sneaking sympathy for this pair of horrified villains. Their plans to marry her off to Diocletian's son have fallen apart and neither actually intends matters to end in martyrdom. Under Julian the Apostate, the rioting group of pagan women who wield their spindles against the martyrs of Gaza are distinguishable from the men in the mob only by their choice of weapons.[17] The adultery of the wife of Paul the Simple, Antony of Egypt's disciple, conveniently frees him from family responsibility to pursue his chequered ascetic career.[18] Such stories provide what little information on social status is available from the *Synaxarion*. Finally the devoted Lycaonian lady who accompanied St Papas as he was driven from town to town and collected the blood pouring from his many wounds on a cloth defies categorization.[19] Her tale should be related to the cult of Papas' relics. It is a rare variant on the common topos of Christian devotees who collect martyrs' remains by night and may link with stories like that of St Deborah and the face-cloth.

Table 16.5 draws on both main and subordinate entries. Explicit evidence of social status is uncommon and usually relates to martyrs. The higher classes predominate, and would do so still more if some of the more atmospheric evidence from the narratives had been admitted to the database. The only two women of low class who are not slaves or prostitutes are wives of Egyptian monks – one of them Paul the Simple's lady.[20] However, servile origins interest the hagiographer and affect the narrative. The slave's role is always positive,

*Table 16.5*    Information on social status of women mentioned in the
           *Synaxarion*: approximate figures only

| Category | Number | Additional information |
|---|---|---|
| Imperial family | 8 | Mostly fourth-century or later eastern, but includes fictitious daughter of Trajan |
| Foreign royalty | 2 | 1 Armenian, 1 Persian |
| Roman race (explicitly) | 2 | This underestimates the number of martyrdoms set in Rome, but the inclusion of the phrase seems to indicate high birth |
| Senatorial | 5 | – |
| Well-born | 11 | – |
| Well-born and wealthy | 4 | 1 of these, on being widowed, falls into servile poverty |
| Wealthy | 3 | – |
| Military family | 2 | The wives of the NT centurion and of St Eustathios |
| Pagan priestly family | 1 | – |
| Medical family | 2 | 1 purports to be a doctor herself |
| Humble origins | 3 | Includes 2 wives of (subsequent) Egyptian anchorites. A rare motif for a female saint, where only elevated birth is regularly mentioned |
| Prostitute | 4 | 1 *hetaira*, 2 *pornai* and one would-be *hetaira* |
| Nurse | 1 | – |
| Slave | 5 | 2 as *doule*, 3 as *oiketis* |
| Total | 53 | This figure represents just under a third of the entries in the database; the relative rarity of such information in hagiography generally may be compounded by the excerpting process |

sometimes sentimental. For example, the devoted slave (*oiketis*) of Severianus of Sebasteia resurrects her own slave-husband's corpse so that he may serve at his martyred master's tomb.[21] Eroteis is freed by her free-speaking mistress Capitolina only to follow her mistress' example and join her in martyrdom.[22] Most sentimental of all is the tale of the heart-broken senator Claudianus, to whom Domitian writes demanding that he hand over his slave-girl Charitine for punishment.[23] In an inversion of their normal social roles, it is she who comforts her master. Perhaps not coincidentally, Charitine's martyrdom is one of the most grotesque and involved.[24] The motif can be reversed. St Ariadne is turned in by her master Tertylus[25] and St Agathoclea suffers repeated torment and eventually death at the hands of her Christian master's spiteful pagan wife in a horrific *ménage à trois*.[26]

In monastic stories sex is overtly at issue as battered slave-girls are replaced by their generic equivalent, reformed dancing girls and prostitutes, here the high-class Pelagia of Antioch[27] and the rather humbler Taesia who was born into her mother's business.[28] These share their feast-day with the two martyred Pelagias, one of Antioch and one of Tarsos, along with Peter's daughter Petronia and an unnamed group of certain other female martyrs. Two men, the elderly martyrs Artemon and Nicodemus, look distinctly uncomfortable in this company, and such a grouping is rare.[29] Women ascetics' favoured disguise, as eunuchs in male monasteries, receives its due attention. When all goes well, the secret is usually revealed only once risk of child-bearing is over, or indeed at death. Euphrosyne on 25 September is a good example of both. After thirty-eight years of searching for his lost daughter, her father consults the saintly 'eunuch' Smaragdus. *She* answers 'Don't grieve, father, or seek your child. I am she' and gives up the ghost.[30] Odder and potentially nastier variants can be found: a woman betrays the monk Susanna's sex and so precipitates her ordination as a deaconess and indirectly her martyrdom.[31]

In their different ways these monastic accounts reflect on the perilous nature of women from the perspective of the early desert fathers, none more so than two curiosities dealing with anonymous women. In the first, a girl is brought to the anchorite Jacob (because she continually cries out his name) to have the assumed demon cast out.[32] Then her naive parents leave her with him to make sure that the cure has taken. Jacob struggles in vain against the devil and then rapes and kills her. Yet this narrative is less concerned with Jacob's sin than with the temptation posed by the girl, for the monk repents and ascends to great heights of asceticism. In the second story Abraamius is faced with caring for his orphaned niece's education.[33] An enclosed hermit himself, he very naturally walls her up too in the cell next door. All goes well until at the age of twenty she departs to the bright lights of the nearest brothel. Nothing daunted, her uncle puts on his armour and rides off to hale her back to her cell again. She too later achieves marvels of asceticism, yet her uncle's sanctity is what interests the excerptor.

A certain even-handedness here does not obscure the fact that in both tales the women are viewed as threatening and suspect. Such stories began as cautionary tales dealing with the desirability and the perils of monasticism for both men and women, particularly when there was any contact between the sexes. Their fairy-tale equivalent of living happily ever after is not marriage but the attainment of chastity. To a twentieth-century mind concerned with the most basic psychology or with the horrors of abused women, the *Synaxarion*'s summaries seem by turns naive – how could they have left the girl there given her symptoms, and where did Abraamios get the horse and armour?[34] – or downright horrific, one girl raped and murdered, the other reduced to viewing a brothel as a women's refuge. Clearly neither reaction matches that assumed in the original written context or in that of its reuse and repetition down to the tenth century. Yet were those one and the same? As time went by this sort of monastic story pattern became fixed. The ideal may have remained chastity and withdrawal from the world and these were a recognizable if increasingly organized reality throughout the period, yet in time it may be correct to think more in terms of the glamourizing of a model or pattern by hagiographical association.

The strong influence of monastic example upon Imperial women is a case in point. September and October include Pulcheria, the Emperor Marcian's 'wife' in name alone,[35] and the sixth-century Febronia, princess and ascetic,[36] both of whom receive low-key entries, although Pulcheria certainly exploited her lifestyle to political ends. However, among the January entries, Apollinaria, grand-daughter of Leo the Great,[37] runs away to Egypt, disguises herself as a monk and ends up with a complexion shrivelled like a tortoise shell. Under 18 April, Anthousa, the determinedly and irritatingly virginal daughter of Constantine Copronymous,[38] provides another example of an Imperial monastic lady whose story rivals the most novelistic of the humbler versions.

We come back to all those martyrs. The stories are straight-forward enough: persecution by pagan emperor or foreign ruler, trial, refusal to recant, imprisonment, torture, eventually death. The basic format is historical – many Christians died in this way – yet many surviving passions are largely fiction built merely on a name. The *Syriac Martyrology*[39] of 411's format of name, place, occasionally status and method of execution, testifies to the determination of the early church to record and remember. Yet its compiler would have been astounded at some of the lengthy accounts developed and embroidered between the fourth and sixth centuries. The function of such writings is likely to have been repeatedly and some-times drastically modified, affecting not only their content but their impact. With few exceptions they exploit the church's history, not its present, and the process of rewriting is very clear. If some martyr-doms under Decius, Valerius and during the Great Persecution of the first decade of the fourth century are grounded in sound histor-ical sources, little else is so certain. Increasingly it was on the very early years of the church that the most fantastical constructs were focused and some of the activities attributed to Trajan are quite extra-ordinary.[40]

For women martyrs the emphasis on threatened virginity is increas-ingly stressed. For all martyrs the emphasis on torture, particularly multiple and horrific torture, is increased. At certain stages this may have been linked to rivalry between cult centres, a desire to stress the miraculous and to claim the local hero or heroine as an alpha-class saint through an elaborate account. Later on one should perhaps think more in terms of literary and liturgical competition.[41] Certainly in the East, the proliferation, survival and repeated recompilation of the passions of the martyrs is in some sense a commentary on the history of Byzantium and the continual renewal of their relevance would repay further study. Iconoclasm is one case in point. Rather than viewing its existence as a barrier to the survival and continuity of the veneration of martyrs, it might be better to view its removal as a spur to subsequent revival and to the tenth-century vogue of which the *Synaxarion* is only one example.[42]

Within such a context the *Synaxarion*'s heavy emphasis on the details of torture requires comment. So emphatic is it that a specialist Greek vocabulary is required in order to follow. Whatever else the excerptor omits, the gory, grisly and revolting details are impassively charted one by one. Recently the sexual aspects of some longer hagiograph-ical accounts of the torture of women have been receiving scholarly attention.[43] Yet this aspect does not appear to be central to the excerptor's concerns.

Take the elaborate sufferings of Charitine, her of the grieving master Claudianus.[44] She was beaten and thrown into the sea with a millstone chained to her neck; the chains parted and she walked on the water. She was confined in an iron dog collar, had coals heaped on her head and then vinegar poured over her, yet was released by prayer. Her breasts were branded, the skin scraped from her ribs which were then cauterized; she was fixed naked on a wheel over hot coals but an angel quenched the coals and prevented the torturers from rolling the wheel. Her finger- and toe-nails were torn out, also her teeth. Finally, like many an unkillable martyr she prayed for death and had her prayer granted. Her body was put into a sack full of sand and thrown into the sea, only to be washed up miraculously three days later unharmed for secret burial.

Certainly there are sexual aspects to such an account. Yet the genre, particularly in this excerpted form, presents it as all very much par for the course. Apart from the mutilation of Charitine's breasts, most of the tortures are found often identically excerpted in comparable lengthy accounts of male martyrdom. Women's breasts are mutilated by torturers.[45] Again the threat of rape, not usually its execution, is found in female martyrdoms. Stripping naked is used to humiliate men and women alike. This happens in life, not just in hagiography. Hagiography deals with sexual insult to women as one aspect of the personal violation of either sex by means of violence and its chief concern is with the failure of violence against the defiance of a saint. When a long account of torture is written or excerpted, a particular worst-case scenario may be chosen or handed down that matches the sex of the victim. Charitine does not give in and so she wins her crown, dies happily ever after. Had she been rescued and carried off to safety, she would have failed. Because she returns repeatedly of her own free will to face martyrdom, she wins. The worst-case scenario for a woman functions in hagiography primarily to vindicate her triumph – in this example both as a woman and as a slave-girl, an outsider in earthly society turned into the ultimate insider in the ranks of the saints.

From the safety of western Europe it has sometimes been possible to view torture as a thing of the past or of far-distant places, although rather less so in the light of recent events. While I have stressed the fictitious nature of many of these compilations, martyrs, torture and violence were realities, as in some places they still are; the techniques described in the *Synaxarion* were in use. To celebrate not merely the martyr but the desire for martyrdom may be a concept foreign, even repugnant, to the western nature, yet there is little doubt that this response has a long history. If the *Synaxarion* is not entirely immune from the tendency to dwell on the sufferings of women, it makes violence against either sex one of its chief concerns. Neither Late Antiquity nor Byzantium was a stranger to violence, at home or abroad. Down the centuries martyr passions and works like the *Synaxarion* may often have served to focus strong responses to the threats of a hostile world, responses that may have varied at different times and in different places. Yet the primacy of martyrdom as a road to sanctity remains an important constant and the disturbing questions that this provokes cannot be escaped. The authors and excerptors of martyr acts do not merely record – they both glamourize and trivialize. In their insistence on the enumeration of ever more horrific detail, whether historical or not, they end by conniving at brutality. Even as they condemn the torturers, they elicit from their audience acceptance and admiration for the unacceptable until more and worse horrors are required before that admiration is forthcoming. Any single act of torture or cruelty lies or should lie beyond the pale. Ultimately the issue does not concern gender but the perverted morality of a literary genre that celebrates human suffering in a manner repugnant to the religion that it claims to serve.

## NOTES

1 Ed. Delehaye 1902. References to saints in this work are given by month, day and entry number. Where material from Delehaye's apparatus drawn from other manuscripts is used (*Synaxaria Selecta*), column and line number are given. Note the following abbreviations: *AASS*: *Acta Sanctorum . . . quae collegit J. Bollandus*, Antwerp and Brussels 1643–; *PG*: J.-P. Migne (ed.), *Patrologiae Cursus Completus, Series Graeco-Latina* 1–166, Paris 1844–1864; *PO*: R. Graffin and F. Nau (eds) *Patrologia Orientalis*, 1–, Paris 1903–.

2 The first point can be checked where a comparison is possible, for example, between Mart. 11.3 (Pionius) and the early *Acta Pionii* (Musurillo 1972: 136–166). On the same day the style, vocabulary and rather sophisticated tone of the entry on Sophronios of Jerusalem (*ob.* 638, Mart. 11.2) match its period, as do the more jejune and circumstantial language and information on George the 'Newly-appearing' (Mart. 11.4) the very late date of his entry.

3 Information for all the following tables was drawn from Delehaye 1902: 2–184. Table 16.1 is based on a straightforward count of the entries for all categories of saint across the first two months. For the remaining tables a database was constructed using Locoscript's *Locofile*.

4 Sept. 24.1.
5 Characteristically, the *Synaxarion* opts for the doubtful Greek variant in which Thecla is martyred rather than dies in old age (Sept. 24.1).
6 For example, Palladius *HL* 54–61 (Butler 1904).
7 For example Oct. 28.1, Terentius, Neonilla and their children Nitas, Sarbelus, Theodulus, Hierax, Bele, Photas, Euneice, of whom only Photas is out of place. Occasionally the narrative order will affect the order of the names. The New Testament pairing of Joachim and Anna, parents of the Virgin, of course reverses the emphasis when it comes to the actual narrative.
8 Oct. 23.3 (Procopia and Michael as parents of Ignatius, future patriarch of Constantinople, and Theodora, Empress at the time of his elevation). Oct. 4.4 (Constantine's sister and Callisthene); Oct. 6.2 (Irene and the exiled Nicetas).
9 Sept. 14.1. At Oct. 28.10 she figures again in a subordinate role to Cyriacus, martyred Bishop of Jerusalem, who revealed the true cross to her. She is celebrated in her own right at Mai 22.1.
10 Sept. 21.3 (Philippa, mother of the military martyr Theodore of Perge).
11 Oct. 24.1. The whole entry is unusual, an account of the wartime massacre of 1,250 Christians at Nagran when the city was taken by the Himyarites in 523.
12 Oct. 12.2.
13 Oct. 11.1 as an anonymous group, but at Sept. 4.4 one is named as Hermione.
14 Oct. 30.3.
15 Sept. 17.3.
16 Oct. 8.2.
17 Sept. 21.4. Cf. Sozomen, *Historia Ecclesiastica*, 5.9.
18 Oct. 5.6.
19 Sept. 14.2.
20 Oct. 5.6.
21 Sept. 9.2.
22 Oct. 27.2.
23 Oct. 5.1.
24 Below, p. 244.
25 Sept. 18.5.
26 Sept. 17.2. The motif is an expanded doublet of the treatment of Sabina (later Theodote) at the hands of the wicked Politta at *Acta Pionii* 9 (Musurillo 1972: 147).
27 Oct. 8.1.
28 Oct. 8.4.
29 Oct. 8.2, 8.3, 8.7, 8.8; the two men at 8.4, 8.5. The grouping of the three Pelagias, for once reasonably well sorted out, looks deliberate, yet the procedure is slightly at odds with the efforts at Oct. 17.2, Nov. 1.1 to deal with the various sets of Cosmas and Damian one at a time on their relevant day. Taesia certainly seems to have been attracted to Oct. 8 by the presence of Pelagia the *hetaira*. Theoretically, saints are celebrated on the anniversary of their death, but occasionally one finds evidence of more systematic grouping. The two groups of martyrs from

Marcianopolis, for example, are unlikely to have died on the same day several centuries apart. Monks too show a general tendency to clump: the precise day of their deaths may have lacked the traditional significance of that of martyrs and the monastic sources are not always informative about dates of death. Yet the main reason is probably the use by the compilers of collections of monastic lives or anecdotes. There is interesting work to be done on the evidence for several hands at work in the editorial process.

30  Sept. 25.3.
31  Sept. 19.2.
32  Oct. 10.3.
33  Oct. 29.2.
34  The latter point is in fact explained in the full length version of the *Life of Abraamios*, Brock and Harvey 1987: 27–39. A comparison of the full account with the *Synaxarion*'s summary reveals particularly clearly the distortions of emphasis as well as of simple facts that result from this process.
35  Sept. 10.3.
36  Oct. 27.3. This is the daughter of Heraclius, not the martyred nun of Iun. 25.1, for whom she was most probably named.
37  Jan. 5.1.
38  Apr. 18.5.
39  *AASS* Nov II ii; F. Nau *PO* x.1 1–163. The work draws on mid- or late fourth-century sources.
40  Drusilla's martyrdom is a prime example: Sept. 22.2 with Mart. 22, *Synax. Select.* 553.11–556.47.
41  The latter aspect was still operating at Constantinople itself when the *Synaxarion* was compiled, and is clearly visible in its handling of the many sanctuaries throughout the city in which the different saints were celebrated. Yet it has a history going back to the fourth-century traffic in relics.
42  Symeon Metaphrastes' painstaking rewriting of full-scale passions for each month of the ecclesiastical calendar is another major example, *PG* 114–116.
43  See Brock and Harvey 1987 for the Syriac tradition; Malamud 1989: 149–180 on Prudentius *Peristephanon* 13, as an explicitly erotic treatment of the martyrdom of St Agnes. In an unpublished paper, 'Blood wedding, Prudentius on the martyrdoms', delivered at the University of Keele in May 1993, Gillian Clark put forward interesting insights on the topic with regard to both Syriac and Latin texts.
44  Oct. 5.1.
45  Mastectomy is not uncommon. Occasional horrifying references to bleeding milk rather than blood are more complex. They describe the same torture applied to nursing mothers, but this is not usually made explicit in the *Synaxarion*; instead the phrase's miraculous overtones suggest a female equivalent of the water and blood of the Crucifixion.

# Select bibliography

Alexiou, M. (1974) *The Ritual Lament in Greek Tradition*, Cambridge.

d'Ambrosio, A. and de Caro, S. (1987) 'La necropoli di Porta Nocera, Campagna di Scavo 1983', in *Römische Gräberstrassen, Bayerische Akad. der Wiss*, NF 46, H. Hesberg and P. Zanker (eds) Munich

Anderson, W.S. (1982) *Essays on Roman satire*, Princeton, NJ

Ardener, E. (1975a) (1972) 'Belief and the problem of women' in J.S. LaFontaine (ed.) *The Interpretation of Ritual*, London: 135–158

—— (1975b) 'The "Problem" revisited', in S. Ardener (ed.) *Perceiving women*, London: 19–27

Ardener, S. (1987) 'A note on gender iconography: the vagina', in Caplan, P. (ed.) *The Cultural Construction of Sexuality*, London: 113–142

Ariès, P. (1962) *Centuries of Childhood: A Social History of Family Life*, trans. Boldick, R., London

Arthur (Katz), M.B. (see also Katz) (1976) 'Review essay: classics', *Signs* 2: 382–403

—— (1982a) 'Cultural strategies in Hesiod's *Theogony*: law, family, society', *Arethusa* 15: 63–81

—— (1982b) 'Women and the family in ancient Greece', *Yale Review* 71: 532–547

—— (1983) 'The dream of a world without women: poetics and the circles of order in the *Theogony* Proemium', *Arethusa* 16: 97–116

—— (1994) (1977) 'Politics and pomegranates: an interpretation of the Homeric Hymn to Demeter', in Foley, H. (ed.) *The Homeric Hymn to Demeter. Translation, Commentary, and Interpretative Essays*, Princeton, NJ: 214–242

d'Avino, M. (1967) *The Women in Pompeii*, Naples

Balsdon, J.P.V.D. (1962) *Roman Women: Their History and Habits*, London

Bauman, R.A. (1992) *Women and Politics in Ancient Rome*, London

Beard, M. (1980) 'The sexual status of Vestal Virgins', *JRS* 70: 12–27

—— (1994) 'The Roman and the foreign: the cult of the "Great Mother" in Imperial Rome', in Thoman, N. and Humphrey, C. (eds) *Shamanism, History and the State*, Ann Arbor, Mich.: 164–90

Becker, W.A. (1866) *Charicles or Illustrations of the Private Life of the Greeks*, trans. Metcalfe, F., London

Beloch, J.K. (1912, 1914, 1922, 1925) *Griechische Geschichte*, 2nd edn, Strasbourg and Berlin

Berard, Cl. (1983) 'Le corps bestial', *Etudes de lettres*: 432–354

Bergren, A. (1983) 'Language and the female in early Greek thought', *Arethusa* 16: 69–95

Bernal, M. (1987) *The fabrication of Ancient Greece*, vol. 1: *Black Athena: The Afroasiatic Roots of Classical Civilization*, London

Bernstein, F.S. (1988) 'Pompeian women and programmata', *Studia Pompeiana and Classica in Honour of W. Jashemski*, New York: 1–18

Bisel, S. (1986) 'The people of Herculaneum AD 79', *Helmantica* 37: 11–23
—— (1987) 'Human bones at Herculaneum', *Rivista di Studi Pompeiani* 1: 123–9

Blok, J. (1987) 'Sexual asymmetry: a historiographical essay', in Blok, J. and Mason, P. (eds) *Sexual asymmetry: studies in ancient society*, Amsterdam: 1–57; first published in Dutch 1984

Blok, J. and Mason, P. (eds) (1987) (1984) *Sexual Asymmetry: Studies in Ancient Society*, Amsterdam

Boardman, J. (1988) 'Sex differentiation in grave vases', *AION* 10: 171–179

Boedeker, D. (1983) 'Hecate: a transfunctional goddess in the *Theogony?*', *TAPHA* 113: 79–93

Böhnert, K.-J. and Hahn, G. (1990) 'Phytotherapie in Gynäkologie und Gerburtshilfe: vitex agnus-castus (Keuschlamm). Eine alte Kultur- und Arzneipflanze', *Erfahrungsheilkinde* 39: 494–502

Bookidis, N. (1993) 'Ritual dining at Corinth', in Marinatos, N. and Hägg, R. (eds) *Greek Sanctuaries: New Approaches*, London: 45–61

Bookidis, N. and Stroud, R.S. (1987) *Demeter and Persephone in Ancient Corinth*, Princeton, NJ

Bosch, L.P. van den and Bremmer, J.N. (1994) *Between Poverty and the Pyre: Moments in the History of Widowhood*, London

Boswell, J. (1988) *The Kindness of Strangers: The Abandonment of Children in Western Europe from Late Antiquity to the Renaissance*, New York
—— (1990) 'Concepts, experience, and sexuality', *Differences* 2.1, special issue on 'Sexuality in Greek and Roman society': 67–87

Botsford, G. (1909) *The Roman Assemblies from their Origin to the End of the Republic*, New York

Böttiger, K.A. (1837) (1796) 'Were Athenian women spectators at dramatic festivals?', paper reprinted (1837) in Böttiger, K.A. *Kleine Schriften* 1, ed. Sillig, J., Leipzig: 295–307

Bottigheimer, R.B. (1987) *Grimm's Bad Girls and Bold Boys: The Moral and Social Vision of the 'Tales'*, New Haven, Conn.

Bourriot, F. (1976) *Recherches sur la nature du genos*, Paris

Bradeen, D.W. (1974) *The Athenian Agora*, vol. 1: *Inscriptions: The Funerary Monuments*, Princeton, NJ

Bradley, K.R. (1991a) *Discovering the Roman Family*, New York
—— (1991b) 'Remarriage and the structure of the upper-class Roman family', in Rawson, B. (ed.) *Marriage, divorce and children in ancient Rome*, Oxford: 79–98

Braund, S.H. (1988) *Beyond anger*, Cambridge
—— (ed.) (1989) *Satire and Society in Ancient Rome*, Exeter
—— (1992) 'Juvenal – misogynist or misogamist?', *JRS* 82: 71–86

Braund, S.H. and Cloud, J.D. (1981) 'Juvenal: a diptych', *LCM* 6: 195–208
Bremen, R. van (1983) 'Women and wealth', in Cameron, A. and Kuhrt, A. (eds) *Images of women in antiquity*, London: 223–242
Bremmer, J. (1994) 'Pauper or patroness: the widow in the early Christian Church', in Bosch, L.P. van den and Bremmer, J.N. *Between Poverty and the Pyre: Moments in the History of Widowhood*, London: Ch. 3.
Brock, S. and Harvey, S.A. (1987) *Holy Women of the Syrian Orient*, Berkeley, Calif.
Brodie, J. Farrell (1994) *Contraception and Abortion in Nineteenth-Century America*, Ithaca, NY
Brown, L.M. and Gilligan, C. (1992) *Meeting at the Crossroads: Women's Psychology and Girls' Development*, Cambridge, Mass.
Brumfield, A.C. (1981) *The Attic Festivals of Demeter and their Relation to the Agricultural Year*, Salem, NH
Burkert, W. (1979) *Structure and History in Greek Mythology and Ritual*, Berkeley, CA
—— (1984) *Greek Religion*, Oxford
Burton, A. (1989) *Davidis Prolegomena et in Porphyrii Isagogen Commentarium*, Berlin
Butler, C. (1904) *Palladius, The Lausiac History*, in *Texts and studies* 6, Cambridge
Cameron, A. and Kuhrt, A. (eds) (1993) (1983) *Images of Women in Antiquity*, rev. edn, London
Cantarella, E. (1987) *Pandora's Daughters: The Role and Status of Women in Greek and Roman Antiquity*, trans. Fant, M.B., Baltimore, Md. and London
Carcopino, J. (1939) *La vie quotidienne à Rome à l'apogée de L'Empire*, Paris; trans. Lorimer, E.O. (1940) as *Daily Life in Ancient Rome*, New Haven, CT
Carson, A. (1990) 'Putting her in her place: woman, dirt, and desire', in Halperin, D.M., Winkler, J.J. and Zeitlin, F. (eds) *Before Sexuality: The Construction of Erotic Experience in the Ancient Greek World*, Princeton, NJ: 135–169
Castrén, P. (1983) *Ordo Populusque Pompeianus: polity and society in Roman Pompeii*, *Acta Inst. Finl.* 8, 2nd edn, Rome
de Cazanove, O. (1987) 'Exesto. L'incapacité sacrificielle des femmes à Rome', *Phoenix* 41: 159–173
Clairmont, C. (1970) *Gravestone and Epigram: Greek Memorials from the Archaic and Classical Period*, Mainz
Clark, G. (1989) *Women in the Ancient World, Greece and Rome, New Surveys in the Classics* 21, Oxford
—— (1993) *Women in late Antiquity*, Oxford
Clinton, K. (1988) 'Sacrifice at the Eleusinian Mysteries', in Hägg, R., Marinatos, N. and Nordquist, G.C. (eds) *Early Greek Cult Practice, Fifth International Symposium*, Swedish Institute at Athens, Stockholm: 69–80
—— (1992) *Myth and Cult: The Iconography of the Eleusinian Mysteries*, Stockholm
—— (1993) 'The sanctuary of Demeter and Kore at Eleusis', in Marinatos, N. and Hägg, R. (eds) *Greek Sanctuaries: New Approaches*, London: 110–24
Cohen, D. (1989) 'Seclusion, separation, and the status of women in classical Athens', *G & R* 36: 3–15
—— (1991a) 'Adultery, women, and social control', in Cohen, D. *Law, Sexuality, and Society: The Enforcement of Morals in Classical Athens*, Cambridge: 133–70
—— (1991b) 'Debate (with Clifford Hindley): law, society and homosexuality

in classical Athens', *Past and present* 133: 167–194

—— (1991c) *Law, Sexuality, and Society: The Enforcement of Morals in Classical Athens*, Cambridge

—— (1991d) 'Law, social control, and homosexuality', in Cohen, D. *Law, Sexuality, and Society: The Enforcement of Morals in Classical Athens*, Cambridge: 171–202

—— (1991e) 'The law of adultery', in Cohen, D. *Law, Sexuality, and Society: The Enforcement of Morals in Classical Athens*, Cambridge: 98–132

Cohen, J. (1989) *'Be fertile and increase, fill the earth and master it': The Ancient and Medieval Career of a Biblical Text*, Ithaca, NY

Cole, S.G. (1994) 'Demeter in the ancient Greek city and its countryside', in Alcock, S.E. and Osborne, R. (eds) *Placing the Gods: Sanctuaries and Sacred Space in Ancient Greece*, Oxford: 199–216

Collignon, M. (1904) 'Matrimonium 1. Grèce', Daremberg, Ch. and Saglio, E. *Dictionnaire des antiquités grecques et romaines d'après les textes et les monuments*, 3.2, Paris 1877–1919: 1639–54

Colton, R.E. (1965) 'Juvenal's Second Satire and Martial', *CJ* 61: 68–71

Corbier, M. (1987) 'Les comportements familiaux de l'aristocratie romaine (II<sup>e</sup> siècle avant J.-C.–III<sup>e</sup> siècle après J.-C.)', *Annales ESC*: 1267–1285; republished in *Parenté et stratégies familiales dans l'antiquité romaine (Actes de la table ronde des 2–4 octobre 1986)*, Rome 1990: 225–249 = 'Family behaviour of the Roman aristocracy', in Pomeroy, S. (ed.) *Women's History and Ancient History*, Chapel Hill, NC 1991: 173–196

—— (1990) 'Construire sa parenté à Rome', *Revue historique*, 575: = 3–36 = 'Constructing kinship in Rome. Marriage and divorce. Filiation and adoption' (abbreviated version), in Kertzer, D.I. and Saller, R.P. (eds) *The History of the Family in Italy from Antiquity to the Present*, New Haven, Conn. and London: 127–144

—— (1991) 'Divorce and adoption as Roman familial strategies', ('Le divorce et l'adoption' amplified), in Rawson, B. (ed.) *Marriage, Divorce and Children in Ancient Rome*, Oxford: 47–78

—— (1994a) 'A propos de la *Tabula Siarensis*: le Sénat, Germanicus et la domus Augusta', in González, J. (ed.) *Roma y las provincias: realidad administrativa e ideologia imperial*, Madrid: 39–85

—— (1994b) 'La maison des Césars', in Bonte, P. (ed.) *Epouser au plus proche. Inceste, prohibitions et stratégies matrimoniales autour de la Méditerranée*, Paris: 243–91

Corte, M. della (1965) *Case ed abitanti di Pompei*; 3rd edn, Naples

Courtney, E. (1980) *A Commentary on the Satires of Juvenal*, London

Crawford, P. (1978) 'Attitudes to pregnancy from a woman's spiritual diary, 1687–8', *Local Population Studies* 21: 43–45

—— (1981) 'Attitudes to menstruation in seventeenth-century England', *Past and Present* 91: 47–73

—— (1994) 'Sexual knowledge in England, 1500–1750', in Porter, R. and Teich, M. (eds) *Sexual Knowledge, Sexual Science*, Cambridge: 82–106

Crook, J.A. (1967) *Law and Life of Rome*, London

Culham, P. (1986) 'Ten years after Pomeroy: Studies of the image and reality of women in Antiquity', *Helios*, new series 13: 9–30

Davies, C. (1980) *Rewriting Nursing History*, London

Davies, J.K. (1971) *Athenian Propertied Families*, Oxford
—— (1988) 'Religion and the state', in Boardman, J., Hammond, N.G.L., Lewis, D.M. and Ostwald, M. (eds) *Cambridge Ancient History*, 2nd edn, Cambridge, 4: 368–388
Davis, N. Zemon (1976) ' "Women's history" in transition: the European case', *Feminist Studies* 3: 83–103
Dean-Jones, L.A. (1992) 'The politics of pleasure: female sexual appetite in the Hippocratic Corpus', *Helios* 19: 72–91
Delaney, C. (1986) 'The meaning of paternity and the Virgin Birth debate', *Man* 21: 494–513
—— (1991) *The Seed and the Soil: Gender and Cosmology in Turkish Villa Soceity*, Berkeley, CA
Delehaye, H. (ed.) (1902) *Synaxarium Ecclesiae Constantinopolitanae e codice Sirmondiano*, in *Propylaeum ad Acta Sanctorum Novembris*, Brussels
Demand, N. (1986) 'The relocation of Priene reconsidered', *Phoenix* 40: 35–44
Detienne, M. (1972) *Les jardins d'Adonis*, Paris (1977) *The Gardens of Adonis: Spices in Greek Mythology*, trans. Lloyd, J., Atlantic Highlands, NJ
—— (1979) (1977) *Dionysos slain*, trans. Muellner, M. and L., Baltimore, Md.
—— (1989) 'The violence of wellborn ladies: women in the Thesmophoria', in Detienne, M. and Vernant, J.-P. *The Cuisine of Sacrifice Among the Greeks*, trans. Wissing, P., Chicago, Ill. and London: 129–147
Diels, H. (1929) *Doxographi Graeci*, Berlin
Diels, H. and Kranz, W. (1964) *Die Fragmente der Vorsokratiker*, 11th edn, Zurich
Dixon, S. (1983) 'A family business: women's role in patronage and politics at Rome 80–44 BC', *C & M* 34: 91–112
Douglas, M. (1966) *Purity and Danger: An Analysis of the Concepts of Pollution and Taboo*, London
—— (1975) *Implicit Meanings: Essays in Anthropology*, London
Dover, K.J. (1973) 'Classical Greek attitudes to sexual behavior', *Arethusa* 6: 64–5
Dow, S. and Healey, R.F. (1965) *A Sacred Calendar of Eleusis*, Harvard Theological Studies 21, Cambridge, Mass. and London
Dowden, K. (1989) *Death and the Maiden: Girls' Initiation Rites in Greek Mythology*, London and New York
—— (1992) *The Uses of Greek Mythology*, London duBois, P. (1982) *Centaurs and Amazons: Women and the Prehistory of the Great Chain of Being*, Ann Arbor, Mich.
—— (1988) *Sowing the Body: Psychoanalysis and Ancient Representations of Women*, Chicago, Ill.
Duby, G. and Perrot, M. (eds) (1991) *Histoire des femmes*, vol. 1: *L'antiquité*, Paris
Dupont, F. (1992) *Daily life in Ancient Rome*, Oxford
Dyson, S.L. (1992a) 'Age, sex and status: the view from the Roman Rotary Club', *EMC* 36: 369–395
—— (1992b) *Community and Society in Roman Italy*, Baltimore, Md.
Eck, W. (1993) 'Das *s.c de Cn. Pisone patre* und seine Publikation in der Baetica', *Cahiers du Centre G. Glotz* 4: 189–208
Edwards, C.H. (1993) *The Politics of Immorality in Ancient Rome*, Cambridge
Eilberg-Schwartz, H. (1990) *The Savage in Judaism: An Anthropology of Israelite*

*Religion and Ancient Judaism*, Bloomington, Ind.

Ery, K.K. (1969) 'Investigations on the demographic source value of tomb-stones originating from the Roman period', *Alba Regia* 10: 51–67

d'Escurac, H. Pavis (1974) 'Pour une étude sociale de l'Apologie d'Apulée', *Antiquités Africaines* 8: 68–101

Evans, J.K. (1991) *War, Women and Children in Ancient Rome*, London

Fantham, E. (1991) '*Stuprum*: public attitudes and penalties for sexual offences in Republican Rome', *EMC*, new series, 10: 273–282

Farber, A. (1975) 'Segmentation of the mother: women in Greek myth', *Psychoanalytic Review* 62: 29–47

Farnell, L.R. (1896–1909) *Cults of the Greek States*, 4 vols, Oxford

Flacelière, R. (1964) *Daily Life in Greece at the Time of Pericles*, London

Flower, M.A. (1985) '*IG* II² 2344 and the size of Phratries in classical Athens', *CQ*, new series, 35: 232–235

Foley, H.P. (ed.) (1981a) *Reflections of Women in Antiquity*, New York

—— (1981b) 'The conception of women in Athenian drama', in Foley, H.P. (ed.) *Reflections of Women in Antiquity*, New York: 127–168

—— (ed.) (1994) *The Homeric Hymn to Demeter*, Princeton, NJ

Forbes, H.A. (1982) *Strategies and Soils: Technology, Production and Environment in the Peninsula of Methana, Greece*, Ann Arbor, Mich.

Forbis, E.P. (1990) 'Women's political image in Italian honorary inscriptions', *AJPh* 111: 493–512

Foucault, M. (1985) *The Use of Pleasure*, trans. Hurley, R., New York

Foxhall, L. (1989) 'Household, gender and property in classical Athens', *CQ*, new series, 39: 22–44

Foxhall, L. and Forbes, H.A. (1982): 'Sitometreia: the role of grain as a staple food in classical antiquity', *Chiron* 12: 41–90

Franklin, J.L. Jr (1980) *Pompeii: the Electoral Programmata, Campaigns and Politics, AD 71–79*, Papers and Monographs of the American Acad. in Rome 28, Rome

French, V. (1986) 'Midwives and maternity care in the Roman world', in *Rescuing Creusa: New Methodological Approaches to Women in Antiquity*, special edition of *Helios* 13, 69–84

—— (1988) 'Birth control, childbirth and early childhood', in Grant, M. and R. Kitzinger (eds) *Civilization of the Ancient Mediterranean. Greece and Rome*, vol. 3, New York, 1355–62

Furth, C. (1986) 'Blood, body, and gender: medical images of the female condition in China', *Chinese Science* 7: 43–66

Fustel de Coulanges, N.D. (1980) (1864) *The Ancient City*, trans. from *La cité antique*, Baltimore and London

Gaertringen, H. von (1906) *Die Inschriften von Priene*, Berlin

Gardner, J. (1986) *Women in Roman Law and Society*, London and Sydney

—— (1993) *Being a Roman Citizen*, London

Garnsey, P. (1988) *Famine and Food Supply in the Graeco-Roman World*, Cambridge

Gasparro, G. Sfameni (1986) *Misteri e culti mistici di Demetra*, Rome

Giordano, C. and Casale, A. (1990) 'Iscrizioni pompeiane inedite scoperte tra gli anni 1954–1978', *Atti della Accademia Pontiana*, new series, 39, Naples: 273–378

Gleason, M. (1990) 'The semiotics of gender: physiognomy and self-fashioning in the second century CE', in Halperin, D.M., Winkler, J.J. and Zeitlin, F. (eds) *Before Sexuality: The Construction of Erotic Experience In the Ancient Greek World*, Princeton, NJ

Golden, M. (1985) ' "Donatus" and Athenian Phratries', *CQ*, new series, 35: 9–13

—— (1988) 'Male chauvinists and pigs', *EMC* 32: 1–12

Golden, M.P. and N.H. (1975) 'Population policy in Plato and Aristotle: some value issues', *Arethusa* 8: 345–358

Gomme, A.W. (1937) (1925) 'The position of women in Athens in the fifth and fourth centuries BC', *CPh* 20: 1–25; reprinted in Gomme, A.W. *Essays in Greek History and Literature*, Oxford: 89–115

Gould, J. (1980) 'Law, custom and myth: aspects of the social position of women in classical Athens', *JHS* 100: 38–59

Gourevitch, D. (1968) 'Pudeur et pratique médicale dans l'antiquité classique', *La presse médicale* (2 March): 544–545

—— (1987) 'La mort de la femme en couches et dans les suites de couches', in *La mort, les morts et l'au-delà dans le monde romain*, Caen, *Actes du colloque de Caen, 20–22 novembre, 1985*, 187–93

—— (1990) 'Se marier pour avoir les enfants: le point de vue du médecin', in Andreau, J. and Bruhn, H. (eds) *Parenté et stratégies familiales dans l'antiquité romaine*, Rome, 139–51

—— (1994) 'La cuisine du corps féminin: l'eau dans le Livre III du traité gynécologique de Soranus d'Ephèse', in Guimier-Sorbets, A.M., Ginouvès, R., Jouanna, J. and Villard, L. (eds) *Colloque* CRNS (Nov.): *L'eau, la santé et la maladie dans le monde grec*, *BCH* Suppl. 28, Paris: 95–108

Green, M.H. (1989) 'Women's medical practice and health care in medieval Europe', *Signs* 14: 434–473

Griffith, M. (1983) 'Personality in Hesiod', *CA* 2: 37–65

Grmek, M.D. (1988) *Nuove prospettive per la storia delle malattie antiche*, Naples: 59

Gründel, R. (1967) 'Wahlpropaganda post eventum', *Acta of the Fifth International Congress of Greek and Latin epigraphy*, Cambridge: 225–227

Gutiérrez, R. (1991) *When Jesus Came, the Corn Mothers Went Away: Marriage, Sexuality and Power in New Mexico, 1500–1846*, Stanford, CA

Hadas, M. (1936) 'Observations on Athenian women', *CW* 29 (3 February): 97–100

Hallett, J.P. (1984) *Fathers and Daughters in Roman Society*, Princeton, NJ

—— (1989) 'Female homoeroticism and the denial of Roman reality in Latin literature', *Yale Journal of Criticism* 3: 209–227

Halperin, D.M. (1992) *One Hundred Years of Homosexuality and Other Essays on Greek Love*, New York

Halperin, D.M., Winkler, J.J. and Zeitlin, F. (eds) (1990) *Before Sexuality: The Constrction of Erotic Experience in the Ancient Greek World*, Princeton, NJ

Hanson, A.E. (1987) 'The eight months' child and the etiquette of birth: *Obsit omen!*', *Bulletin of the History of Medicine* 61: 589–602

—— (1990) 'The medical writers' woman', in Halperin, D.M., Winkler, J.J. and Zeitlin, F. (eds) *Before Sexuality: the Construction of Erotic Experience in the Ancient Greek World*, Princeton, NJ: 309–337

—— (1991a) 'Continuity and change: three case studies in Hippocratic gynecological therapy and theory', in Pomeroy, S.B. (ed.) *Women's history*

*and ancient history*, Chapel Hill, NC: 73–110
—— (1991b) 'The logic of gynecological prescriptions', in Lopez Ferez, J.A.
(ed.) *Tratados Hipocraticos: Actas del VII* Colloque internationale hippocratique 1990, Madrid: 235–250
—— (1992) 'Conception, gestation, and the origin of female nature', *Helios*
19:31–71
Hanson, A.E. and Armstrong, D. (1986) 'Vox virginis', *BICS* 33:97–100
Harris, W. (1983) 'Literacy and epigraphy 1', *ZPE* 52:87–111
Hayduck, M. (1982) *Simplicii in libros Aristotelis De Anima Commentaria*,
Berlin
—— (1887) *Ioannis Philoponi in Aristotelis De Anima libros Commentaria*, Berlin
—— (1891) *Alexandri Aphrodisiensis in Aristotelis Metaphysica Commentaria*,
Berlin
Henderson, J. (1989) 'Satire writes "woman" gendersong', *PCPhS* 35: 50–80
Hoffmann, G. (1986) 'Pandora, la jarre et l'espoir', *Quaderni di storia* 24: 55–89
Hopkins, K. (1983) *Death and Renewal, Sociological Studies in Roman History* 2,
Cambridge
Horowitz, M.C. (1976) 'Aristotle and woman', *Journal of the History of Biology*
9:183–213
Hughes–Hallett, L. (1990) *Cleopatra. Histories, Dreams and Distortions*, London
Humbert, M. (1972) *Le remarriage à Rome*, Milan
Humphreys, S.C. (1983) '*Oikos* and *Polis*', in Humphreys, S.C. *The Family,
Women and Death: Comparative Studies*, London: 1–21
—— (1991) 'Public and private in classical Athens', in Cohen, D. (ed.) *Law,
Sexuality, and Society: The Enforcement of Morals in Classical Athens*, Cambridge
—— (1993) *The Family, Women and Death*, Ann Arbor, Mich. 2nd edn
Jacobs, F. (1930) 'Beiträge zur Geschichte des weiblichen Geschlechtes', in
*Abhandlungen über Gegenstände des Alterthums, Vermischte Schriften* 4; *Leben und
Kunst der Alten* 3, Leipzig: 157–554
Jameson, M. (1990) 'Private space and the Greek city', in Murray, O. and
Price, S. (ed.). *The Greek City from Homes to Alexander*, Oxford: 171–195
Johansen, J. Prytz (1975) 'The Thesmophoria as a women's festival', *Temenos*
11:78–87
Jongman, W. (1988) *The Economy and Society of Pompeii, Dutch Monographs on
Ancient History and Archaeology* 4, Amsterdam
Jouanna, J. (1984) 'Rhétorique et médicine dans la collection hippocratique:
contribution à l'histoire de la rhétorique au Vᶜ siècle', *REG* 97: 26–44
Jouanna, J. and Taillardat, J. (1980) 'Une voix nihili, ΦΗΡΕΑΤΙΚΛΞΣ
dans le *Glossaire hippocratique* de Galien (Kühn XIX, 151, 3)', *REG* 93:
126–135
Just, R. (1975) 'Conceptions of women in classical Athens', *Journal of the
Anthropological Society of Oxford* 6: 153–170
—— (1989) *Women in Athenian Law and Life*, London, and New York (1991)
Kajanto, I. (1965) *The Latin Cognomina. Comm. Humanarmum Litterarum* 36.2,
Helsinki
—— (1969) 'On divorce among the common people of Rome', *REL: Mélanges
Marcel Durry* 47 *bis*: 99–113
Kakridis, J.T. (1971) *Homer revisited*, Lund
Kampen, N. (1981) *Image and Status: Roman Working Women in Ostia*, Berlin

Katz, M.A. (see also Arthur) (1989) (1990) 'Sexuality and the body in ancient Greece', *Métis. Revue d'anthropologie du monde grec ancien* 4: 155–179; reprinted in *Trends in History* 4: 97–125

—— (1992) 'Ideology and "the status" of women in ancient Greece', *History and Theory*, Beiheft 31, *History and Feminist Theory*, Middletown, CT: 86–92

Kearns, E. (1985) 'Change and continuity in religious structures after Cleisthenes', in Cartledge, P.A. and Harvey, F.D. (eds) *Crux*, London: 189–207

Kerenyi, K. (1933), 'Satire und Satura', *Studi e materiali di storia delle religioni* 9: 129–156

Kertzer, D.I. and Saller, R.P. (eds) (1991) *The Family in Italy*, New Haven, CT

Keuls, E. (1985) *The Reign of the Phallus: Sexual Politics in Ancient Greece*, New York

King, H. (1989a) 'La femme dans la médicine grecque', *La recherche* 209 (April): 462–469

—— (1989b) 'The daughter of Leonides: reading the Hippocratic corpus', in Cameron, A. (ed.) *History as text*, Chapel Hill, NC: 11–34

—— (1991) 'Using the past: nursing and the medical profession in ancient Greece', in Holden, P. and Littlewood, J. (eds) *Anthropology and Nursing*, London and New York: 7–24

—— (1993a) (1983) 'Bound to bleed: Artemis and Greek women', in Cameron, A. and Kuhrt, A. (eds) *Images of women in antiquity*, rev. edn, London

—— (1993b) 'Once upon a text: hysteria from Hippocrates', in Gilman, S.L., King, H., Porter, R., Rousseau, G.S. and Showalter, E. *Hysteria Beyond Freud*, Berkeley, Calif. and London: 3–90

—— (1995) 'Medical texts as a source for women's history', in Powell, A. (ed.) *The Greek World*, London and New York

Kirschner, J. and Wemple, S. (1985) *Women of the medieval world*, Oxford

Kitto, H.D.F. (1951) *The Greeks*, Harmondsworth

Kleiner, D.E.E. (1977) *Roman Group Portraiture: The Funerary Reliefs of the Late Republic and Early Empire*, New York

—— (1987) *Roman Imperial Funerary Altars with Portraits*, Rome

Konstan, D. (1993) 'Sexuality and power in Juvenal's second Satire', *LCM* 18.1: 12–14

Koppelman, A. (1992) 'Sex equality and/or the family: from Bloom vs. Okin to Rousseau vs. Hegel', *Yale Journal of Law and Humanities* 4: 399–432

Kraus, T. (1960) *Hekate: Studien zu Wesen und Bild der Göttin in Kleinasien und Griechenland*, Heidelberg

Kroll, W. (1899–1901) *Proclus Diadochus: in Platonis Rem Publicam Commentarii*, 2 vols, Leipzig

—— (1902) *Syrianus: in Aristotelis Metaphysica Commentaria*, Berlin

Kron, U. (1988) 'Kultmahle im Heraion von Samos archaischer Zeit. Versuch einer Rekonstruktion', in Hägg, R., Marinatos, N. and Nordquist, G.C. (eds) *Early Greek Cult Practice, Fifth International Symposium*, Swedish Institute at Athens, Stockholm: 135–148

—— (1992) 'Frauenfest in Demeterheiligtümern: das Thesmophorion von Bitalemi', *Archäologischer Anzeiger*: 611–650

Lacey, W.K. (1968) *The Family in Classical Greece*, Ithaca, NY

Lambropoulou, S. (1976) *Women in the Pythagorean Societies*, Athens

Langholf, V. (1990) *Medical Theories in Hippocrates: Early Texts and the 'Epidemics'*, Berlin

Laqueur, T. (1986) 'Orgasm, generation, and the politics of reproductive biology', *Representations* 14: 1–41

—— (1990) *Making Sex: Body and Gender from the Greeks to Freud*, Cambridge, Mass.

Ledl, A. (1907) 'Das attische Burgerrecht und die Frauen, I', *WS* 29: 173–227

Lefkowitz, M.R. (1981) *Heroines and Hysterics*, Baltimore, Md. and London

—— (1986) *Women in Greek Myth*, Baltimore, Md. and London

—— (1993) 'Influential women', in Cameron, A. and Kurht, A. (eds) *Images of women in antiquity*, rev. edn, London: 49–64

Lefkowitz, M.R. and Fant, M.B. (1992) *Women's Life in Greece and Rome: a Source Book in Translation*, 2nd edn, London

Le Guin, U.K. (1990) *Tehanu: The Last Book of Earthsea*, London

—— (1992) *Searoad: Chronicles of Klatsand*, London

Lewis, J. (1981) 'Women, lost and found: the impact of feminism on history', in Spender, D. (ed.) *Men's Studies Modified: the Impact of Feminism on the Academic Disciplines*, New York: 55–72

Lévi–Strauss, C. (1983) *Le regard éloigné*, Paris

—— (1990) 'Maison', in P. Bonte and M. Izard (eds) *Dictionnaire de l'anthropologie*, Paris

*Lexicon Iconographicum Mythologiae Classicae*, Zurich and Munich 1981– (= *LIMC*)

Littré, E. (trans.) (1839–1861) *Oeuvres complètes d'Hippocrate*, Paris

Lloyd, G.E.R. (1979) *Magic, Reason and Experience*, Cambridge

—— (1983a) *Science, Folklore and Ideology: Studies in the Life Sciences in Ancient Greece*, Cambridge

—— (1983b) 'The female sex: medical treatment and biological theories in the fifth and fourth centuries BC', in Lloyd, G.E.R. *Science, Folklore and Ideology: Studies in the life sciences in ancient Greece*, Cambridge: 86–94

Locke, J. (1967) *Two Treatises of Government*, ed. Laslett, P., 2nd edn, Cambridge

Lonie, I.M. (1981) *The Hippocratic Treatises 'On Generation', 'On the Nature of the Child', 'Diseases IV'*, Berlin and New York

Loraux, N. (1978) (1981, 1993) 'Sur la race des femmes et quelques-unes de ses tribus', *Arethusa* 11: 43–87; reprinted in Loraux, N., *Les enfants d'Athéna: idées athéniennes sur la citoyenneté et la division des sexes*, Paris 1981: 75–117; trans. by Levine, C. as 'On the race of women and some of its tribes: Hesiod and Semonides', in Loraux, N. *The Children of Athena: Athenian Ideas about Citizenship and the Division between the Sexes*, Princeton, NJ 1993: 72–110

—— (1989a) 'Le lit, la guerre', in Loraux, N. *Les expériences de Tirésias*, Paris: 29–53, 305–317

—— (1989b) *Les expériences de Tirésias*, Paris

—— (1989c) '*Ponos*: sur quelques difficultés de la peine comme nom du travail', in Loraux, N. *Les expériences de Tirésias*, Paris: 29–53, 54–76

Lowe, N.J. (1994) 'Thesmophoria and Haloa: myth, physics and mysteries', in Blundell, S. and Williamson, M. (eds) *The Sacred and the Feminine*, London

Mabey, R. (1988) *The Complete new Herbal*, London

McCullough, C. (1987) *The Ladies of Missalonghi*, London

McIntyre, A. (1988) *Herbs for Pregnancy and Childbirth*, London

McLaren, A. (1984) *Reproductive Rituals: The Perception of Fertility in England from the Sixteenth to the Nineteenth Century*, London and New York
—— (1990) *A History of Contraception from Antiquity to the Present Day*, Oxford
—— (1994) ' "Not a stranger: a doctor": medical men and sexual matters in the late nineteenth century', in Porter, R. and Teich, M. (eds) *Sexual Knowledge, Sexual Science*, Cambridge: 267–283
McManus, B. (1990) 'Multicentering: the case of the Athenian bride', *Helios* 17: 230–1
Macmullen, R. (1982) 'The epigraphic habit in the Roman Empire', *AJPh* 103: 233–246
Malamud, M.A. (1989) *A Poetics of Transformation, Prudentius and Classical Mythology*, Cornell Studies in Classical Philology 49, New York
Mann, A. (1858) (1969) *Die auf gekommenen Schriften der Kappadocier Aretaeus, aus dem griechischen übersetzt*, Halle, reprinted Wiesbaden
Manuli, P. (1980) 'Fisiologica e patologia del femminile negli scritti ippocratici dell'antica ginecologia greca', in Grmek, M.D. (ed.) *Hippocratica: Actes du colloque hippocratique de Paris, 1978*, Paris: 393–408
——(1983) 'Donne mascoline, femminine sterile, vergine perpetue. La ginecologia greca tra Ippocrate e Sorano', in Campese, S., Manuli, P. and Sissa, G. (eds) *Madre materia: sociologica e biologia della donna greca*, Turin: 147–192
Marquardt, P. (1981) 'A Portrait of Hecate', *AJPh* 102: 243–260
Marshall, B. (ed.) (1905) *Memoirs of Lady Fanshawe*, London and New York
Matthieu, N.-C. (1973) 'Homme – culture et femme – nature?', *L'homme* 13: 101–113
Mau, A. (1889) 'Bibliografia Pompeiana', *MDAI(R)* 4: 298–305
Meiners, C. (1788–1800) *History of the Female Sex*, Hanover, trans. Shoberl, F. (1808) London
Mezzadri, B. (1987) 'La pierre et le foyer: notes sur les v. 453–506 de la *Théogonie* hésiodique', *Métis* 2: 215–220
Mikalson, J.D. (1975) *The Sacred and Civil Calendar of the Athenian Year*, Princeton, NJ
—— (1983) *Athenian Popular Religion*, Chapel Hill, NC and London
Mills, S. (1992) *Woman Medicine: vitex agnus-castus*, Christchurch, Dorset
Mirrer, L. (1992) *Upon my Husband's Death: Widows in the Literature and Histories of Medieval Europe*, Ann Arbor, Mich.
Mossé, C. (1983) *La femme dans la Grèce antique*, Paris
Mouritsen, H. (1988) *Elections, Magistrates and Municipal Élite. Studies in Pompeian Epigraphy*, Analecta Rom. Inst. Dan. Suppl. 20, Rome
Murray, O. and Price, S. (eds) (1990) *The Greek City from Homer to Alexander*. Oxford
Musurillo, H. (ed.) (1972) *Acts of the Christian Martyrs*, Oxford
Mylonas, G. (1961) *Eleusis and the Eleusinian Mysteries*, Princeton, NJ
Nagy, G. (1982) 'Hesiod', in Luce, T.J. (ed.) *Ancient Writers: Greece and Rome*, 2 vols, New York: vol. 1: 43–73
Nau, F. (1915) 'Martyrologes et ménologes orientaux 1–XIII: un martyrologe et douze ménologues syriaques', in Graffin, R. and Nau, F. (eds) *Patrologia Orientalis* 10.1, Paris: 28

Nevett, L.C. (1994) 'Greek households under Roman hegemony', in Samson, R. (ed.) *Proceedings of the Third Theoretical Roman Archaeological Conference*, Glasgow

Nickel, F. (1979) 'Berufsvorstellungen ueber weibliche Medizinalpersonen in der Antike', *Klio* 61: 515–518

Nilsson, M.P. (1906) *Griechische Feste von religiöser Bedeutung*, Leipzig

—— (1932) *The Mycenaean Origins of Greek Mythology*, Berkeley, Calif. and London

—— (1964) (1925, 2nd edn, 1951) *A History of Greek Religion*, New York

Noica, S. (1984) 'La boîte de Pandore et "l'ambiguité" de l'Elpis', *Platon* 36: 100–124

Nutton, V. (1979) *Galen on Prognosis*, *CMG* 5.8.1, Berlin

—— (1985) 'The drug trade in antiquity', *Journal of the Royal Society of Medicine*, 78: 138–145

Okin, S.M. Moller (1979a) 'John Stuart Mill, liberal feminist', in Okin, S.M. Moller *Women in Western Political Thought*, Princeton, NJ: 197–223

—— (1979b) *Women in Western Political Thought*, Princeton, NJ

Olender, M. (1990) 'Aspects of Baubo: ancient texts and contexts', in Halperin, D.M., Winkler, J.J. and Zeitlin, F. (eds) *Before Sexuality: The Construction of Erotic Experience in the Ancient Greek World*, Princeton, NJ: 83–113

Opie, I. and P. (eds) (1974) *The Classic Fairy Tales*, Oxford

Osborne, M. (1988) 'Attic epitaphs – a supplement', *Anc Soc* 19: 5–60

—— (1993) 'Women and sacrifice in classical Greece', *CQ* 43: 392–405

Parker, R. (1987) 'Festivals of the Attic Demes', *Boreas* 15: 137–147

—— (1991) 'The *Hymn to Demeter* and the Homeric Hymns', *G & R* 38: 1–17

Parkin, T.G. (1992) *Demography and Roman Society*, Baltimore, Md.

Pateman, C. (1989) *The Disorder of Women*, Stanford, Calif.

Penglase, D. (1994) *Greek Myths and Mesopotamia: Parallels and Influences in the Homeric Hymns and Hesiod*, London

Peradotto, J. and Sullivan, J.P. (eds) (1984) *Women in the Ancient World: The Arethusa Papers*, New York

Perrot, M. (ed.) (1984) *Une histoire des femmes est-elle possible?*, Paris

Peschlow–Bindokat, A. (1994) 'Demeter and Persephone in der attischen Kunst des 6. bis 4 Jahrhunderts v. Chr.', *JdI* 87: 60–156

Philippson, P. (1936) *Genealogie als Mythischie form*, Oslo

Phillips, A. (1992) 'Universal pretensions in political thought', in Barrett, M. and Phillips, A. (eds) *Destabilizing Theory: Contemporary Feminist Debates*, Stanford, Calif.: 10–30.

Pigeaud, J. (1981) 'Le rêve érotique dans l'antiquité gréco-romaine: l'oneirogmos', *Litt., Méd., Société (Nantes)* 3: 10–23

Pollard, A.R. (1984) *Politics and Property*, Gloucester

Pomeroy, S.B. (1975), *Goddesses, Whores, Wives, and Slaves: Women in Classical Antiquity*, New York and London

—— (1984) *Women in Hellenistic Egypt: From Alexander the Great to Cleopatra*, New York

—— (ed.) (1991) *Women's History and Ancient History*, Chapel Hill, NC

—— (forthcoming) *The Family in Classical and Hellenistic Greece*, Oxford

Porter, R. (ed.) (1985) *Patients and Practitioners: Lay Perceptions of Medicine in*

*Pre-industrial Society*, Cambridge
Porter, R. and Teich, M. (eds) (1994) *Sexual Knowledge, Sexual Science*, Cambridge
Potterton, D. (ed.) (1983) *Culpeper's Colour Herbal*, London
Pucci, P. (1977) *Hesiod and the Language of Poetry*, Baltimore, Md.
Rabe, H. (1906) *Scholia in Lucianum*, Leipzig
Rabinowitz, N. Sorkin and Richlin, A. (eds) (1993) *Feminist Theory and the Classics*, London
Radermacher, L. (1928) 'Die Stellung der Frau innerhalb der griechische Kultur', *Mitteilungen des Vereins der Freunde des Humanistischen Gymnasiums* 27
Raeder, J. (1983) *Priene: Funden aus einer griechischer Stadt*, Berlin
Raepsaet–Charlier, M.–T. (1987) *Prosopographie des femmes de l'ordre sénatorial (I^er-II^e s.)*, Louvain
Rawson, B. (1966) 'Family life among the lower classes at Rome in the first two centuries of the Empire', *CPh* 61: 71–83
—— (1974) 'Roman concubinage and other *de facto* marriages', *TAPhA* 104: 279–305
—— (ed.) (1991) *Marriage, Divorce and Children in Ancient Rome*, Oxford (reprinted 1992)
—— (1990) '*Spurii* and the Roman view of illegitimacy', *Antichthon* 23: 10–41
Renard, L. (1834) *Arétée, traité des signes*, Paris
Rhodes, P.J. (1981) *A Commentary on the Aristotelian Athenaion Politeia*, Oxford
Rich, J. and Wallace–Hadrill, A. (eds) (1991) *City and Country in the Ancient World*, London
Richardson, L. (1988) *Pompeii: An Architectural History*, Baltimore, Md.
Richardson, N. (1974) *The Homeric Hymn to Demeter*, Oxford
Richlin, A. (1983) *The Garden of Priapus*, New Haven, Conn.
—— (1984) 'Invective against women in Roman satire', *Arethusa* 17: 67–80
—— (ed.) (1992) *Pornography and Representation in Greece and Rome*, New York
—— (1993) 'Not before homosexuality: the materiality of the *Cinaedus* and the Roman law against love between men', *Journal of the History of Sexuality* 5: 41–54
Richter, D.C. (1971) 'The position of women in classical Athens', *CJ* 67: 1–8
Riddle, J. (1992) *Contraception and Abortion from the Ancient World to the Renaissance*, Cambridge, Mass.
Ridgway, B.S. (1964) 'Kindergräber im Kerameikos', *MDAI (A)* 79: 85–104
—— (1991) 'Ancient Greek women and art: the material evidence', *AJA* 91: 397–409
Riley, D. (1988) '*Am I That Name?' Feminism and the Category of 'Women' in History*, Minneapolis, MN
Robertson, N. (1992) *Festivals and Legends: The Formation of Greek Cities in the Light of Public Ritual*, Toronto, Buffalo, NY and London
Rolley, C. (1965) 'Le sanctuaire des dieux Patrooi et le Thesmophorion de Thasos', *BCH* 89: 441–483
Roscalla, F. (1988) 'La descrizione del sé e dell'altro: api ed alveare da Esiodo a Semonide', *QUCC* 29: 23–47
Rousseau, J.J. (1925) *Émile, or Éducation*, trans. Foxley, B., New York, London and Toronto
—— (1978) *The Social Contract*, trans. Cranston, M., Baltimore, Md.: 64–65

Roussel, D. (1976) 'Tribu et cité', *Annales littéraires de l'Université de Besançon* 23, Paris

Rousselle, A. (1980) 'Images médicales du corps'. Observation féminine et idéologie masculine: le corps de la femme d'après les médicins grecs', *Annales ESC* 35: 1089–1115

—— (1988) *Porneia: on desire and the body in antiquity*, trans. of *Porneia. De la Maîtrise du corps à la privation sensorielle*, Paris 1983, trans. Pheasant, F., New York and Oxford

Rudhardt, J. (1982) 'De l'inceste dans la mythologie grecque', *Revue française de psychanalyse* 46: 731–763

—— (1986) 'Pandora': Hésiode et les femmes', *MH* 43: 231–246

Ruschenbusch, E. (1966) *SOLONOS NOMOI: Die Fragmente des Solonischen Gestzeswerkes mit einer Text- und Überlieferungsgeschichte. Historia Einzelschr.* 9, Wiesbaden

Russ, J. (1981) 'Recent feminist utopias', in Barr, M.S. (ed.) *Future Females: A Critical Anthology*, Bowling Green, OH: 71–80

Said, E. (1978) *Orientalism*, New York

Saller, R.P. (1986a) 'Men's age at marriage and its consequences for the Roman family', *CPh* 82: 21–34

—— (1986b) '*Patria potestas* and the stereotype of the Roman family', *Continuity and Change* 1: 7–22

Saller, R.P. and Shaw, B.D. (1984) 'Tombstones and family relations in the Principate: civilians, soldiers and slaves', *JRS* 74: 124–156

Sanders, G.M. (1972) 'Gallos', in Klauser, Th. and Dassman, E. (eds) *Reallexikon für Antike und Christentum* 8, Stuttgart

Saxonhouse, A. (1985) *Women in the History of Political Thought*, New York

Scafuro, A.C. (1990) 'Discourse of sexual violation in mythic accounts and dramatic versions of "The Girl's Tragedy"' *Differences* 2.1, special issue on 'Sexuality in Greek and Roman society': 126–159

Scalera, A. (1919) 'Le donne nelle elezioni municipali a Pompei', *Rend. d. Reale Acc. dei Lincei, Cl. sc. mor. stor. fil.*, series 5, 28: 387–405

Scarborough, J. (1991) 'The pharmacology of sacred plants, herbs, and roots', in Faraone, C.A. and Obbink, D. (eds) *Magika Hiera*, New York: 138–174

—— (1992) 'Sexual anatomy: the "Parts (female)"', in Scarborough, J. *Medical Terminologies: Classical Origins*; Norman, Okla.

Scheid, J. (1992) 'The religious roles of Roman women', in Schmitt-Pantel, P. (ed.) *A History of Women in the West*, Cambridge, Mass. and London

Scheper-Hughes, N. (1987) ' "Basic strangeness": maternal estrangement and infant death – a critique of bonding theory', in Super, C.M. (ed.) *The role of Culture in Developmental Disorder*, San Diego, Calif.: 131–151

Schlörb–Vierneisel, B. (1964) 'Zwei klassische Kindergräber im Kerameikos', *MDAI (A)* 79: 85–104

Schmitt–Pantel, P. (1984) 'La différence des sexes: histoire, anthropologie et cité grecque', in Perrot, M. (ed.) *Une histoire des femmes: est-elle possible?*, Paris: 98–119

—— (ed.) (1992a) *A History of Women in the West*, vol. 1: *From Ancient Goddesses to Christian Saints*, Cambridge, Mass. and London

—— (1992b) 'Women and ancient history today', in Schmitt-Pantel, P. (ed.) *A History of Women in the West*, Cambridge, Mass. and London: 464–471

Schuller, W. (1985) *Frauen in der griechischen Geschichte*, Constance
Schwabl, H. (1966) *Hesiods Theogonie. Evie Unitarisclie Analyse*, Vienna
Seltman, C. (1955) 'The status of women in Athens', *G&R*, series 2: 119–124
Shaw, B.D. (1987) 'The age of Roman girls at marriage: some reconsiderations', *JRS* 77: 30–46
Shaw, B.D. and Saller, R.P. (1984) 'Close-kin marriage in Roman society?', *Man* 19: 432–444
Shero, L.R. (1932) 'Xenophon's portrait of a young wife', *CW* 26 (17 October): 17–21
Simon, E. (1983) *Festivals of Attica*, Madison, Wisc.
Sissa, G. (1990) *Greek Virginity*, trans. Goldhammer, A., Cambridge, Mass.
—— (1992) 'The sexual philosophies of Plato and Aristotle', in Schmitt-Pantel, P. (ed.) *A History of Women in the West*, Cambridge, Mass. and London
Skinner, M. (1987) 'Classical studies, patriarchy and feminism: the view from 1986', *Women's Studies International Forum* 10: 181–186
Sokolowski, F. (1969) *Lois sacrés des cités Grecques*, Paris (= *LSCG*)
Solin, H. (1982) *Die griechische Personennamen in Rom: ein Namenbuch*, Berlin
—— (1983) 'Juden und Syren im westlichen Teil der röm. Welt: eine ethnisch-demographische Studie mit bes. Berücksichtigung der sprachlichen Zustände', *ANRW* 2.29.2: 587–789
Sourvinou–Inwood, C. (1978)(1991) 'Persephone and Aphrodite at Locri: a model for personality definitions in Greek religion', *JHS* 98: 101–121; reprinted in Sourvinou–Inwood, C. *'Reading' Greek Culture: Texts and Images, Rituals and Myths*, Oxford: 147–188
—— (1987) *Studies in Girls' Transitions: Aspects of the Arkteia and Age Representation in Attic Iconography*, Athens
—— (1991) *'Reading' Greek Culture: Texts and Images, Rituals and Myths*, Oxford
Sozomen *Historia ecclesiastica*, in Migne, J.-P. (ed.) *Patrologiae Cursus Completus, Series Graeco–Latinia* 1–166, Paris 1844–1864, 67: 843–1630
von Staden, H. (1992a) 'Spiderwoman and the chaste tree: the semantics of matter', *Configurations* 1: 23–56
—— (1992b) 'The mind and skin of Herakles: heroic diseases', in Gourevitch, D. (ed.) *Mélanges Grmek*, Paris and Geneva: 131–150
—— (1992c) 'Women and dirt', *Helios* 19: 7–30
Staveley, E. (1972) *Greek and Roman Voting Assemblies*, London
Stengel, P. (1910) 'Gamelia', *RE* 7.1, Stuttgart: cols 691–692
Stewart, M. (1988) *Thornyhold*, London
Stone, L. (1987) *The Past and the Present Revisited*, London
Strauss, B. (1993) *Fathers and Sons in Athens: Ideology and Society in the Era of the Peloponnesian War*, London
Sussman, L. (1984) 'Workers and drones: labor, idleness and gender definition in Hesiod's beehive', in Peradotto, J. and Sullivan, J.P. (eds) *Women in the Ancient World: The Arethusa Papers*, New York: 79–84
Syme, R. (1984) *Roman Papers 3*, ed. Birley, A.R., Oxford
Taggart, J.M. (1990) *Enchanted Maidens: Gender Relations in Spanish Folktales of Courtship and Marriage*, Princeton, NJ
Taylor, L.R. (1966) *Roman Voting Assemblies from the Hannibalic War to the Dictatorship of Caesar*, Ann Arbor, Mich.
Taylor, T. (1965) *Iamblichus' Life of Pythagoras*, London

Temkin, O. (trans.) (1956) *Soranus' Gynecology*, Baltimore, Md.
Thesleff, H. (1965) *The Pythagorean Texts of the Hellenistic Period*, Abo
Thorp, J. (1992) 'Review article: the social construction of homosexuality', *Phoenix* 46: 54–61
Töpperwein–Hoffmann, E. (1971) 'Terracotten von Priene', *MDAI (I)* 21: 125–160
Travlos, J.T. (1988) *Bildlexicon zur Topographie des antiken Attika*, Tübingen
Treggiari, S. (1991a) 'Divorce Roman style: how easy and how frequent was it?', in Rawson, B. (ed.) *Marriage, divorce and children in ancient Rome*, Oxford: 31–46
—— (1991b) *Roman marriage: Iusti Coniuges from the Time of Cicero to the Time of Ulpian*, Oxford
Turner, F.M. (1981) *The Greek Heritage in Victorian Britain*, New Haven, Conn.
Turner, V.W. (1960) 'Muchona the hornet, interpreter of religion', in Casagrande, J.B. (ed.) *In the Company of Man: Twenty Portraits by Anthropologists*, New York: 333–355
—— (1969) *The Ritual Process*, London
Väänänen, V. (1937) *Le latin vulgaire des inscriptions pompéiennes*, Helsinki
Verbeke, G. (1973) *Corpus Latinum Commentariorum in Aristotelem Graecorum*, trans. Moerbeke, G. de, 1: Themistius, 2: Ammonius, 3:I. Philoponus, Leiden
Verdenius, W.J. (1985) *A Commentary on Hesiod: Works and Days, vv. 1–382*, Leiden
Vernant, J.-P. (1955) 'Hestia–Hermès. Sur l'expression religieuse de l'espace et du mouvement chez les Grecs', Vernant, J.-P. in *Mythe et pensée chez les Grecs*, Paris: 155–201
—— (1980a) *Myth and Society in Ancient Greece*, trans. Lloyd, J., London
—— (1980b) 'The myth of Prometheus in Hesiod', in Vernant, J.-P. *Myth and Society in ancient Greece*, trans. Lloyd, J., London: 168–185
—— (1989) 'At man's table: Hesiod's foundation myth of sacrifice', in Detienne, M. and Vernant, J.-P. *The Cuisine of Sacrifice Among the Greeks*, trans. Wissing, P., Chicago, Ill. and London: 21–86, 224–237
Versnel, H.S. (1992) 'The festival for Bona Dea and the Thesmophoria', *G & R* 39: 31–55
—— (1993) *Inconsistencies in Greek and Roman Religion* vol. 2: *Transition and Reversal in Myth and Ritual*, Leiden
Vestergaard, T., Bjertrup, L., Harsen, M.H., Nielsen, T.H. and Rubinstein, L. (1985) 'A typology of the women recorded on gravestones from Attica', *AJAH* 10: 178–190
Veyne, P. (1991) 'La famille et l'amour sous le haut-empire romain', *Annales* 33: 35–63
Wachsmuth, C. and Hense, O. (1968) *Ioannis Stobaei Anthologium*, 2nd edn, Berlin
Wagner–Hasel, B. (1982) *Zwischen Mythos und Realität: Die Frau in der früh-griechischen Gesellschaft* (Diss Berlin 1980), Frankfurt am Main
—— (1988) 'Das Private wird politisch', in Becher, U.A.J. and Rüsen, J. (eds) *Weiblichkeit in geschichtlicher Perspektive*, Frankfurt am Main
—— (1989) 'Frauenleben in orientalischer Abgeschlossenheit? Zur Geschichte und Nutzanwendung eines Topos', *Der altsprachliche Unterricht* 2: 18–29
Waithe, M.E. (1987) *A History of Women Philosophers*, vol. 1, Boston, Mass.

Walcot, P. (1958) 'Hesiod's hymns to the Muses, Aphrodite, Styx and Hecate, *SO* 34: 5–14
—— (1984) 'Greek attitudes towards women: the mythological evidence', *G&R* 31: 37–47
—— (1991) 'On widows and their reputation in antiquity', *Symbolae Osloenses* 66: 5–26
Walker, S. (1993) 'Women and housing in classical Greece', in Cameron, and Kuhrt, A. (eds) *Images of Women in Antiquity*, rev. edn: 81–91
Ward, J.C. (1992) *English Noblewomen in the Later Middle Ages*, London
Weaver, P.R.C. (1991) *Familia Caesaris: A Social Study of the Emperor's Freedmen and Slaves*, 2nd edn, Cambridge
Wehrli, F. (1944) *Die Schule des Aristoteles: Texte und Kommentar*, 1 Dikaiarchos, Basle
West, M.L. (1966) *Hesiod, Theogony*, Oxford
Wiegand, T., and Schrader, H. (1904) *Priene: Ergebnisse der Ausgrabungen und Untersuchungen in den Jahren 1895–1898*, Berlin
Will, E. (1979) 'Women in Pompeii', *Archaeology* 32: 34–43
Willems, P. (1887) *Les élections municipales à Pompéi*, Paris
Wilson, N.G. (1975) *Prolegomena de Comoedia Scholia in Acharnenses, Equites, Nubes*, 1B: *Scholia in Aristophanis Acharnenses*, Groningen
Winkler, J. (1990a) 'Listening to the laughter of the oppressed: Demeter and the Gardens of Adonis', in Winkler, J. *The Constraints of Desire: The Anthropology of Sex and Gender in Ancient Greece*, New York and London 188–209
—— (1990b) *The Constraints of Desire: The Anthropology of Sex and Gender in Ancient Greece*, New York and London
Winkler, M.M. (1983) *The Persona in Three Satires of Juvenal*, Hildesheim
Wollstonecraft, M. (1988) (1792) *A Vindication of the Rights of Woman: An Authoritative Text, Backgrounds. The Wollstonecraft Debate, Criticism*, ed. Poston, C.H., New York
Wyke, M. (1992) 'Augustan Cleopatras: female power and poetic authority', in Powell, A. (ed.) *Roman Poetry and Propaganda in the Age of Augustus*, London: 98–140
Zanker, P. (1988) *The Power of Images in the Age of Augustus*, Ann Arbor, Mich.
Zeitlin, F.I. (1978) (1984) 'The dynamics of misogyny: myth and mythmaking in the Oresteia', *Arethusa* 11: 149–184; reprinted in Peradotto, J.J. and Sullivan, J.P. (eds) *Women in the Ancient World: The Aresthusa Papers*, Albay, NY, 1984: 159–194
—— (1982) 'Cultic models of the female: rites of Dionysos and Demeter', *Arethusa*, 15.1 and 2: 129–157
—— (1985) 'Playing the Other: theater, theatricality, and the feminine in Greek drama', *Representations* 11: 63–94
—— (1986) 'Configurations of rape in Greek myth', in Tomaselli, S. and Porter, R. (eds) *Rape*, Oxford: 122–161
—— (1995) 'Signifying difference: the case of Pandora', in Zeitlin, F.I. *Playing the Other: gender and society in classical Greek literature*, Chicago, Ill.
Zipes, J. (1987) *The Complete Fairy Tales of the Brothers Grimm*, New York
Zivanovic, S. (1982) *Ancient Diseases: The Elements of Palaeopathology*, London

# Index